The First Modern Campaign

The First Modern Campaign

Kennedy, Nixon, and the Election of 1960

Gary A. Donaldson

ROWMAN & LITTLEFIELD PUBLISHERS, INC.
Lanham • Boulder • New York • Toronto • Plymouth, UK

ROWMAN & LITTLEFIELD PUBLISHERS, INC.

Published in the United States of America
by Rowman & Littlefield Publishers, Inc.
A wholly owned subsidiary of The Rowman & Littlefield Publishing Group, Inc.
4501 Forbes Boulevard, Suite 200, Lanham, Maryland 20706
www.rowmanlittlefield.com

Estover Road
Plymouth PL6 7PY
United Kingdom

British Library Cataloguing in Publication Information Available

Library of Congress Cataloging-in-Publication Data:
Donaldson, Gary.
  The first modern campaign : Kennedy, Nixon, and the election of 1960 / Gary A.
Donaldson.
      p. cm.
  Includes bibliographical references.
  ISBN-13: 978-0-7425-4799-5 (cloth : alk. paper)
  ISBN-10: 0-7425-4799-X (cloth : alk. paper)
  ISBN-13: 978-0-7425-4800-8 (pbk. : alk. paper)
  ISBN-10: 0-7425-4800-7 (pbk. : alk. paper)
  1. Presidents—United States—Election—1960. 2. Kennedy, John F. (John Fitzgerald),
1917–1963. 3. Nixon, Richard M. (Richard Milhous), 1913–1994. 4. Presidential
candidates—United States—Biography. 5. Political campaigns—United States—
History—20th century. 6. Democratic Party (U.S.)—History—20th century. 7.
Republican Party (U.S. : 1854–)—History—20th century. 8. United States—Politics
and government—1953–1961. 9. United States—Politics and government—
1961–1963. I. Title.
  E837.7.D66 2007
  324.973'0921—dc22   2007004168

Printed in the United States of America

∞™ The paper used in this publication meets the minimum requirements of
American National Standard for Information Sciences—Permanence of Paper
for Printed Library Materials, ANSI/NISO Z39.48-1992.

~

Contents

~

Preface

Following World War II the American political process began going through a series of changes that, by 1960, finally evolved into the modern presidential election campaign. The first postwar election, in 1948 between President Harry Truman and the Republican challenger Thomas Dewey, is often described as the "last campaign," the last of the old style presidential elections.[1] Truman won that year the way candidates had won elections for decades. He built a coalition, pandered for endorsements from party bigwigs, labor leaders, and urban machines; and he made deals behind the scenes and in smoke-filled rooms. To cap off his campaign, he took to the political hustings by train, speaking to the nation and making news from the platform of the rear car. His celebrated whistle-stop tour was a rousing success; he saw the people, and they saw him, as he moved through the nation stopping at little towns and crossroads. The crowds grew through the fall, and on Election Day the effects were felt at the polls. No other presidential candidate in American history had done more to take his campaign to the people. That campaign, so prominent in election lore, was not the last time a candidate would use a train to campaign, but it was the last time a campaign would be won from a train's rear platform, and it was the last time a candidate would base his campaign almost solely on a series of train trips. The age of the whistle stop ended with Truman's 1948 victory. By 1960, candidates would campaign on television, travel on jet airplanes to speaking engagements, and engage in long drawn-out primary campaigns. And by then, the candidates' images had gone a long way toward replacing campaign issues. It was that presidential campaign, between Richard Nixon and John Kennedy, that changed the American campaign process. It was the nation's first modern presidential campaign.

The most obvious distinction of the 1960 campaign was the importance that image played in the outcome; for the first time in American history a candidate's image was a deciding factor in an election. John Kennedy, really a little known senator from Massachusetts with a reputation for personal wealth and a lack of experience, made extensive use of television to present himself to the American public, to put his face into America's living rooms. It was the first campaign covered extensively by television, and the result was the emergence of an indelible and popular image. Some of it was manufactured by public relations people, and it was mostly favorable. Kennedy was portrayed as a war hero. He presented the image of vigor, youth, and activism to follow his slogan of getting the nation "moving again." He was handsome; he had a wife who looked like a movie star; he had kids. It was all a wonderful image, and the American people were fascinated and charmed by the entire package.

One person who became enamored with the Kennedy image and its accompanying mystique was the journalist Theodore White. White wrote the Pulitzer Prize–winning *The Making of the President, 1960*, which was published a year after the election. His writing on the 1960 campaign is a wonderful addition to political reportage, but White is often charged with flawed journalism for his biased reporting and selective use of sources.[2] While writing his book on the 1960 campaign, White was drawn very close to the Kennedy camp, particularly to Jackie Kennedy. For that reason he is often criticized for being a shaper of the Kennedy image; but he was, in fact, shaped by it—in much the same way the nation was aroused by the Kennedy image. White was star-struck by the Kennedys.[3] Consequently, he saw only good in Kennedy, the candidate who did everything right and won the hearts, minds, and votes of the American people. In contrast, he disliked Nixon—and mostly everything about him. According to White, all that Nixon did was wrong, and thus he lost the election. Image played a deciding role in the 1960 campaign, and it played a key role in White's book.

Image is just part of the story of the 1960 campaign, but because of image, as it was played that year, American elections would never be quite the same again. Growing directly out of this election would be the manufactured candidate, someone who could look good for the cameras, whose image could be manipulated for American voters, a candidate who could be made to appear to be something he was not. Under the obvious assumption that a strong image does not necessarily translate into strong leadership, it must be assumed that the introduction of image as a primary factor into the American electoral process is detrimental to that process. The 1960 campaign, the first modern campaign, opened those floodgates.

CHAPTER ONE

~

The "Modern Republicanism" of Eisenhower and the GOP Split in the Fifties

When Dwight Eisenhower defeated Adlai Stevenson in November 1952, it ended a Republican drought that had lasted a very long twenty years. Except for a short moment when the Republican 80th Congress (between 1947 and 1949) did little more than give Harry Truman a whipping boy for the 1948 campaign, the Republicans had sat on the sidelines of the American political system while the New Deal-Fair Deal juggernaut ran Washington and expanded American liberalism. "For most of a full generation," a conservative Republican leader wrote years later, the Republican Party had been little more than "the shapeless, gutless alternative to well-formed, principled Democratic programs and candidates."[1] Stanton Evans, another leader on the GOP Right in this period, called the Republican Party in the FDR-Truman years "a satellite of the Democratic Party, a political doppelgänger that moves only with the impulse of its original."[2]

The most conservative Republicans in Congress were particularly powerless, almost always pushed out of the loop when the Democrats and moderate Republicans found some common ground in proposing and supporting legislation. And it was the moderate Republicans, at least in part because of their willingness to work with the Democrats on some issues, who at least found some place within the structure of the decision-making processes. Not surprisingly, it was this group that soon captured the nominating apparatus of the Republican Party from their more conservative brethren. These moderates presented the nation's voters with a series of presidential and congressional candidates who promised to do the job in Washington better, more efficiently, and with greater anticommunist fervor than the Democrats. The 1940 Republican candidate, Wendell Willkie, had, in fact, voted for Roosevelt in the 1936 Democratic landslide—a point the Republicans made often in hopes of pulling moderates away from Roosevelt. In 1944, and then again in 1948, the Republicans nominated Tom Dewey, and often referred to him as a liberal. Dewey, the governor of New York, maintained strong ties to organized labor and civil rights leaders and was sensitive to such national problems as housing and job shortages.

But after two defeats, one at the hands of Roosevelt in 1944 and another against Truman in 1948, Dewey became, to GOP conservatives, the party's symbol of failure. They argued with some affect that Dewey lost because he was too liberal, too willing to accept the foundations of the New Deal, too eager to pander to Northeastern liberals, and too accepting of the foreign policy of engaged internationalism that most GOP conservatives hated.

Much of this frustration revolved around Dewey's upset in the 1948 presidential election. In the immediate postwar years it seemed that the political tide was turning toward the GOP. With the depression and the war over, with Roosevelt gone, and Truman's popularity at an all-time low, it appeared that the Republicans were on the ascent; their time had come again. And so, when the GOP took control of the House following the 1946 midterm elections, both Democrats and Republicans prepared for the beginning of a new Republican age in Washington. *Newsweek* speculated that the New Deal was at its end and announced, "An Era Begins."[3] And *U.S. News* reported that the Republicans could be expected to remain in office for up to sixteen years.[4] In January, the GOP members of the new Congress arrived on the House floor armed with brooms. They refused to explain their strategy, but the press speculated that the brooms were intended to sweep out the New Deal. Their optimism, however, was premature. Two years later, Harry Truman rallied the Democratic faithful once again and won the presidency along with a Democratic majority in Congress. The defeat devastated the Republicans. The voters, it seemed, had reaffirmed the New Deal and rejected the Republican alternative.

Following each GOP loss through the 1940s, the conservative wing of the party succeeded in gaining immediate control of the party structure and began devising a strategy to run one of their own in the next election. But in each instance, as the election approached, the moderate wing of the party grabbed control of the convention apparatus and won the nomination with a candidate who was generally repugnant to the party's right wing. The candidate would then control the platform committee, and the party would head into the campaign with another moderate candidate and a moderate platform. Conservative Republicans continually argued that their party was losing ground to the Democrats because it offered a political philosophy that was only barely distinct from the Democratic line. What the voters would respond to, they argued, was a conservative alternative to the liberalism of the Democrats. These conservatives believed that if the Republicans held to the staid conservative principles of lower taxes, a balanced budget, less government spending, less federal interference in state and local affairs, a tough stance on communism, and a strong (though unilateral) national defense, a conservative alternative to the Democratic liberal agenda would be a winner at the polls.

One primary problem that the GOP Right faced with this strategy was that they were never able to present the party, and the nation, with an electable candidate. They had never had a standard-bearer who was charismatic, a character who could excite the masses and send voters to the polls in big numbers. The isolationist Robert Taft was the Republican Right's leader through the 1940s and into the early 1950s; and he ran for his party's nomination in 1940, 1948, and again in 1952. But in each campaign year he was pushed aside by the party's moderates who nominated one of their own, someone who was at least perceived as having more vote-getting power than Taft. Taft simply was not an electable figure. He was often described as dour, aloof, and cold. He was no hand-shaker and no baby-kisser. It was a common refrain among Republicans in Washington that "Taft can't win," that he was simply too plain to excite voters and get votes—at least outside of his home state of Ohio. In an attempt to polish up his image, Taft, in preparation for the 1948 campaign, hired a professional image-maker to turn his stiff personality into something that voters would see as an appealing fatherly type. The effort was a dismal failure, and Taft was crushed in the early primaries.[5] At the 1952 GOP convention in Chicago, Senator John Bricker of Ohio, a long-time Taft supporter, withdrew Taft's name from consideration for the third time in twelve years. Taft made his strongest bid yet for the nomination that year, but for the fifth time in as many elections, Republican conservatives were forced to get behind a moderate candidate for president—another "me-too" candidate, as they called Eisenhower.

The election of Eisenhower in 1952 was a long awaited rebirth for Republicans, and even for conservatives like Taft, the election of any Republican was preferable to the election of any Democrat. In addition, Ike's coattails were enormous; he brought with him a Republican Congress—the first since 1946, and before that since 1928. But Eisenhower presented two problems for Republicans. First: Did the American voters like the Republicans and their policies, or did they just like Ike? That question was answered abruptly when, in the 1954 midterm elections, the Democrats again grabbed control of both houses of Congress. And then in 1956, Eisenhower won a second term, carrying a whopping 58 percent of the vote. Apparently, it was Ike and not the Republicans that the nation's voters liked. That presented an immediate concern for the 1960 campaign. How would Republicans transfer the Eisenhower magic to the much less appealing vice president, Richard Nixon? Second: Eisenhower proved to be a moderate (disgruntled conservatives in the party called him a liberal), and in fact, continued to keep Dewey at his side. Through Ike's two administrations, his moderate policies slowly split the Republican Party between the conservatives on the Right and the moderates on the Left. That split, as the party headed into the 1960 campaign, threatened to be debilitating.

Eisenhower called his moderate political philosophy "Modern Republicanism," or "The Middle Way," a plan that conservatives snubbed as little more than a validation of the New Deal plus a foreign policy of internationalism. This Modern Republicanism is difficult to define, at least in part because Eisenhower never really defined it himself. In 1954 Ike remarked to his press secretary James Hagerty that he was looking for a word "to put ahead of Republican—something like 'New' or 'Modern' or something."[6] During Eisenhower's second term, a few Republicans (who believed they thought like Eisenhower) tried to give Modern Republicanism some credence and specificity, but their ideas were never really accepted by Eisenhower or the moderate wing of the party. Several Republicans, such as George Aiken of Vermont, insisted that the party drop the term entirely, because without any specific program to define it, Modern Republicanism was subject to any number of interpretations.[7] In fact, it is difficult to see any move by Eisenhower in his second term that was substantially new or different from his first term. He remained generally where he had always been—in the middle of the road—and most observers passed off Modern Republicanism as a political catch phrase with no real meaning. The phrase, however, stuck in the craw of the Republican Right. When Ike refused to define the term, party conservatives placed their own definition on it, and Modern Republicanism became the culmination of Eisenhower's moderation, his middle-of-the-road stance that they hated. To right-wingers like writer William Rusher, "middle-of-the road" was little more than cavorting with liberals. It became an increase in welfare spending, an expanded role of the government in the lives of individuals and institutions, reduced military spending, and a peaceful coexistence with the Soviet Union. By 1957, Modern Republicanism had been defined, but it was never Eisenhower's definition. By then Rusher and others had added to the list such things as the president's handling of the Suez Crisis, his failure to aid the Hungarian Revolution, and even his mishandling of *Sputnik*. Modern Republicanism became all that the GOP Right opposed in the party—and it became the battle line within the party as the 1960 campaign approached.[8]

The 1952 election also revealed that the South was beginning to find its way into the Republican Party. The South had made up the conservative wing of the Democratic Party since the end of Reconstruction. At various times in the late 1920s and again in the late 1930s, the South had exhibited discontent with their fellow Democrats, but until 1948 they had stayed in the party, voting almost solidly Democratic in each presidential election. In 1948 Truman made a bid for the northern urban black vote by supporting a civil rights agenda. Many white southerners, however, refused to tolerate Truman's overtures to civil rights and at the party convention in Philadelphia, Alabama and Mississippi delegates walked out to form the third party Dixiecrats and nominate Strom Thurmond for president. Thurmond's message of states' rights appealed to the white South, and he took four southern states in the November election. Truman won the election while still managing to hold most of the South—and winning large numbers of African-American voters in several key northern urban areas. But these events meant that the Democrats had chosen northern urban black votes over southern white votes, and that left large numbers of southern whites without a political home. In 1952 Eisenhower saw the cracks developing in the Solid South and campaigned for southern votes. In that election, he took seven southern states, mostly in the Deep South, plus the border states of Kentucky and West Virginia. The Republicans would have trouble hanging on to the South in the next two elections, but it was clear—after the 1948 and 1952 elections—that the South was no longer in the bag for the Democrats, that under certain circumstances, at least, the South would follow their conservative noses and vote with the Republicans.

When Eisenhower came to office in January 1953, the members of the Republican Right expected their new president to lead them in a point-by-point dismantling of New Deal programs, something Taft and others on the Right had promised to do at least since the war. The president, however, wanted to lead his party and the nation down the middle of the road. In fact, he wanted to work with Democrats, build a bipartisan consensus, and emerge as a national president. He had no intention of going to war with the Democrats over domestic issues. The Republicans on the Right simply found this intolerable. The more Ike continued his middle-of-the-road traverse, the more the Right chafed. Through issue after issue, the two wings of the party clashed—and then pulled back in the name of party unity. By the time of the

1960 campaign, the Right was weak and leaderless, while the moderates fell in behind the New Nixon—a much more moderate Nixon than in his early days, a Nixon who could demand an endorsement from the still-popular Ike.

Another aspect of the Left-Right division within the GOP revolved around the issue of communism—both foreign and domestic. The Far Right had become nearly engulfed in a highly visible and highly charged anticommunist crusade. Led by Wisconsin senator Joseph McCarthy and a few others from the party's right wing in both Houses, they conducted hearings and investigations in their relentless search for communists and communist sympathizers inside the federal government (most specifically in the State Department). For many of these conservatives, Eisenhower lacked the aggression they believed was necessary to deal with international communism and with the communist conspiracies they were looking for in the United States. In an attempt to push the president to be more aggressive, the conservatives, at the 1952 GOP convention, forced a plank into the party platform that called the Democratic Party's foreign policy of containment "negative, futile and immoral," because it "abandons countless human beings to a despotism and godless terrorism." In place of containment they called for a new, more aggressive policy they called "liberation."[9] Eisenhower never embraced liberation as an aspect of his own foreign policy, probably understanding that liberation and invasion were much the same. Republican conservatives, however, saw Eisenhower's lack of aggression as weakness and appeasement of the communist enemy. The difference in strategy further divided the conservative Right and the Eisenhower Modern Republicans.

McCarthy had been holding Senate hearings since 1950, accusing federal employees of being communists or communist sympathizers. The president disapproved of McCarthy, but because of the influence of the Right in his party and because of the general popularity of McCarthy's antics, Eisenhower was forced to lay low on the issue to avoid a party split. But as McCarthy's investigations progressed, the president's disapproval grew into hatred. "Eisenhower grew to loathe McCarthy," Stephen Ambrose has written, "almost as much as he hated Hitler."[10] At the same time, Eisenhower was confronted with McCarthy's popularity, and that made it difficult to reprimand the senator. As late as January 1954 a full 50 percent of Americans polled by the Gallup organization approved of what McCarthy was doing, while only 29 percent disapproved.[11]

The McCarthy episode, probably more than anything, made the rift in the Republican Party most visible. Certainly the president saw it. He wrote to a friend near the end of McCarthy's run: "[T]he Republican Party has got for once and for all to make up its mind whether to follow the ludicrous partnership of the Old Guarders and the McCarthyites (one of my friends had called it a 'marriage of convenience'), or whether it is going to stand behind the program of the Administration and the middle-of-the-road philosophy in which we firmly believe."[12] To another friend he wrote, "There is a certain reactionary fringe of the Republican Party that hates and despises everything for which I stand. . . ."[13]

Eisenhower's "hatred" of McCarthy, as Ambrose describes the president's feelings, resulted mostly from McCarthy's almost foolish attack on George Marshall, Eisenhower's friend and mentor. Marshall had openly supported Truman's firing of Douglas MacArthur in 1951 (as had Omar Bradley and the other Joint Chiefs of Staff) when the president and the general clashed over the war strategy in Korea. On the Senate floor, McCarthy attacked Marshall, accusing him of being associated with "a conspiracy so immense and an infamy so black as to dwarf any previous such venture in the history of man."[14] The statement surely infuriated the president, but again, McCarthy's popularity kept Eisenhower from acting. "Nothing would probably please him more," Eisenhower wrote a friend, "than to get the publicity that would be generated by public repudiation by the President."[15] He could not, however, sit idly by and allow McCarthy to carry on as he wished. From behind the scenes (where Eisenhower often felt the most comfortable dealing with sensitive issues), the president quietly exerted significant pressure, mostly through executive privilege, and denied McCarthy's committee access to the executive branch of government, including both records and people. In a similar, but uncoordinated effort, Lyndon Johnson, the Senate Majority Leader, was carrying out an almost parallel strategy of denying McCarthy and his people access to Senate files and documents. This two-pronged strategy of information strangulation—along with McCarthy's own harsh image as he appeared on television—brought down the Wisconsin senator. In early December 1954, the Senate censured McCarthy and that chapter in American history came to an end.

From the standpoint of Republican politics, the McCarthy episode was even more significant. Because Eisenhower was able to maintain an image of staying above the McCarthy fray, the entire incident damaged the Republican Right badly. When McCarthy collapsed without any visible attack directly from the White House, congressional conservatives were left holding the bag on the issue, and they received much of the blame for McCarthy's actions. In the 1958 midterm elections, and again in the 1960 general election, the GOP Right suffered at the polls, while Eisenhower and the moderates—generally unscathed by the McCarthy episode—maintained a tight grip on the party machinery. As these events unfolded through the 1950s, Richard

Nixon, who had made a political name for himself as a communist hunter in the McCarthy mold, saw his future more along Eisenhower's middle-of-the-road, and as far away as possible from his old haunting grounds with his party's right wing. He quickly moderated his positions (as some would see it, reinvented himself) and moved to the middle ground. He did not want to run in 1960 with the albatross of McCarthyism around his neck.

Eisenhower and his party's right wing banged heads during his administrations over a number of issues, but one of the most telling came almost immediately after Ike's first inauguration over his choice of Charles "Chip" Bohlen as ambassador to Moscow. Bohlen had been a career officer in the State Department—precisely the place where Joe McCarthy was insisting there were communists giving away secrets—and he had been Roosevelt's translator at the Yalta Conference in February 1945. To the GOP Right, Yalta had become the "Great Betrayal," the Democratic Party's delivery of Eastern Europe to the Soviets as reward for aiding in the defeat of the Germans. To make matters worse, Bohlen had testified at his confirmation hearing that the problem at Yalta had not been the Yalta agreement, but that Stalin had broken the agreement—precisely the argument made by the Democrats.[16]

It appeared that the Bohlen appointment would further drive a wedge between the party's Left and Right wings when Taft stepped in to make peace. Taft expected to lead the Republican Congress in the present session, and the last thing he needed was a Republican Party split over an ambassadorial appointment. He agreed to accept Bohlen, but he made it clear to Ike that he did not like the choice and that he would not stand for similar appointments in the future. His message to Ike made it clear: "No more Bohlens!"[17] In the final confirmation vote on the Senate floor, only eleven Republicans voted against the confirmation. Of that group, the president wrote in his diary, "There were only two or three who surprised me by their actions; the others," he added, "are the most stubborn and essentially small-minded examples of the extreme isolationist group in the Party."[18] The quarrel over the Bohlen appointment convinced Republicans on the Right that Eisenhower would be following the internationalist foreign policy that was being pushed by Republican moderates like Dewey, Henry Cabot Lodge, and John Foster Dulles.

Mostly because of the Japanese attack on Pearl Harbor and the obvious need for engagement during World War II, the Republican Right had abandoned their decades-old isolationism for a new policy that was customarily called "unilateralism." This policy rejected most world diplomatic engagement as well as multilateral, United Nations–style military involvement in world affairs—in exchange for a go-it-alone strategy. During the war, Eisenhower had embraced multilateralism and the need for a unified military effort to stop aggression in the world and rejected the unilateralism touted by the Republican conservatives. Again, a wedge was driven between the two divisions of the party.

More problems emerged over the handling of the Korean War. As Eisenhower had promised during the 1952 campaign, he brought a speedy end to the war—much to the disgust of the GOP Right. They saw the armistice, signed in April 1953 with the North Koreans and the Chinese Communists, as the worst kind of appeasement: the acceptance of a near status quo ante and an unwillingness by the administration to confront and defeat the enemy. The armistice also seemed to be an acceptance by Eisenhower that Truman's firing of Douglas MacArthur was justified. MacArthur, himself an ardent right wing Republican, had wanted to take the war to the Chinese, and even to the Soviets if necessary, in order to win the war. But Truman intended to contain the war on the Korean peninsula and bring it to an honorable conclusion. The two clashed, and Truman fired MacArthur. To the Republican Right, MacArthur became a martyr, and they complained that Truman was appeasing the communists and that MacArthur should have been given free reign to crush the communists once and for all. When Eisenhower signed the armistice in April 1953, he seemed to be taking Truman's side on the issue. Conservatives in the Senate like William Jenner of Indiana and George Malone of Nevada insisted that the armistice was a victory for international communism and a defeat for the Free World. William Knowland of California even contended that the armistice would cause the United States to "lose the balance of Asia."[19]

Eisenhower and the Republican Right also developed differences over the United Nations and the administration's willingness to compromise U.S. foreign policy in order to coordinate with UN objectives. To the Republican Right, America's foreign policy should be unilateral—the United States should not predicate its foreign policy based on permission to act from the United Nations or any other international organization. This new isolationism had evolved from the old prewar "Fortress America" principle, an argument that was destroyed by the chief lesson of World War II that nonintervention can lead to a dangerous world order that is counter to American interests. During the war, Eisenhower had, of course, been the very personification of international cooperation in his planning for the D-Day invasion and the following march to Berlin. In the early-to-mid-1950s, Ike could only respond to his party's detractors on the Right by insisting that the United States simply could not "go it alone" in foreign affairs. The Republican Right, with Taft in the lead, prepared to mount a full-scale attack on Eisenhower's internationalism with a potential of causing a severe party split if the president refused to follow Taft's lead. But Taft fell ill with the cancer that would finally take his life, and without Taft's leadership the conservatives pulled back from the issue.

Eisenhower was also unwilling to push hard for a balanced budget. The GOP Right had considered a balanced budget as a top priority at least since Roosevelt began accumulating big deficits in the early 1930s. At the 1952 Republican convention, Taft and the GOP Right pushed into the platform a plank calling for reduced government spending and a lowering of taxes. But in April 1953, in a budget briefing, Ike admitted that he would not be able to balance his first budget. Taft was livid. He jumped up and pounded the table: "The primary thing we promised the American people was reduction of expenditures! With a [budget] like this, we'll never elect a Republican Congress in 1954!" Then he cut hard at Ike: "You're taking us down the same road Truman traveled!" Both Ike and Taft had notorious tempers, and the fragile Republican coalition might have ended there in a shouting match. "[T]he ludicrous part of the affair came," the president wrote in his diary that evening, "when several of my close friends around the table saw that my temper was getting a little out of hand. . . ." But the president remained calm and explained to Taft the need for certain expenditures, particularly military expenditures to maintain U.S. strength abroad. He then promised to balance the 1954 budget—presumably after the war in Korea was brought to an end. Taft calmed down, and again the split never came. But Eisenhower, continuing his diary entry, made it clear that the event had made him mad. "I think that everyone present was astonished at the demagogic nature of [Taft's] tirade, because not once did he mention the security of the United States. . . . He simply wanted expenditures reduced, regardless."[20]

These events in the spring of 1953 had taken Eisenhower to the edge. His party's right wing had opposed his administration by making it clear that they would fight for their agenda and oppose any plan he might have to move to the center. In another diary entry, made even before the clash with Taft, the president was so frustrated by the difficulties of working with his party's right wing that he even contemplated appealing to his party's moderates to form a new political party that would purge the Right. "Of course," he wrote of his problems with the Right, "if this kind of thing were often repeated, it would give some weight to an argument that . . . I should set quietly about the formation of a new party. The method would be to make a personal appeal to every member of the House and Senate; to every Governor, and to every National Committeeman whose general political philosophy and purpose seem to belong to that school known as 'The Middle Way.' It may come about that this will be forced upon us, but . . . if we can possibly bring about a better solidarity among Republicans, if we can get them more deeply committed to teamwork and party responsibility, this will be a much better way."[21]

Eisenhower and Taft never quite worked well together. But by the summer of 1953 both men had been to the brink of a divide and concluded that they needed to keep the party united. Taft expected to be the driving force behind the 82nd Congress, and he wanted that Congress to be a success in his hands. He could not succeed without the White House and the support of Republican moderates in Congress. So Taft worked to heal the wounds and bridge the breach. Eisenhower knew, of course, that without the support of his party's right wing that his initiatives and programs would have a difficult time on Capitol Hill. So, despite their animosity toward each other, the two titans of the Republican Party in the 1950s joined efforts and began working together. In order to be a part of the plan and maintain party harmony, Nixon abandoned his right wing roots and embraced the approach.

Eisenhower believed that the American people wanted him to be a consensus president, and in response he continued to run down the middle of the road on most issues. Often that meant working with Democrats, especially conservative Democrats in the Senate. Again, members of the Republican Right cringed at conspiring with the opposition. Eisenhower proposed, for instance, expanding Social Security, the very program that the Republican Right despised as the essence of creeping socialism. The plan would have added ten million workers to the Social Security rolls, but congressional right-wingers worked to defeat it in 1953. A year later, with the midterm elections on the horizon and the Democrats poised to make big gains in Congress, the bill passed over objections from the GOP Right.

In late July 1953 Robert Taft died of cancer. His death dealt the nation's conservatives a severe blow that damaged their cause for at least the remainder of the Eisenhower administration. Taft may not have been presidential material, but he had built extraordinary power. He was the Right's ideological center, and had been since before the war. He was powerful enough to demand the president's ear; and through Taft, conservatives could be sure that their side would at least be heard. Also, it was Taft who had maintained the close relationship with conservative Democrats. Taft's death cut conservative power on Capitol Hill almost immediately. With no real leadership, Eisenhower and the Republican moderates overran the Right. By 1956 Eisenhower loyalists controlled two-thirds of the Republican National Committee—a traditional bastion of the Right—and forty-one state chairmanships. The primary leaders of the Right, men like Everett Dirksen, Joseph Martin, and William Knowland had fallen in behind Eisenhower and were voting the moderate Republican line. The *National Review* complained bitterly that those who refused to support Eisenhower were being "consigned to outer darkness. . . . With such skill have [Eisenhower] and his associates conducted the movement [that] it has become quite clear what the Republican Party is not: It is not the Party of Senator Taft."[22]

Eisenhower's strength within his own party (and the decline of the Right) became most apparent in 1955 when the president announced he would attend the Geneva Conference for the purpose of pursuing a policy of "peaceful coexistence" with the Soviets. For the Right, this was heresy—the pursuit of an accommodating relationship with international communism. McCarthy introduced a bill to tie the president's hands at Geneva that would allow him to discuss only the liberation of Eastern Europe. The bill reached the floor of the Senate and only four Republicans voted for it. The vote left the GOP Right gasping for air. At no time since the 1920s had the Republicans been so united—united behind the president and not the party's right wing.

This shift in power was felt by Vice President Richard Nixon more than any other member of the Republican Party. Nixon had been tapped by Ike in 1952 to appease the Right. But by 1956 Nixon was keenly aware of the shift away from conservative dominance in the party to Eisenhower's moderation. He responded by reinventing himself in the Eisenhower mold and supporting the administration's initiatives through the first term. Nixon had political aspirations beyond the vice presidency, and with Ike at the peak of his popularity in the mid-1950s, Nixon surly realized that if he could position himself as the natural outgrowth of the Eisenhower administration—the successor to it—he could win the nomination easily in 1960 and have a very good chance of becoming president. So, through the 1950s, Nixon did all he could to shed his conservative trappings to be one of the Eisenhower loyalists.

In September 1955, about a year before the 1956 election, Eisenhower suffered a heart attack, and it appeared that American politics might change dramatically. Ike had made himself the great leader of the moderates—and the unifier of the party under that banner. Without Eisenhower, the power of the moderates would certainly diminish significantly, possibly leading to a party split. On the very day of Eisenhower's attack, a struggle developed between Eisenhower's closest allies, led by the president's chief of staff Sherman Adams and the party's Right that began to coalesce around Nixon. Several press stories reported that party moderates were doing all they could to keep Nixon out of the picture, while leaders on the Right were encouraging Nixon to exert power and lead—in anticipation of Ike's death.[23] Within days, Eisenhower, considering the possibility that he might not be able to run in 1956, suggested to James Hagerty that Dewey might be the right person to run on the Republican ticket. "He represents my way of thinking," Ike told Hagerty. But Hagerty realized what might happen to the party in such a case and argued that if Dewey ran for the nomination, the Right would revolt and possibly even name their own candidate and split the party. Ike relented. "I guess you're right." The discussion turned to Nixon, but both men agreed that Nixon was not up to the job.[24]

The GOP Right saw an opportunity in Eisenhower's heart attack. If Ike decided not to run in 1956 (and there was plenty of speculation even before his attack that he might not), then the conservatives hoped to be ready to place one of their own in to play.[25] The problem was that they really had no one. Since Taft's death, no one had really stepped forward to fill his sizeable shoes. California senator William (Big Bill) Knowland had taken the role as the leader of the Right, but Knowland was really no more presidential timber than Taft had been. Nevertheless, with Ike recuperating and making no announcements for his own political future, Knowland took a step forward and offered himself as the champion of the Right to make a run in 1956 if Ike demurred.

Knowland first made his intentions known in an article in the *National Review,* and it seems clear that the editors of that conservative magazine, particularly William F. Buckley, Jr., had convinced Knowland to make the run. In the *National Review*'s first issue (which came out in November 1955, just two months after Eisenhower's heart attack), Knowland berated the president for going to Geneva and seeking peaceful coexistence with the Soviets. Then on the floor of the Senate, he made continued references to the "Trojan Horse of Coexistence," and he often called for a blockade of China and an American withdrawal from the UN.[26]

Eisenhower considered not running in 1956. In fact, he told his friends and his brother, Milton, often that he would not run under any circumstances. Ike told Milton in 1953 that "if ever for a second time I should show any signs of yielding to persuasion, please call in a psychiatrist." Then, just a few days later he sent a note to his friend Swede Hazlett that concluded, "I shall never again be a candidate for anything."[27] But Eisenhower had been making statements like that since 1946. According to Sherman Adams, it was not at all difficult to convince Ike to make another run in 1956. Those closest to him simply convinced the president that if he left the arena and did not run, all he had worked for would be lost. In addition, it was quite possible that a candidate like Knowland might get the nomination, and Eisenhower could not abide what he considered the isolationists in the party like Knowland. As Adams recalled, "The Republicans were isolationist. Their leadership was isolationist. He looked at the people that ran the Congress after he was elected, and he saw a bunch of isolationists."[28] Eisenhower decided, again, that the nation needed him. All the jockeying for position ended in February when the president, looking thin but fit, appeared on television and made it clear that he wanted a second term.

With that question answered, another question immediately arose: Would Nixon be kept on the ticket? There were several people, a few very close to the president, who wanted Nixon out, particularly Harold Stassen, Christian Herter, and Arthur Goldsmith. But the vast majority of those who opposed Nixon kept their own counsel; Nixon, after all, was only a heartbeat away from the presidency and tremendous political power. Those who did oppose Nixon saw him as a conduit to the Right, really the last vestiges of the right wing that held any power in the party or the administration—despite Nixon's attempts to shift to the Eisenhower center. Of course, the decision was the president's, and he refused to decide. Ike's indecision on the point cut deeply at Nixon, who believed he had been a loyal soldier. Eisenhower continually insisted that Nixon might be better off somewhere else, at one point suggesting that Nixon take a cabinet post in the administration, even secretary of state or defense. In his diary, the president wrote of the situation: "[My] concern is where is Nixon going to be 4 years from now [in 1960]? What does 8 years in the job do for him? In the long run, he is thought of as the understudy to the star of the team, rather than being a halfback in his own right."[29] The situation must have been agonizing for Nixon. One problem was that he had nowhere else to go. In 1952, if he had been passed over for the job, he could have retained his seat in the Senate and probably have been no worse off for the effort. But in 1956 there were fewer choices: he could fight to stay in the administration or return to California and practice law. So Nixon stayed the course and did all he could to hang on to his job.

One reason that Eisenhower made the choice to run for a second term was that he felt he had no successor; or more exactly, as he wrote Swede Hazlett, "I had failed to bring forward and establish a logical successor for myself."[30] At the same time, Eisenhower liked Nixon. As Stephen Ambrose has pointed out, Ike appreciated a subordinate who had served him loyally and to the best of his ability. And Nixon had certainly done that. But Ike clearly understood that his health might keep him from completing his second term. And there is little question that the president did not feel that Nixon was presidential timber. So, with the president conflicted on the point, Nixon sat on a bubble. He had Ike's respect and admiration, but he did not have his support—a problem that would plague him through the 1960 campaign. One of Nixon's good friends told Earl Mazo (Nixon's 1960 campaign biographer) that Eisenhower's failure to endorse Nixon was "one of the greatest hurts of

[Nixon's] whole career. . . . But Nixon had a much shrewder judgment and reached the conclusion very early in the whole episode that either he had to go all the way and win . . . or get out and be finished."[31]

On March 13, Eisenhower wrote in his diary his likes and dislikes about his vice president. "I am happy to have him as an associate," he wrote, "and I am happy to have him in government." However, he added, "That still doesn't make him vice president. He has serious problems. . . . I am not going to say he is the only individual I would have for vice president. There is nothing to be gained politically by ditching him. He is going to be a 'comer' four years from now. I want a bevy of young fellows to be available [then]. Nixon can't always be the understudy to the star."[32]

Eisenhower probably would have liked to dump Nixon from the ticket, *and* he may well have thought Nixon would do better as a future candidate if he gained some experience at a cabinet post. He believed, and he was certainly being advised, that Nixon would hurt him in the South, and that if the president brought in a more moderate running mate he would pull votes from independents and Democrats and be the centrist president that he had wanted to be since 1952. Perhaps most importantly, however, Eisenhower clearly did not think that Nixon had the ability to be president in 1956, and considering the president's health that was, most likely, how Eisenhower was viewing the situation. He was also slowly coming to the conclusion that he had chosen Nixon in 1952 and he was stuck with him in 1956.[33]

Through most of the spring, Eisenhower responded to the constant questioning by the press on the issue. "I am very happy that Richard Nixon is my friend," he said in a press conference in late March. "I am very happy to have him as an associate in government. I would be happy to be on any political ticket in which I was a candidate with him. Now, if those words aren't plain, then it is merely because people can't understand the plain unvarnished truth. I have nothing further to add."[34] That may have seemed pretty "plain," but it was not an official announcement. Finally, on April 26, Nixon took events into his own hands and called on the president at the Oval Office and announced that he would be "honored to continue as vice president under you." Nixon added that he had waited so long because he did not want to appear to be forcing himself onto the ticket. Eisenhower responded that he wondered why Nixon had taken so long to say so. The decision was announced that day. The press treated the announcement as a matter of political course and never bought Nixon's insistence that he had considered the ticket above his own interests, and that he had actually considered not running.[35]

⌒

The two divisive wings of the Republican Party pulled together in the spirit of unity for an instant at the 1956 Republican National Convention, staged at the Cow Palace in San Francisco. The Right demanded its place in the sun with several speeches honoring "the spirit of Bob Taft." The general mood of the convention was that the president would beat the Democrats again in a landslide, and that his coattails would be generous. There were many in the party who continued to oppose Ike's moderation, but they had to realize that (at least for many of them) he kept them in office. Near the end of the convention, California governor Goodwin Knight announced that the Republicans would leave the Cow Palace "marching arm in arm."[36] As the campaign got underway, Republicans of all types rode the Eisenhower bandwagon to victory. *Life* magazine thought it recognized a "New Republican Harmony."[37] But the party had serious problems.

Eisenhower did win big in November. He carried 57.3 percent of the popular vote and took 457 electoral votes from forty-one states. The Democratic candidate, Adlai Stevenson, carried only seven states in the South. But the president's coattails were not quite as long as the party had hoped. In a major setback, the GOP lost control of Congress again. It was an agonizing thought to most Republicans, but again the message from the voters was all too clear: They liked Ike, but they did not necessarily like the Republicans. It was, in fact, the first time since 1848 that voters presented a newly elected president with a Congress in which his party controlled neither house. And in that 1848 election, a popular general, Zachary Taylor, headed a political party, the Whigs, that was essentially in its death throes.

Congress changed little as a result of the 1956 election. The Democrats picked up one Senate seat, giving them a slight edge of forty-nine to forty-seven. In the House, they picked up two seats, holding their substantial majority of 232 to 199. What was remarkable, however, was that the Democrats made any gains at all given the magnitude of Eisenhower's victory. The president was clearly basking in the rays of a successful presidency, while congressional Republicans were still answering for the excesses of McCarthyism.

On election night, Eisenhower made his acceptance speech and then headed off for an extended vacation. But in his speech he left something for the GOP Right to ponder. "America," he said, "has approved Modern Republicanism."[38] This was Eisenhower ascendant. To him, the Election-Day mandate was clear, and he was now powerful enough to push the troublesome (and quickly weakening) right wing aside and move forward with his own agenda.

Eisenhower's 1956 victory left the Republican Right weak and almost helpless. And they still lacked significant leadership. Big Bill Knowland could not fill Taft's shoes, and he lacked popular appeal. In addition, the president disliked him—a fact well known on Capitol Hill. "It is a pity," the president wrote of Knowland in his diary, "that his wisdom, his judgment, his tact, and his sense of humor lag so far behind his ambition. . . ."[39] Knowland had other problems. There were rumors that his wife hated Washington so much that she threatened to return to California and file for divorce if Big Bill insisted on running for the Senate again in 1958. Apparently to save his marriage, Knowland resigned his Senate seat and jumped into the California governor's race. To most conservatives this actually made good political sense. He would run for president in 1960 from the California governor's chair rather than as a Washington insider from the Senate—which would appeal to conservatives who distrusted the power of the federal government. Goodwin Knight, the sitting California governor, even accommodated the strategy by stepping aside and agreeing to run for Knowland's Senate seat. Both men lost—and Knowland's wife divorced him anyway.[40]

The 1958 midterm election was a disaster for the Republicans. It exposed the party as divided and in disarray. It also seemed to reveal that the nation was on a leftward swing leading up to the 1960 campaign. The party suffered a net loss in the House of forty-eight seats and thirteen in the Senate. It was, in fact, the biggest Democratic gain since Roosevelt's 1936 landslide. The GOP also lost thirteen of twenty-one gubernatorial contests and nearly seven hundred seats in state senates and lower houses.[41] The nation's political mood seemed to be shifting.

Not only did the Republicans lose nationwide, but the GOP Right took the biggest hit. Party conservatives like John Bricker, Knowland, William Jenner, Joseph Martin, McCarthy, and Nevada's George W. "Molly" Malone were all put out. Of the Republicans who survived the bloodletting, most were moderates—Eisenhower Modern Republicans. To Brent Bozell at the *National Review*, the election was a disaster. "Let us conservatives not look for a silver lining," he wrote. "There is none."[42] In fact, there was a significant silver lining. Between 1932 and 1952 the Republicans were a minority party, often sitting so far outside the realms of power in Washington that many thought the nation was on its way to a one-party system. Eisenhower changed all that. As a result of Ike's successes (that included building a strong base in several new demographic areas including the rising suburban vote and the white South) the Republican Party could now claim parity with the Democrats. Much of that, of course, was based on Eisenhower's own popularity. The Republicans had also, finally, shaken the twenty-year-old accusation that they were the party of depression, that they had brought on the Great Depression through their own laissez-faire economic policies. The question, then, for Republicans was: Could they move forward and capitalize on the Eisenhower mystique? Could they take the party into the next decade and maintain it as a majority party? Or would the Republicans again slip back into its old position as the loyal opposition?

The Eisenhower presidency set the stage for the coming modern Republican Party. The age-old Right-Moderate split grew increasingly wider and more antagonistic during the Eisenhower years. After decades on the sidelines, the leaders on the GOP Right demanded a leadership role in the party and, finally, a presidential candidate of their own. It may not have been apparent yet, but the nation was on its way to becoming increasingly conservative. The nation's suburbs were growing rapidly, and by the late 1960s it would be apparent that suburban America had become the focus of a new conservatism. The American South, always conservative, would soon complete its slow relocation into the Republican Party. Although it would not be visible for some time, the new Republican Right, with its true origins in the Eisenhower fifties, would soon become powerful enough to divest itself of the Moderates and build a new conservative coalition that would take back the party and then finally the federal government.

As the Eisenhower era came to a close, the Republicans looked to its future—and saw only Richard Nixon. Could he rally the faithful and unite the party? Would his rebirth as an Eisenhower moderate satisfy the Right and the South while keeping the party base in line? Could he lead? Could he govern? After eight years in Ike's shadow, Richard Nixon was still an enigma, an unknown commodity to most Republicans and to most of the nation. But the nomination was his, and the GOP would have to find accommodations.

CHAPTER TWO

~

The Democrats Endure
the Eisenhower Years

To anyone with the slightest eye toward politics or history, 1948 was going to be the year of the Republicans. The Depression was over; the war had ended; Roosevelt was dead, and the era of the New Deal had, it seemed, run its course. A tidal wave of conservatism was expected to rush over Washington. Everyone knew it, and everyone began to prepare for the changing of the guard.

Everyone at least except President Harry Truman—and there is some evidence that even he was not so certain. In the 1948 campaign, the ever-feisty Truman cobbled together a tenuous coalition that had its roots in the Roosevelt coalition of 1936. It included traditional liberals, organized labor, and northern African-Americans, and it gave Truman one of the greatest political upsets in American history; and it was a solid victory. Although the popular vote was close, Truman won big in the Electoral College with a substantial margin of 303 to 189. The Democrats also regained control of Congress. The Democratic victory left the Republicans in disarray, pointing fingers and divided.

It was quickly apparent, however, that the Democratic Party victory was the result of little more than a talented campaigner and politician pulling together the party's disparate parts—for one moment in time—to defeat the Republicans. The Democrats were at least as badly divided as the Republicans, and when the election dust settled, the Democrats' old wounds began to fester again. One of the most divisive issues was race and civil rights for African-Americans—a battle that the Democrats had been fighting since

Reconstruction. As the 1948 campaign approached, Truman and his advisors had concluded that black voters in the northern urban areas were far more important than white voters in the South. Black voters in Chicago, Cleveland, and Los Angeles, for instance, might be instrumental in delivering the electoral votes of Illinois, Ohio, and California. Those three states alone would deliver seventy-eight electoral votes, nearly twenty more than the entire Deep South combined. The strategy was a good one and it helped Truman pull his 1948 upset, but it divided the party by alienating the white South.

Roosevelt had been a master at walking the fence between white southerners (who wanted to maintain segregation) and black leaders (who wanted civil rights). During the 1948 campaign, Truman attempted to follow FDR's lead by trying to keep both groups satisfied and inside the party loop. But that strategy had become nearly impossible by 1948. The issue of civil rights for African-Americans had simply become too volatile; neither side was willing to compromise on the issue. African-Americans had grown tired of waiting for the fulfillment of promises, and white southerners had begun to see any concession to civil rights as a slippery slope to racial equality. In addition, Truman lacked Roosevelt's charm—his amazing ability to satisfy opposing groups and to keep the party together. By the summer of 1948, Truman's strategy had done little more than alienate both sides. His modest civil rights concessions did not satisfy African-Americans, and any movement toward civil rights immediately angered southern whites. At the Democratic National Convention in Philadelphia, party liberals (led by Minneapolis mayor Hubert Humphrey) pushed a strong civil rights plank into the party platform, and most of the Alabama and the entire Mississippi delegations bolted the convention. We have been "instructed," an Alabama delegate bellowed from the convention floor, "never to cast [our] vote for any candidate with a civil rights program such as adopted by this convention. We bid you goodbye!"[1] The result was the formation of the States' Rights Democrats, better known as the "Dixiecrats." It appeared that the Democrats had split in the face of a strong Republican surge. Victory in November would be next to impossible.

The Dixiecrats nominated South Carolina governor Strom Thurmond as their presidential candidate. But despite all their bluster, they had little impact on the election. In fact, they aided in Truman's victory by energizing the black vote throughout the nation for Truman who was able to cast himself as the civil rights candidate standing in opposition to the racist Dixiecrat ticket.

One result of this was that the powerful southern leaders in Congress concluded that Truman had neglected their needs during the campaign and at the convention, and they turned against the president. Since at least the late 1930s, a loose coalition had existed between the minority Republican Party and conservative southern Democrats. That coalition had often been brought together to aid the South in defeating civil rights measures and, in turn, aiding the Republicans on various antilabor bills and other probusiness initiatives before Congress. But following the 1948 election, the loose coalition turned into a southern rebellion against the administration. Southern Democrats often ignored the administration's initiatives and voted with the Republicans to kill Truman's Fair Deal programs. Despite a Democratic majority in Congress, the administration could not move its agenda. By 1952 the party was in disarray and about to face a formidable Republican Party ticket of Eisenhower and Nixon. A changing of the guard was about to take place in Washington—a change that most pundits had predicted four years earlier.

Truman had no intention of running in 1952. His wife, Bess, wanted to return to their Missouri home; there was a scandal brewing in his administration, and the war in Korea was beginning to generate public discontent. So Truman pushed back from running again and settled on naming an heir, someone who would succeed him in office and continue his policies and legacy. He first approached his friend Chief Justice of the Supreme Court Fred Vinson. But Vinson refused the offer and immediately turned the tables by trying to convince Truman to make another run. Truman then turned to Illinois governor Adlai Stevenson. Stevenson had won an overwhelming victory in the 1948 Illinois gubernatorial race and immediately became one of the up-and-coming stars in the Democratic Party. In January, Truman invited Stevenson to the president's temporary residence at Blair House and suggested he consider becoming a candidate. Stevenson insisted he was not interested.[2]

With no one willing to accept his offer, Truman began to reconsider his decision and took another look at making a run himself, but advisors such as Clark Clifford and Charles Murphy contended that the tide the president had so skillfully pushed back in 1948 would swamp him in 1952. Finally in late March, Truman announced that he would not run.[3] He still had no heir apparent.

Through 1952, Stevenson continued to turn down all offers to run for the Democratic nomination. Even on the very day the Republicans nominated Eisenhower and Nixon, he announced that he was not a candidate for the presidency. But his protests were never heeded. On July 21, at the Democratic Convention, the Democrats drafted Stevenson on the third ballot.[4] It was supposedly a "genuine draft," a demand that Stevenson pick up the gauntlet, unite the party, and engage the Republicans. It was not quite that; Stevenson had been campaigning for at least a year while, at the same time, insisting that he would not run. Nevertheless, the Democrats had their man.

Stevenson was billed as an intellectual and a liberal; he was really neither. He often called himself a moderate. The *New York Times* tried to describe him as "slightly to the right—enough to the right to satisfy the center, but not far enough mortally to offend the left or to please the right. . . ." His intellectual persona came mostly from his education (Choate and then Princeton and Northwestern Law) and an effective speaking style that exhibited an uncanny use of the language and a well-developed dry wit. From all this, the American press donned Stevenson the "egghead."[5]

As a candidate, Stevenson opposed public housing, federal aid to education, federally funded medical care, and he even refused to support the repeal of Taft-Hartley, the Republican-sponsored law that the nation's labor leaders called the "slave labor" bill. He was weak on civil rights and even forced his party in 1952 to resend the 1948 civil rights plank in favor of a more moderate plank that would satisfy the southern delegations at the convention. All this alienated liberals in the party, but those same liberals seemed to think that with the proper advice and advisors, Stevenson would prove to be liberal enough if he won the election.

But he did not. Eisenhower's infectious personality, along with the nation's growing fear of communism (and the Republicans' more aggressive efforts at stopping its growth), and the nagging anxiety over the war in Korea pushed Eisenhower to an impressive victory in 1952 that brought in a Republican Congress and even cracked the South. For the first time since 1930, the Republicans held both houses of Congress and the White House.

The 1952 election revealed a shift in the Democratic Party. Eisenhower campaigned in the South and took seven traditionally Democratic states there: Texas, Tennessee, Virginia, Maryland, Oklahoma, Missouri, and Florida. At least on the federal election level, white southerners were beginning to make a slow transition into the Republican Party and away from their traditional home in the Democratic Solid South. On the other side of the coin, African-Americans had begun to abandon the party of Lincoln and move into the Democratic Party in big numbers. Much of this had to do with the New Deal and its positive impact on black Americans, the Great Migration to northern urban areas where labor unions influenced black workers, and even Eleanor Roosevelt's sympathy for African-Americans. In 1948, Truman seemed to capitalize on all this with mostly minor overtures to civil rights that produced the result of strong African-American support, stronger by far than any Democrat in American history. But in 1952 Stevenson turned his back on most of Truman's civil rights initiatives; he even chose a southerner, John Sparkman of Alabama, as his running mate. Nevertheless, a full 73 percent of African-Americans voted for Stevenson.[6] The Democratic Party had become the party of civil rights, and the white South was becoming more and more comfortable with the conservatives in the Republican Party.

At the same time, President Eisenhower did not ignore civil rights. He desegregated Washington, DC, and he supported legislation to end lynchings and the poll tax in the South. But he always made it clear that he did not believe in the power of the federal government to solve race problems; and when the *Brown* decision was handed down in 1954 he commented immediately, "I don't believe you can change the hearts of men with laws or decisions."[7] For white southerners who wanted to maintain the white-dominated way of life in the South, Eisenhower sounded like a states' righter, and for a growing number of white southerners, that was enough.

The loss of the South—or at least part of it—frightened Democratic Party leaders and following the 1952 defeat, they set out to mend fences. The party platform in 1956, in its only reference to civil rights, rejected "all proposals for the use of force to interfere with the orderly determination of these matters by the courts." Stevenson, again the party candidate, danced around most civil rights issues, and when southern governors and congressional leaders issued a "Southern Manifesto" in opposition to the *Brown* decision, Stevenson said, "[T]he 'Declaration of Constitutional Principles' [the "Southern Manifesto"] includes distinguished, responsible leaders of a great region of our country [and] it is a reflection of the gravity of the racial tensions that have arisen in the South."[8] With the Democrats backing away from civil rights, Eisenhower had little need to engage the issue and through both of his terms he continued to assure southern leaders that he had no intention of forcing desegregation on the South. Even at Little Rock in the fall of 1957, when Eisenhower sent in federal troops to end the disturbances there, he followed up in a number of statements that he was only fulfilling his constitutional obligations as president of the United States to keep the peace, and that his actions in Little Rock were in no way intended as support by his administration for desegregation of southern schools.[9]

～

By 1954 Lyndon Johnson had emerged as the leading light of the Democratic Party. As Majority Leader in the Senate, he had pushed through legislation with an amazing ability of persuasion, compromise, and political maneuvering. One of Johnson's several biographers, Robert Dallek, describes his qualities: "Johnson's mastery of the Senate came not only from knowledge of other senators but also a skillful use of Senate rules. Unanimous consent agreements, aborted quorum calls, night sessions, and periods of inaction alternating with bursts of frenetic activity were Johnson's principal weapons in driving bills through. . . . And the outcome was a Senate following Lyndon's lead. On bill after bill, resolution after resolution, Lyndon dominated the 84th Congress."[10] Johnson had also pulled the party together from the disarray that followed the 1952 defeat. "[A]t that moment," George Reedy, one of Johnson's chief advisors, recalled in an interview later in his life, "there was a great conflict in the party between the northern liberals and the southern conservatives. By 1955, LBJ had pulled the party together and there was no question that he could run the Senate."[11] One of Johnson's tactics was what is famously known as "the treatment," the manner in which Johnson persuaded an opponent that he should come to his side on a particular issue. There are a number of well-known descriptions of this "treatment." George Reedy's recollection is that it was "an incredibly potent blend of badgering, cajolery, promises of favors, implied threats" leaving the victim "absolutely helpless. . . . [I]t was just all of a sudden this stream would come out, it would be like standing under Niagara Falls. . . . It was just unbelievably potent. Sometimes I think he did it just for practice."[12]

Much of Johnson's effort in the Senate revolved around trying to drive a wedge between the Eisenhower moderates and the GOP conservatives. But that strategy often translated into a willingness to compromise and work with the president and Republican moderates to get legislation passed—often at the expense of the conservatives in the GOP. For example, when Democrats asked for a federal housing bill that would provide for 135,000 units to be built, Johnson worked with Republican moderates for a bill authorizing 70,000 units. To Johnson and his supporters in the Senate, this was "half a loaf," and half a loaf, he argued often, was always better than none. At the same time, the compromise isolated the GOP conservatives who opposed both aspects of the bill. Liberals, on the other hand, saw this type of wheeling and dealing as sleeping with the enemy, and Johnson's tactics began to drive a wedge between the moderates and liberals in his own party. "There was a certain point," Reedy recalled, "at which Johnson's tactic of supporting Eisenhower against the Republicans was becoming damn embarrassing. . . ." As the 1956 election approached, Reedy continued, it became necessary for both Eisenhower and Johnson to put on "a display of antagonism at that certain point," to satisfy the Democratic Left and the Republican Right that their party leadership was confronting the other side with sufficient strength.[13]

As a result of Johnson's successes as Senate leader, his name began to be bandied about as a possible presidential candidate for the upcoming 1956 campaign. But in the summer of 1955, a serious heart attack ended much of the talk. Oddly enough, within months, in September, Eisenhower would also suffer a heart attack. Most likely, much of the nation counted both men out, but they recovered quickly and reentered the fray.[14]

Johnson began to position himself to run, but he continued to insist that he was not a candidate beyond running as a favorite son from his home state of Texas.[15] His plan was that the convention would be wide open (with no obvious winner), and that he could turn his favorite son status into a nomination. His biggest supporters were the big names in Washington, senators or former senators from all over the nation, often personal friends who owed him favors. The most important names among these supporters were the true lions of Congress, Speaker of the House Sam Rayburn from Texas and Georgia Senator Richard Russell. But convention nominations are almost always in the hands of local politicians, governors, party bosses, and municipal leaders, not senators. Johnson refused to enter any primaries, and he did not campaign. He believed that his accomplishments as Majority Leader in an open convention would catapult him to the top of the heap as the best candidate, and he would win the nomination, possibly as a compromise candidate.

Johnson may also have been reticent about openly campaigning because, through his entire life, he harbored a terrible fear of personal failure. He reacted much the same as the 1960 campaign approached, and even as president of the United States after November 1963, he was constantly afraid that he would fail. Here was a man who excelled at the machinations of politics-but who refused to bring his political power to bear in a presidential bid. As George Reedy later recalled, Johnson's noncampaign did not bring him support: "[N]obody took his campaign seriously as a campaign for the presidency. . . . There were no serious efforts [to nominate Johnson] and certainly nothing sparked by him." Reedy also recalled, "I think that that psychological complex . . . that inferiority complex did inhibit any serious drive on [Johnson's] part for the presidency."[16]

~

At nearly the moment Eisenhower suffered his heart attack in September 1955 (followed by the widespread speculation that he would not run for a second term), John Kennedy determined that his political prospects had brightened. In October, Kennedy's father, Joseph Kennedy, contacted Johnson and suggested that the Kennedy family finance Johnson's candidacy. It was apparently the senior Kennedy's plan to facilitate the nomination for

Johnson who would then choose Jack as his running mate. After eight years as vice president, at age forty-seven, Jack could then run for the White House in 1964 from a very advantageous position. But Johnson declined the offer, insisting that he had no intention of running, realizing fully that the offer was little more than a plan to further Jack's presidential ambitions. Robert Kennedy, John's younger brother, considered Johnson's refusal to be an affront to the Kennedy family's generosity, and this incident may possibly have been the origins of the Bobby-Lyndon feud that continued unabated until Bobby's death in 1968.[17]

As the 1956 campaign approached, Stevenson abandoned his 1952 strategy of waiting for a party draft. In fact, he might have realized that one reason his 1952 campaign failed so miserably was that he did not organize his campaign until after the convention. Through the summer of 1955, Stevenson held a series of campaign organizational meetings at his farm near Springfield, Illinois. Among the ideas to come from these meetings was that the Eisenhower administration was vulnerable on foreign affairs because of cutbacks in military spending that had "gravely weakened our military forces and particularly our air power."[18] This group also tried to determine why the nation was so clearly Democratic (they controlled both houses of Congress) yet so enamored with Eisenhower. They concluded what might well have been so. The president was a man of such evident goodwill and trust that the people of the nation were relieved of the necessity of following day-to-day political developments. They described this as "apathy," finally determining that "The popularity of Eisenhower is thus one side of the coin; the flight from politics is the other." Then in the final analysis, the strategists concluded the obvious. "There can be no question, in short, that the country likes both the Democratic Party and Eisenhower."

Stevenson and his advisors also concluded that part of their problem was Johnson and his collaborative strategies. They determined, in a series of memos most of which were written by Arthur Schlesinger, that Johnson's backroom dealings had taken the political process out of the line of sight of the people, which, they argued, simply "promoted and fortified the political apathy which is Eisenhower's main strength." They then called for a "vigorous and unrelenting opposition [to the Republican agenda] in the next session."[19]

But any possibility of a victory over Eisenhower was a long shot at best, and that kept several candidates out of the field and packing their war chests for 1960. But all that changed when Eisenhower had his heart attack in September 1955. Almost immediately, New York governor Averell Harriman announced that he would make a run, and there were rumors that Tennessee senator Estes Kefauver might also be preparing to enter the race. When

Stevenson announced in November, he also announced that he would run in five primaries: Illinois, Minnesota, Pennsylvania, Florida, and California.[20] Stevenson had always resisted primary runs; he simply did not have the demeanor to slog through a primary campaign. But if he wanted the nomination, he would have to show his party regulars that he was a man of the people, and that he could pull voters to the polls.

Stevenson's announcement immediately brought a challenge from Kefauver to engage the campaign in Minnesota. That state allowed crossover voting, and a strong Republican stop-Stevenson vote resulted in an embarrassing defeat for Stevenson and rewarded Kefauver with the state's thirty delegates to the convention.[21] Stevenson responded with a strong campaign that brought him victories in the District of Columbia, New Jersey, Illinois, Oregon, and Florida. In Florida, Stevenson and Kefauver squared off for a debate, the first ever on both national radio and television. In California, Stevenson scored a knockout punch with a two-to-one victory over Kefauver and, in July, Kefauver dropped out, throwing his support to Stevenson. Only Harriman and Johnson remained. Harriman was working to collect delegates in nonprimary states, and Johnson was still running his noncampaign and refusing to commit beyond his favorite son candidacy in Texas. As the convention in Chicago approached, Johnson announced that he would run, and Truman jumped in and endorsed Harriman, insisting that Stevenson was not experienced enough to be president.[22]

By the time the convention convened, however, Stevenson had the nomination sewn up. Johnson tried to salvage his situation by handing his Texas delegates over to Stevenson in exchange for southern concessions on civil rights, but Stevenson refused. He was nominated on the first ballot before the roll call reached Pennsylvania.

The first order of business for the Democrats was to keep the South in line—mostly by giving southern leaders what they wanted on civil rights. Everyone knew, particularly Stevenson, that the party could not afford to lose the South, to let it dribble into the Republican Party as it had done in 1952. Just before the convention, John Sparkman, Alabama senator and 1952 vice presidential candidate, called a meeting of southern delegates "to work out our problems within the party rather than to walk out or to bolt," as he explained the situation to a colleague. Among those delegates was a young Eugene "Bull" Conner from Birmingham, who, some nine years later, would defend that city against Martin Luther King's marches; and a young George Wallace, then a judge from Clayton, Alabama.[23] As the party began to devise its platform, even the party's most liberal figures and civil rights advocates seemed to be willing to trade civil rights advances for southern votes.

Hubert Humphrey, who built a reputation as a strong supporter of civil rights and for pressing the party to accept the mantle of civil rights for African-Americans, insisted that the 1956 platform be "acceptable to the South." Even Eleanor Roosevelt called for reconciliation: "I think understanding and sympathy for the white people of the South," she said, "is as important as understanding and sympathy for the colored people."[24] The result was a weak civil rights plank and a generally satisfied South.

As for any nominating convention, the next big question was who would be the candidate's running mate? Stevenson had been planning for some time to open that decision to the delegates and let them chose by acclamation. His intention, most likely, was to show that the Democrats were more open in their choices than the Republicans who were about to nominate Nixon again even though many in the Republican Party did not want him. For most party members, Stevenson's plan was a ridiculous move. Johnson and Rayburn saw it as a blatant lack of professionalism when the candidate (by carefully choosing a running mate) could do a great deal toward uniting the party. As Reedy recalled, "nobody wants a fight over the vice presidency."[25] The numbers quickly narrowed to Kefauver and John Kennedy.

Joseph Kennedy had pushed his son hard to withdraw from the contest, insisting that a Stevenson-Kennedy ticket was a loser and ultimately a detriment to Jack's political future. But the young Kennedy pressed on against his father's wishes.[26] His staff people had distributed a memo early in the campaign that argued that Kennedy's religion would actually aid the 1956 ticket rather than hurt it, mostly because Catholics were beginning to trickle out of the Democratic Party at least in part because the Republicans were seen as standing stronger against communism. Kennedy, the memo argued, would bring Catholics back into the fold. But Stevenson was never convinced that a Catholic on the ticket would be anything but a detriment, and he continued to believe (as he had believed in 1952) that he needed a southerner on the ticket—or at least someone from a border state. Several New England governors continued to push Kennedy, but party bigwigs like Sam Rayburn (who had never liked Kennedy, calling him a "little piss-ant") continued to counsel Stevenson to look for someone else. Stevenson finally decided to ask Kennedy to nominate him at the convention, but he probably never seriously considered him for his running mate. At the same time, Stevenson had never cared much for Kefauver.[27]

The voting on the floor, mostly between Kennedy and Kefauver, went back and forth for most of an afternoon. Kennedy was hurt by his religion and an open lack of support from Eleanor Roosevelt. He had also failed to support a Democratic Party-sponsored bill to raise farm price supports and that hurt him with delegates from the farm states. In the final analysis, it was assumed that Kennedy would hurt the ticket in the farm states and rural areas where Kefauver was the strongest. Kefauver won. He was the candidate who Stevenson probably disliked more than any other in the running. Stevenson was still annoyed at Kefauver's challenges in the primaries; and he was, as both Rayburn and Johnson put it, "the most hated man in the Senate."[28] Kennedy then went before the convention to ask the delegates for a unanimous vote of support for Kefauver. The events at the 1956 convention raised Kennedy's stock in the party a great deal. He went to the convention generally an unknown commodity in his own party; he left a familiar figure, the representation of the party's future.

Arthur Schlesinger, Jr., wrote in A Thousand Days that Kennedy always believed that had he won the nomination for vice president in 1956 and then gone down to ignominious defeat with Stevenson, that he would never have been elected in 1960. At the same time, according to Schlesinger who was close to both men, Stevenson always believed that by asking Kennedy to nominate him, he had given the thirty-nine-year-old first-term senator an opportunity to impress the convention and the nation, and that Kennedy should be appreciative. "Up to that time," Schlesinger wrote, "the two men, without knowing each other well . . . had had the friendliest feelings for each other. Now their relationship began to take on a slight tinge of mutual exasperation." The event was also the beginning of Kennedy's personal characterization of Stevenson as indecisive and wishy-washy on issues.[29]

Kennedy immediately began campaigning for the Stevenson-Kefauver ticket, but he seemed at least as much interested in gaining national recognition for himself as campaigning for the candidates. He also began building a strategy for 1960. Robert Kennedy probably got more out of the 1956 Stevenson campaign than Jack. He traveled the nation with Stevenson at the candidate's request, learning mostly how not to run a campaign. He complained that Stevenson did everything wrong, from reading speeches when he should have spoken extemporaneously, to wasting time on the tiny details of the campaign that he should have delegated to subordinates. To Robert, the Stevenson campaign was "the most disastrous operation" he had ever seen.[30] The learning experience in the Stevenson campaign would serve Jack's 1960 campaign well.

By the time the convention convened in the summer of 1956, Jack had already published Profiles in Courage about independence demonstrated by the careers of eight U.S. senators, most of whom had jeopardized their political careers by taking unpopular political stands. It was not, however, until the spring of 1957 that the book was awarded a Pulitzer Prize and reached national popularity. It was good timing. The book was seen almost universally as a call to a greater national commitment, particularly among the nation's public servants. The book and the prize also allowed Kennedy to carry the mantles of statesman and liberal intellectual, despite his young age. There were rumors that he had not written the book, that the Pulitzer was awarded as a result of backroom deals, and that false numbers had been used to keep the book on bestseller lists. Much of that was true. But *Profiles in Courage* seemed to place Kennedy somehow above the other politicians as a man who understood that it was courageous to make the right decision even when it was unpopular and politically unwise.

In early August, just before the convention, Stevenson and his advisors began to map out a national strategy for the general campaign against Eisenhower. Placed in the "safely Democratic" category were every southern state except Texas, Florida, Maryland, and Kentucky. Rhode Island and West Virginia were also added to that category as safe. They classified six states as "safely Republican" and six others as "leaning Republican." Nine states were written off as not worth the effort because their electoral votes were too small, such as North Dakota and Delaware. Everything else was categorized as "battleground states." Those included the big winners in the game: California, New York, Ohio, Pennsylvania, and Texas.[31] It did not take a lot to see from Stevenson's own numbers that he did not stand a chance.

Part of Stevenson's strategy was to portray himself as vigorous and strong in contrast to the ailing and aging president, but it was, in fact, Stevenson who was physically and mentally worn out from the primary fights with Kefauver. During the campaign, he traveled over fifty thousand miles by train, dragging himself from whistle stop to whistle stop, driving himself to the edge of exhaustion. His only real issue was Ike's health (and the concern that Nixon would inherit the office), but attacks on the president's age and health seemed cheap. On Election Day, Eisenhower won by a landslide that was even larger than his 1952 win. At 57.6 percent for Eisenhower-Nixon to 42.1 percent for Stevenson-Kefauver, it was, in fact, the largest popular vote margin in American history. Stevenson took only seven states, all in the South, and seventy-three electoral votes. The only bright spot for the Democrats was that they retained both houses of Congress, making it clear again that the nation was voting for the man and not the party. It may have been that America liked Ike but not the Republicans, but that also meant that they liked the Democrats but not Stevenson.

In May 1956 a series of polls showed that the demographic of the voting population was beginning to change. It revealed that labor union members were starting to slide into the Republican column: 54 percent favored Eisenhower in the coming election. Farmers were making a similar shift. In 1948, 25 percent of the nation's farmers had voted for Truman, 12 percent for Dewey, and 59 percent did not vote. Four years later, 42 percent of farmers said they would vote for Eisenhower, 25 percent would vote for Stevenson, with 32 percent not making the effort. Of groups described as low income, 28 percent voted for Truman in 1948, 16 percent voted for Dewey, with 54 percent not voting. In 1952, 30 percent said they would vote for Eisenhower, 23 percent would vote for Stevenson, while 47 percent would not vote. The polls also showed that Catholics were slowly moving into the Republican ranks, in part because of the communist issue, in part because they were becoming wealthier, or as the data described it, they were becoming "lacecurtainized." In 1948, 25 percent of Catholics voted for Dewey. In 1952 that number jumped to 41 percent for Eisenhower. The poll analysis showed that Democrats were losing ground with several other groups, particularly young people and women. And possibly for the first time, poll numbers picked up the political significance of suburban voters. Between 1947 and 1953, nine million Americans moved to the suburbs. By 1956 it had become clear that suburbanites became Republicans as part of the suburbanization process; and in some areas such as Chicago, the Republican suburban population was beginning to cancel out the urban Democrats.

Pollster Lou Harris began calling Eisenhower the "white collar Roosevelt," and in 1954 he published *Is There a Republican Majority?* His answer was yes. Two years later, political scientist Samuel Lubell published *Revolt of the Moderates* in which he tracked the growth of the nation's middle roaders as they came to dominate the Republican Party.[32] It was all bad news for the Democrats. Eisenhower was building a majority party that was quickly pulling voters away from traditionally Democratic sectors of the electorate. When the 1956 numbers were analyzed, it was clear that there had been a whole series of political shifts, and it all amounted to a bleak future for the Democrats. In fact, it seemed similar in many ways to the political shifts that occurred in the Democrats' favor some twenty years earlier that culminated in the Roosevelt coalition of 1936—an election that revealed several major shifts in national voting patterns.

America was changing, and the changes would have a major impact on the 1960 campaign. The Republicans were rapidly reaching parity with the Democrats for the first time since the late 1920s, and the increase in conservative strength would continue through the next several decades. The 1960s may have been tinged with American liberalism, but the numbers showed that conservatives were catching up in the numbers and poised to overtake the Democrats, who continued to rest on many of their New Deal laurels.

Stevenson took the 1956 defeat hard—particularly its severity. Almost immediately, and then over and over through the next two years, he continued to insist that he had had enough of politics and would never again be a candidate for the presidency. Almost exactly one month after the election, he issued a statement through the Democratic National Committee: "I will not run again for the Presidency." Then in *Time* magazine he was about as unequivocal as possible: "I am not a candidate; I will not be a candidate, and I don't want the nomination." He was quoted in the *Washington Post* just six weeks after the 1956 campaign: "I am not and will not be a candidate."[33] But Stevenson continued to maintain visibility, continued to keep in touch with the party leadership, and continued to speak out on issues. As the Democrats began to look at possible standard-bearers for 1960, Stevenson's name remained in the mix.

Although Stevenson refused to close the door completely, the 1960 Democratic nomination seemed fairly open. Among the several stalkers was Johnson, who again refused to campaign openly, but who again wanted the nomination. He had received some valuable advice from one of the Democratic Party's strategic gurus, James Rowe. Rowe had gained political notoriety by cobbling together a memo in 1946 that explained what Truman had to do to win in 1948. Truman followed the plan and won. Here, as Johnson began thinking of 1960, he listened to what Rowe had to say. "There is danger," Rowe wrote, "that [you] will become . . . a regional candidate, a Southern candidate. . . . If this happens, it will make it almost impossible for [you] to be a candidate in 1960."[34] Johnson took this to heart. He set out to make himself a national candidate, a national leader.

Johnson's first challenge came with the "Southern Manifesto," a statement signed in March 1956 by 101 congressmen and senators pledging to resist the Supreme Court's *Brown* decision. The Manifesto was generated by Georgia senator Richard Russell, mostly at the suggestion of other senators, particularly Strom Thurmond and Harry Byrd. Russell had difficulty wording a document that would satisfy all southern congressmen and senators, but in the end all signed the document except Kefauver, Albert Gore of Tennessee, and Johnson.[35] The Manifesto was designed, at least in part, to show white southerners that their representatives in Congress understood the situation, sympathized with their constituents back home, and were doing something about "the problem," as white southerners saw it.

All this, it seemed, would have placed Johnson in a bad position, but it did not. Russell wanted Johnson to become president, and everyone understood that anyone who signed the Manifesto would alienate key voting sections of the nation outside the South. Russell, the leader of the Southern

Delegation in Congress and one of the most powerful men in Washington, protected Johnson from southern congressmen who wanted Johnson to sign the document and then from criticizing him for not signing. The official reason Johnson gave for not signing the Manifesto was that as leader, he could not be associated with one section of the nation, nor could he come down on one side of such a volatile issue as civil rights and still lead the party. Actually, that was a fairly convincing reason, but it was more important that Russell, and several other powerful southerners, wanted Johnson to be a contender in 1960, and he could not be that if he signed the Manifesto.[36]

There was a prevailing opinion in America in the mid-1950s that the nation's racial problems would disappear if African-Americans in the South could get the vote. That power, as Washington's politicians perceived it, would open doors to everything from ending de jure segregation in the South to fostering equal opportunity and equal rights. To that end, the Eisenhower administration, in 1956, introduced a fairly weak civil rights bill that the president called "non-provocative and moderate in nature."[37] Most Republicans supported the bill; many, in fact, saw it as an excellent means of dividing the Democrats. The bill sped through the House, where it was significantly watered down, and then sent to the Senate.

There, Johnson was persuaded to take leadership of the bill despite its Republican origins. The 1956 campaign and election had just ended, and Johnson wanted badly to get out from under the onus of a southern politician. Perhaps the best route to that end was to support a bill that protected black rights in the South. James Rowe again advised Johnson to become a national leader and take on this bill: "As you probably know," Rowe wrote to Johnson, "both your friends and your enemies are saying that this is [your] Waterloo. They are saying that you are trapped between your southern background and your desire to be a national leader and you cannot escape. . . . To put it bluntly, if you vote against the civil rights bill you can forget your presidential ambitions in 1960." But Rowe went on to add that Johnson might actually benefit from the bill's passage. "As a man with the confidence of the South [you] could urge them to accept a reasonable bill. As a Southerner and a national leader speaking to the North [you] could ask the North . . . to accept less than it could get through the power it has. . . . It would be most important," Rowe continued, "that [you] get all the credit for getting a compromise bill through, with emphasis in the South on compromise, and emphasis in the North on getting a bill."[38] So, Johnson agreed to take on the bill (at least in part) to show northern liberals and African-Americans in the party that he was sympathetic to the civil rights movement.

Johnson had other motives here. Some polls from the 1956 election showed that African-Americans were beginning to backslide into the Republican Party, and Johnson surely saw that a successful civil rights bill passed by the Democrats would stop that shift. He may also have hoped that he could get the North and the South to compromise on the bill, get past the race issue, and finally unite the party as the 1960 election approached. Johnson had always believed that many of the South's problems—poverty, ignorance, poor education—stemmed from the race issue, and that race was holding back the South as the rest of the nation expanded and grew. Certainly, Johnson did not believe that the Civil Rights Act of 1957 would bring an end to race discrimination in the South, but he may have seen it as a first step, one that would isolate the South and bring an end to southern resistance to civil rights actions, at least in Congress.

The bill provided for a new Commission on Civil Rights and for a new attorney general to deal with civil rights issues. The most controversial part of the bill was Title III that gave the Justice Department the power to use injunctions to enforce the equal rights guaranteed by the Fourteenth Amendment, which in turn gave the federal government the power to enforce desegregation. That power, some believed, included military intervention if deemed necessary. Title IV provided for trials without a jury for those who defied federal authority.

The president almost certainly had his own political motives for introducing the civil rights bill. Not surprising to anyone, the bill almost immediately set the Democrats to squabbling over civil rights. Eisenhower insisted that he could not understand what all the fuss was about. In a telephone call to Johnson in June, the president told the leader that he had "devised and approved what he thought was the mildest civil rights bill possible." The president added "that he himself had lived in the South and had no lack of sympathy for the southern position." I was, he said, "a little struck back on [my] heels when [I] found the terrific uproar that was created."[39] The president, however, almost certainly sent the bill to Congress, at least in part, to fan the flames of the age-old sectional conflict in the Democratic Party. He was, most likely, delighted by the "terrific uproar that was created."

Johnson told his constituents in Texas that he opposed the bill, and that it was unfair to the South. At the same time he told southern leaders that it was time for civil rights legislation, and that the bill would pass. The only question to be decided was what kind of bill would become law. Johnson told southern leaders that if they tried to block the bill, the North would exert its greater power, and that would lead to radical civil rights legislation. It would also lead to a further isolation of the South from the entire nation.

Southerners saw the handwriting. They did all they could to weaken the bill and then voted against it, while allowing it to pass. The final bill still provided for the civil rights commission and the civil rights division in the Justice Department, but Title III, the enforcement section, was removed. Just about everyone on both sides recognized that the bill would have never passed with Title III attached, and George Reedy even speculated that Title III had been added only for trading purposes because it was removed so easily and quickly.[40] Title IV remained in the bill, but it included a clever compromise. It provided for jury trials in all criminal contempt trials, which were rare, but allowed for trials without juries for ordinary civil contempt cases, which included most cases.

Johnson pushed through the compromises, and to most observers those compromises emasculated the bill to get it passed. But Johnson accomplished a great deal. He kept his party together in the face of the divisive issue just as it had finished reeling from the 1956 defeat and was preparing for the 1958 midterm elections and looking ahead to 1960. He gained enormous publicity for (what many saw) as an impossible accomplishment. And he enhanced his chances for a presidential nomination in 1960. In fact, as Reedy pointed out, Johnson continually pointed to the possibility that he might one day become president as a means of holding the southern leaders in line. "[I]t would be worth it," Reedy recalled, "to get one southerner from a Confederate state in the White House."[41] Possibly most important, however, (and something that was not apparent to anyone in 1957) Johnson laid the groundwork for much stronger bills that would come later. It was Johnson's half-a-loaf. Civil rights leader Bayard Rustin said later, "I felt that the 1957 civil rights bill was weak, but a very important bill. And while we had considerable questions about it, we all supported it on the basis that this would establish a very important precedent."[42] But not everyone saw it that way. A. Philip Randolph complained "It is worse than no bill at all." Others have argued that no bill could have been passed in 1957 that would have been satisfactory to civil rights leaders and advocates.[43] Senator Harry F. Byrd of Virginia, in possibly the most telling aspect of the nature of the bill, voted against it, and was satisfied that the legislation in its final form was so weak it would be of no significance. The day after the final vote on the bill, Byrd wrote to Johnson: "No one living but yourself could have accomplished what was done last night. It was due to your masterful leadership and strategy. I am glad to have had a small part in this great victory."[44]

Generally, through the 1950s, Democrats handled civil rights badly, mostly for fear of losing the South to the Republicans. As the 1960 campaign approached, the Republicans hoped to make even further inroads into the

South, while the Democrats intended to work hard to keep the South inside the Democratic Party sphere. Democrats, however, also had to continue to appeal to black voters. All this, while the civil rights movement began to heat up and become much more volatile for both parties.

～

As the 1960 campaign approached, the Democrats were faced with a number of serious problems, mostly relating to Eisenhower's two-term successes that could be characterized generally as peaceful and prosperous. His popularity had pulled voters into the Republican Party like never before, and the Democrats felt the shifts in the 1956 election. The bright spot for the Democrats seemed to be that the nation had been enamored with Eisenhower and not really with the Republicans. Eisenhower offered safety, stability, and moderation. As his time ebbed, the Democrats could only hope that the nation would turn back to their party and their policies. Of course, they would need to offer a presidential candidate stronger than Richard Nixon.

CHAPTER THREE

~

Kennedy and the Liberals

One of Kennedy's biggest problems as he headed into the primaries was an almost desperate need to win over the liberals in his party. Without their support, he would have trouble controlling organized labor, which might cost him important industrial states such as Pennsylvania, Michigan, Ohio, and Illinois. Liberal support was also important in winning New York, New Jersey, and several other northeastern states.

The liberals of 1960 believed that they held the legacy of Roosevelt and the New Deal, and they expected their next Democratic Party candidate to carry that mantel. They would expect him to support and expand New Deal programs, be an active president, and carry the liberal flag. Liberals did not make up even a large minority of voting Democrats, but they were one of the most important wings of the party, the most vocal, the intellectuals, the writers, the people who had great influence in the nation. Kennedy would have trouble moving his candidacy forward without them.

Kennedy's principal problem with the liberals was his own less-than-liberal background and voting history. He had, in fact, rubbed liberals the wrong way on a number of issues since he came to Washington in 1948. He had voted to continue funding the anticommunist activities of the House Committee on Un-American Activities (known most commonly by the inaccurate acronym, HUAC), possibly the most offensive to liberals of all government activities. He had supported the Mundt-Nixon Internal Security bill, which, had it passed, would have outlawed the Communist Party and forced communists and communist organizations to register with the federal government. Kennedy had also argued the conservative Republican line that Truman had "lost" China to the Reds in 1949 by not coming to the aid of the anticommunist Nationalist Chinese. And he had supported giving aid to Francisco Franco, the Spanish fascist dictator.

Democratic liberals also held Jack accountable for the sins of his family. The Kennedy family patriarch, Joseph Kennedy, had a very visible falling out with FDR during the war, was a renown anti-Semite, and, as ambassador to England, supported England's appeasement of Hitler in 1938. Joe Kennedy had then turned rabidly anticommunist in the postwar years and had supported the anticommunist activities of the Republican Party. He had also assisted the anticommunism of HUAC, even dispatching Jack to deliver money to HUAC's biggest star in the late-1940s, Richard Nixon. As a one-time Hollywood movie mogul, Joe Kennedy was no stranger to California politics, and he hated the brand of liberal activism embraced by Hollywood actors and writers—many of whom were being investigated by HUAC. He particularly disliked their political darling, Helen Gahagan Douglas, Nixon's liberal opponent in his 1950 bid for his Senate seat. In that campaign, Joe had supported Nixon.[1] Most Democratic Party liberals understood all this and had come to see the Kennedy family as hypocrites who had supported Nixon against one of their own in 1950, but now, as the 1960 campaign approached, saw political advantage in opposing Nixon and had changed their stripes to meet the occasion. It was serious criticism.

John Kennedy also had to answer for his family's association with Joe McCarthy in the early 1950s. When McCarthy, a Wisconsin Catholic, began holding Senate hearings on the pervasiveness of communism in America, Joe Kennedy donated large amounts of cash to the effort. McCarthy often spent time at the Kennedy family compound on Cape Cod, flown there in the family's private plane. He fit in well with the Kennedy kids, participating regularly in the family's grueling weekend sports schedule. He even dated Jack's sister, Pat, for a time. And it was Joe McCarthy who gave Robert Kennedy his first job as the assistant to McCarthy's chief counsel.[2] In February 1952, in a well-publicized event, John Kennedy showed his sympathy for McCarthy by attacking a speaker who had criticized both McCarthy and Alger Hiss in the same comment. "How dare you," Kennedy snapped, "couple the name of a great American patriot with that of a traitor."[3] Then in 1954, when the Senate voted to censure McCarthy, Kennedy, in deference to Boston Catholics, chose to avoid the vote. Liberals simply could not abide this Kennedy-McCarthy association. How could Kennedy have maintained a personal relationship with McCarthy, the liberal nemesis, and then ask for liberal support for his candidacy? By 1960, McCarthy and McCarthyism had been discredited, and Kennedy had to explain to liberals why he had supported the distasteful episode. Pressed about his association, Kennedy could only say "I never said I was perfect."[4]

At the same time, Kennedy clearly understood that no candidate could win the 1960 Democratic nomination without the support of the liberals, and he pandered after their support. In March 1958, on the Sunday morning talk show *Face the Nation*, he was asked, "do you think that the candidate of the Democratic Party would have to be definitely associated with the liberal wing of the party in 1960?" With no hesitation, he answered, "I do." Then when asked, "Do you count yourself a liberal?" He again offered no equivocation, "I do."[5] In October 1959, at the Alfred E. Smith Memorial Dinner in New York, Kennedy used the event to take a liberal stance on anticommunism by portraying Smith (the 1928 Democratic Party candidate and a Catholic) as a politician who repudiated the extreme anticommunism of the 1919 Red Scare. Al Smith, Kennedy noted, had denounced "those who had built this 'red scare' up out of all proportions."[6] The speech earned him praise among some liberals while doing a great deal to separate him from the offending McCarthy connection.

Kennedy's proposed run for the Democratic nomination particularly rankled Eleanor Roosevelt, the doyenne of the party liberal elite. She never forgave Kennedy for being Joe Kennedy's son and for his family's failing to discourage Catholic support for McCarthy. She had come to associate Catholicism directly with McCarthyism, and that made Kennedy guilty by association. She also hated the influence and the money that the Kennedys were spreading around—as she saw it—to ensure Jack's candidacy. As the campaign continued it would be Eleanor Roosevelt, among the nation's liberals, who would continue to be Kennedy's biggest stumbling block; she simply refused to come onboard.

But Eleanor Roosevelt's mistrust of the Kennedys got her into trouble. In December 1958, just as Kennedy was beginning to be noticed nationally as a potential presidential candidate, the former first lady appeared on an ABC television program called *The College News Conference*. In answer to the question, "What do you think of Senator Kennedy?" Mrs. Roosevelt offered what became known in the Kennedy camp as the "oodles statement": "Well, in the first place," she responded, "Senator Kennedy is a charming young man with an enormous amount of charm. His father has been spending oodles of money all over the country and probably has a representative in every state by now." That strategy, she added, was not illegal or even unethical, but the implication was clear, John was still his father's son, and the family was spending what was necessary to win the Democratic nomination in 1960—and that was enough to turn her away from Jack's political ambitions. Then she added, playing on Kennedy's *Profiles in Courage*: "I feel that I would hesitate to face the difficult decisions that have to be taken by the next President . . . with someone who understands what courage is and admires it, but has not quite the independence to have it."[7] Kennedy immediately fired off a letter to Eleanor. It was both firm and cordial. "I am certain," he wrote, "that you are the victim of misinformation; and I am equally certain that you would want to ask your informant if he would be willing to name [for] me one such representative or one such example of any spending by my father around the country on my behalf." Then he added one last point that sounded gracious but was little more than a veiled insult: "Whatever other differences we may have had, I'm certain that we both regret this kind of political practice." To make certain that she realized he meant business, Kennedy added a note at the bottom of the letter that he was sending a copy to Phil Graham at the *Washington Post*.[8]

As it turns out, Mrs. Roosevelt was speaking from speculation and innuendo, with no evidence of any such Kennedy family doings. She was, of course, correct, but she could prove nothing. She knew it, and Kennedy knew it. "If my comment is not true," she wrote back, "I will gladly so state. I was told that your father said openly [that] he would spend any amount of money to make his son the first Catholic President . . . and many people as I travel about tell me of the money spent by him in your behalf. . . . Building an organization," she granted, "is permissible but giving too lavishly may seem to indicate a desire to influence through money."[9] Her admission of no evidence gave Kennedy the opening he needed in the exchange. He shot back: "I am disappointed that you now seem to accept the view that simply because a rumor or allegation is repeated it becomes 'commonly accepted as fact.'" He went on to insist his father had spent no money to further his nomination, and that there were no "paid" representatives working for his nomination in any state. Kennedy ended the note by asking for a retraction in her syndicated newspaper column: "I am confident you will . . . correct the record in a fair and gracious manner." And again, he noted that he was sending a copy to Graham.[10]

Cornered, Mrs. Roosevelt, in her January 6, 1959 column, printed parts of the exchange, including Kennedy's denials from the December 11 letter. She then wrote that she believed this was the best way to deal with the problem.[11] Kennedy, however, was not satisfied, and on January 10 goaded Mrs. Roosevelt once again, complaining in another letter that the article did not deal "with whether the rumors are true. In view of the seriousness of the charge, I had hoped that you would request your informants to give . . . the names of any 'paid representatives' of mine in any State. . . ." Kennedy went on to insist again that there were no such informants, and for that reason "it seemed to me that the fairest course of action would be for you to state that you had been unable to find evidence to justify the rumors." What you have done, he added, merely "leaves the original charge standing." In one last attempt to get off the hook, Mrs. Roosevelt wrote back with a promise: "I will say, when asked, that I have your assurance that the rumors are not true. If you want another column, I will write it—just tell me."[12] And with that, Kennedy let up on the barrage. However, in a telegram of January 29, Mrs. Roosevelt insisted on the last word, again digging at *Profiles in Courage*: "My dear boy," she wrote with a good deal of condescension and reprimand, "I only said these things for your own good. I have found in [a] lifetime of adversity that when blows are rained on one, it is advisable to turn the other profile."[13] A few weeks later on *Face the Nation*, Kennedy was asked that if Mrs. Roosevelt continued to oppose your nomination, "do you think that her opposition to you would be such that it would ruin your chances for nomination? . . ." Kennedy answered abruptly, "No."[14] Mrs. Roosevelt was never satisfied with Kennedy, and at the 1960 convention she continued to throw her support behind the futile draft-Stevenson movement. It was only after Kennedy's nomination that she finally gave her party's candidate her (mostly unenthusiastic) endorsement.

Eleanor Roosevelt was not, however, the only liberal with these complaints. In December 1958, Reinhold Neibuhr wrote in *New Leader* magazine much of what Mrs. Roosevelt had said on television, that Kennedy "is spending too much money." Then he added that Kennedy "hasn't given any vivid proof of possessing the fortitude which he so eloquently extolled in his book."[15] Neibuhr may not have been as well known as Eleanor Roosevelt, but among liberals he was the era's leading theologian of American Protestantism and a chief political thinker of the liberal left. His roots were in the socialism of the thirties and the anti-Nazism of the following decade. He was also one of several founders of the liberal organization, Americans for Democratic Action (ADA), and that organization's forerunner, the Union for Democratic Action. The ADA had counted itself since the war as the harbinger of liberalism, the keeper of the New Deal-Fair Deal flame, and many in that organization had their doubts about Kennedy. In 1944 Neibuhr published *The Children of Light and the Children of Darkness* in which he wrote: "Man's capacity for justice makes democracy possible; but man's inclination to injustice makes democracy necessary." He championed the liberal intellectual and was, in many ways, the conscience of liberalism at midcentury.[16] He was another important key to Kennedy's puzzle for liberal support.

In February, Kennedy sent Neibuhr a letter admonishing him for quoting Mrs. Roosevelt and accepting her words as fact with no evidence. He demanded to see any evidence that Neibuhr could produce.[17] Neibuhr, much less the public figure than Mrs. Roosevelt, felt no need to give in to Kennedy's demands, and responded with a discussion of ethics and politics. He wrote, "it would be wrong to have paid agents, particularly agents paid with family money."[18] Kennedy responded the next day: "I can . . . assure you that no such agents exist," referring to the accusations from Mrs. Roosevelt. Kennedy added that he agreed that paid agents would, in fact, be "highly improper." But he was willing to admit that "in some instances, volunteers can perform some of these functions without compensation." Then Kennedy added, "[A]t the present time I can state with absolute confidence that I have no agents paid from any source in any state of the Union."[19] Obviously, the nation's preeminent liberals like Eleanor Roosevelt and Reinhold Niebuhr were uncomfortable with Kennedy, his money, and his conviction to liberalism.

In the political arena of Democratic Party politics, however, it was Adlai Stevenson who held many of the liberal cards. Stevenson actually was not all that liberal, but he was the titular leader of the liberals in the party, and he had the unconditional support of liberals like Eleanor Roosevelt. He had developed an effective liberal persona and thus received strong liberal support. As his friend Arthur Schlesinger described it, liberals loved him because of "His lofty conception of politics, his conviction that affluence was not enough for the good life, his impatience with liberal clichés, his contempt for conservative complacency, his summons to the young, his demand for new ideas . . . his belief that history afforded no easy answers, [and] his call for strong public leadership. . . ."[20]

If Kennedy could get an endorsement from Stevenson, it would go a long way toward getting party liberals in line behind him. But like Mrs. Roosevelt, Stevenson was a constant problem for Kennedy. Stevenson kept insisting he was not running. At the same time it was clear that he was interested in the nomination, that he would accept a draft if the party wanted him again for a third time. And as long as he wanted to keep that window open, he would not endorse Kennedy.

Stevenson insisted often, following the 1956 campaign, that he would not run for the presidency again, but he usually added that "no man should refuse to serve his country," again, a statement that the press perceived as leaving his options open. When pushed by the press to endorse a candidate, he insisted that he wanted to stay out of the fray and that he would not lend his endorsement to any candidate. *Newsweek* speculated that "perhaps without quite realizing it, Stevenson is hoping for a draft." The *New York Times* political writer, W. H. Lawrence, wrote that "some believe him openly receptive to a draft."[21] "Deep down he wants it," one of Stevenson's closest friends told Theodore White. "But he wants the convention to come to him, he doesn't want to go to the convention."[22]

Several of Stevenson's supporters had been pushing him hard to run ever since his 1956 loss to Eisenhower. They argued, with some reason, that no Democrat could have beaten Eisenhower in 1952 or 1956. But now that Eisenhower was out of the picture, Stevenson might well beat Nixon. Dozens of petitions were signed and sent to Stevenson's offices. But over and over Stevenson continued to deny his candidacy. The major liberal magazines, the *New Republic*, *Nation*, and *Frontier* endorsed him and begged him in their editorials to run. A New York liberal organization took out an ad in the *Saturday Review* telling supporters to write letters to Stevenson supporting his candidacy. By May, Draft-Stevenson groups were in seven states. But Stevenson continued to insist he was not a candidate, while refusing to endorse another.[23]

In mid-May, 1960, Arthur Schlesinger, Jr., a friend of both Kennedy and Stevenson, arranged a meeting of the two men in hopes of convincing Stevenson to endorse Kennedy. Kennedy's objective, Schlesinger wrote Stevenson, will be "to assure his victory [at the Democratic National Convention] in Los Angeles; and he would like to think that he had earned the support of the liberals and particularly of you." Schlesinger continued, arguing that Stevenson's endorsement would have a lot to do with how the campaign is played out. "I think it is most important . . . that his vital backing come from the liberal Democrats and that his vital sense of obligation be to them. The best way to assure these things would be for you to play a leading role in bringing his nomination about. . . ."[24] Following the meeting, Stevenson reported back to Schlesinger that he "wanted to be consistent and did not feel therefore that I could come out for [Kennedy] now," but he promised Kennedy that he would be no part of any stop-Kennedy movements. That, however, did not solve Kennedy's problem; he needed Stevenson's endorsement, and he considered his refusal an affront. I am sorry, Stevenson added, that "Jack seemed 'regretful' about our talk."[25] Yet after a few days of consideration, Stevenson's conciliatory tone changed to a distinct annoyance with Kennedy's lack of gratitude. In a letter of June 7, again to Schlesinger, Stevenson wrote, "I have been reflecting a little about our talk and find myself getting more provoked by the feeling I get from the Kennedy camp that I should do this or that to help if I expect any consideration later for myself. . . ." Then he added, "I have always felt in a way responsible for Jack's recent progress. . . . As a result of the convention in 1956 he [received] a quickly earned national reputation and identification which he has exploited most effectively. Would it have been as easy to exploit it in this campaign year had I chosen to be a candidate or done anything to encourage my friends to promote a third candidacy? . . . With all this in mind, I have found the talk from his camp . . . quite aggravating."[26]

On June 5, Stevenson stayed at Schlesinger's home in Boston, and again Schlesinger tried to push Stevenson to endorse Kennedy—and again Stevenson refused. In a note to Kennedy the next day, Schlesinger wrote, "He [Stevenson] seems to feel that he has told so many people . . . that he would remain neutral that it would be a violation of his word to them if he were now to come out with an endorsement."[27]

To make things worse for Kennedy, on June 10, just a month before the convention, Eleanor Roosevelt officially endorsed Stevenson for president, and then three days later a group of the nation's most influential liberals published a petition (addressed to the Democratic National Committee) endorsing Stevenson for the nomination. Included were the big names of American liberalism: Mrs. Roosevelt, Niebuhr, Archibald MacLeish, Carl Sandburg, John Steinbeck, Harry Belafonte, Harvey Swados, Mrs. Frank Lloyd Wright, Mrs. Marshall Field, Leonard Bernstein, historian Perry Miller, and a number of others.[28]

Kennedy then moved in response by asking several prominent liberals who supported his candidacy to put together a competing statement of endorsement. The result was a Kennedy-supported petition entitled "An Important Message of Intent to All Liberals." Most likely written by Schlesinger, the document touted Kennedy's liberalism, his liberal voting record, and his promises for the future. It was signed by a competing group of the northeastern liberal intellectual elite, including Schlesinger, Joseph Rauh, John Kenneth Galbraith, Arthur Goldberg of the AFL-CIO, Gilbert Harrison of the *New Republic*, and historians Allan Nevins, Henry Steele Commager, and political scientist James MacGregor Burns. "The purpose of this letter," the petition read, "is to urge . . . that the liberals of America turn to Senator Kennedy for President. . . . We are convinced that Senator Kennedy's adherence to the progressive principles which we hold is strong and irrevocable. He has demonstrated the kind of firmness of purpose and toughness of mind that will make him a great world leader." The petition went on to call for desegregation of the South and voting rights for all Americans.[29] With that, the liberals headed to the Los Angeles convention split. Some supported Kennedy; some supported Stevenson. But the result would not be a fight. Kennedy was simply too strong for Stevenson's people to overcome—particularly since Stevenson refused to aid his own candidacy. For most liberals, it would all come down to lukewarm support for Kennedy as the lesser of two evils.

CHAPTER FOUR

~

The Democrats Slug It Out
in the Primary Season

Kennedy had been more or less unofficially running for the presidency since the 1956 campaign. His political organization was unparalleled, and of course his pockets were deep. But it would take more than just good organization and Joe Kennedy's money to make him president. Kennedy had to show the party leadership as well as the rank-and-file party members that he could win votes. The political world was full of Bob Tafts and Stewart Symingtons: capable politicians, men who were smart and who commanded the deepest respect from their peers, but who simply could not awaken the electorate and pull the necessary numbers at the polls. Kennedy had come to believe that the key to demonstrating voter appeal was the primaries, and just after announcing his candidacy, he said that any candidate who avoided the primaries (such as Johnson) did not deserve the Democratic Party's nomination.[1]

It was the use of television that marked 1960 as the first truly modern presidential campaign. During the primary campaigns of that year, television, for the first time, played a major part in giving the candidates—particularly Kennedy—important national exposure. Kennedy recognized this, understanding that the publicity he received from national news reports was much more important than the few convention delegates he collected from winning the primary elections. Consequently, he was just as interested in the nonbinding ("beauty contest") primaries as in state primaries that bound their delegates to the outcome of the primary election.[2] In fact, Kennedy left the delegate collection and counting to his lieutenants while he hit the campaign trail in search of publicity, significant television exposure, and a reputation as a winner. That strategy, which proved extremely successful, changed the nature of American politics. After 1960, candidates would use the primary campaigns, and the television exposure they received in the process, as the builder of momentum that would carry them to a convention victory.

Television had played a part in campaigns before 1960. Eisenhower had used campaign ads fairly effectively in 1952 and again in 1956, but they mostly showed the candidate speaking to crowds, being presidential, smiling into the camera. But by 1960, television allowed candidates to be seen by thousands of Americans as they campaigned across the country, shaking hands, speaking, kissing babies. A good campaigner, who was attractive on camera and who could get his message across to the nation's television watchers could win votes. Old time politicians (like Harry Truman who called primary campaigns "eye wash," meaning that they were of little significance) never quite understood the significance of the medium in the political system. Television exposure in the primaries was particularly important to Kennedy because he was generally unknown outside of New England. For Kennedy to show his face to the voting nation while running in the Wisconsin and West Virginia primaries—and then winning those primaries—was a major advantage over a candidate like Lyndon Johnson who chose to remain in Washington in hopes that his successes in running the Senate would be enough to appeal to voters. Kennedy needed to get his face on television in 1960, and primary campaigns did that. They were, in fact, even better for his campaign than paid advertising.

The 1960 campaign also marked the beginning of image as a major factor in American politics. Image had, of course, played a role in politics before. Eisenhower's image had been an important factor in his elections and in his presidency. But with television to promote and project an image to the American people, or even to change an image, the campaign process changed. Attractive, appealing, candidates gained an immediate edge, while the grizzled, old elder statesman seemed to lose something in the face of the new medium. For the first time, a candidate's physical appearance was a very important factor in a campaign. All this became obvious with Kennedy's 1960 campaign. He seemed to chew up the camera, and America quickly fell in love with him and his family.

As long as Stevenson stayed on the sidelines and insisted he was not a candidate, Kennedy knew that his most significant rival for the nomination was Johnson, but if Johnson refused to come out and fight in the primary battles, Kennedy would battle the man who would fight. That was Hubert Humphrey. And Humphrey wanted to fight in Wisconsin and then in West

Virginia, states where he had certain advantages. Humphrey, from next door in Minnesota, was extremely popular in Wisconsin, possibly revered there more than Wisconsin's own two senators. In West Virginia, Democratic voters were white, Protestant, and strongly influenced by organized labor—all Humphrey strong points. West Virginia Democrats also pined for the reform programs of the New Deal-Fair Deal years, and there was no other politician in 1960 who was more associated with those programs than Humphrey. So, Kennedy reluctantly accepted the challenges against a candidate who was not the real challenger for the nomination, and for no other reason than to prove his worth as a vote getter.

At the same time, Humphrey was not much of a contender. He had no real organization, no money to speak of, and no significant support outside of midwestern liberals, northern urban blacks, and labor—significant voting blocs to be sure, but not enough to take the nomination away from the hard-charging Kennedy. However, if Kennedy did lose, particularly when he was expected to win, it could destroy his candidacy by making it clear to party regulars that he was long on organization and money, but short on voter appeal. Joe Kennedy, who kept up a long-time correspondence with an Italian friend, expressed the consequences of the worst possible scenario: "If we do not do very well [in Wisconsin] we should get out of the fight." He went on to call the Wisconsin primary "the crisis of the campaign."[3]

Joe's worries were unwarranted, and he may well have known that. The Kennedy machine had anticipated the Wisconsin challenge from Humphrey and had laid the groundwork months before. Kennedy men had swamped the state as early as May 1958. Jack had visited the state sixteen times before the primary campaign even began, shaking hands in little towns he had never heard of—from Appleton to Viroqua. He hired a full-time advance man and pulled into his organization the mayor of Madison—a Humphrey stronghold—and the state party chairman.[4]

Although Humphrey had no real chance to win the nomination, he may have hoped to be chosen by the party regulars to lead a stop-Kennedy movement, which might bring him enough support to win the nomination (or possibly the second spot on the ticket) at a deadlocked convention. The press often described Humphrey in this light—the front man for a group of politicians who wanted to put the brakes on Kennedy's steamroller. And Kennedy often complained that he was being ganged-up on by Democrats who opposed his candidacy through their surrogate, Humphrey.[5]

A stop-Kennedy movement did exist, mostly to further Johnson's candidacy, but it was barely organized and Johnson himself did little to advance the effort. Johnson had not yet made the transition to the new politics of television; he campaigned as politicians had campaigned for decades, presenting himself as a statesman and waiting for the campaign and the nomination to come to him. In fact, the two 1960 campaigns of Kennedy and Johnson might be seen as an example of the new style campaign overcoming the old, the future surpassing the past. Four years later, however, Johnson would catch up, and his presidential campaign would change the very nature of campaign advertising on television. But in 1960, his noncandidate campaign strategy would not work, and the stop-Kennedy movement that revolved around Johnson was a failure.

Later in his life Humphrey recalled that he was "about a ten-to-one long shot at best" to win the nomination. His candidacy was inept, by his own admission.[6] One of the great American political errors has been for a candidate to jump headlong into a national campaign organized by local political champions. Barry Goldwater, four years later, would make the same mistake. Humphrey's advisors were all successful Minnesota politicos, friends of the candidate, men who would protect him, men he could trust implicitly, but they had no experience on the national stage. "The heroes of local success," Humphrey recalled in his memoir, "we would be, ultimately, the victims of national ineptitude."[7]

Kennedy refused to confront (or even acknowledge) Humphrey in Wisconsin. But as the campaign continued, it became clear that the two men were getting on each other's nerves. Two of Adlai Stevenson's operatives who were keeping account of events there, saw sparks flying early. "Kennedy and Humphrey seem definitely to be developing some animosity toward one another. . . . Kennedy, not so privately, expresses disgust for Humphrey's 'demagogy.' Humphrey, not so privately, beefs about the slickness and affluence of the Kennedy operation, and about sharp tactics. . . .[8] At the same time, Democratic Party leaders begged the two candidates to avoid the pitfall that had been the party's fate all too often, of destroying themselves in the primary—and then limping, wounded and divided, into the general election.[9]

Just after the Wisconsin primary, Humphrey apparently got fed up with the situation and lost his cool in front of a St. Louis journalist. He charged Kennedy with "racing through the state with a suitcase full of money and an open-end[ed] checkbook trying to buy the . . . election." According to the reporter, Humphrey said that "being born with a silver spoon in one's mouth . . . or attending a great university . . . did not qualify one to be president." "I can't buy an election," Humphrey continued, "and I wouldn't if I could. . . . I can't afford to run through this state with a black suitcase and a checkbook."[10] It was just the kind of interparty attacks that Democrats wanted to avoid.

Possibly the most important outcome of the Wisconsin primary was that Humphrey put all he had into the campaign—and emerged broke. "Money for a campaign," Humphrey later wrote, "is as basic as gasoline for a motor. If you run out, the vehicle stops." He opened offices and then closed them for lack of funds. His phones were cut off; he was unable to pay advertising bills. His television and radio presence in the state barely existed.[11] By mid-April, after the voting in Wisconsin, the Humphrey campaign was $17,000 in debt and had begun the campaign in West Virginia with a measly $2,000 personal loan. When Humphrey cut his campaign staff in half to reduce costs, the press picked up the story that he was both losing in the polls and broke. Humphrey's "chances of nomination never have been great," wrote W. H. Lawrence of the *New York Times*, "but they [are now] reduced almost to zero. . . ."[12]

Despite all that agony in the Humphrey camp, Kennedy managed to portray himself as the underdog in Wisconsin, as the candidate who had to run against Humphrey in his own backyard. In that position, of course, he could claim an excuse if he did badly. But Kennedy was actually better known and more popular than Humphrey in the southern counties of Wisconsin (served by the Chicago print press, radio, and television stations), and in the areas around Milwaukee where the population was largely of Eastern European heritage and Catholic. It was in the rural areas of Wisconsin where Kennedy was not well-known, and the campaigning was often brutally cold—in both weather and reception. Ken O'Donnell recalled a "winter of cold winds, cold towns and many cold people. Campaigning in these rural areas of the state where nobody seemed to care about the Presidential election was a strange and frustrating experience. . . . In some towns, it was difficult to find anybody who was willing to shake hands. . . ." Jack "went into a tavern and approached a booth where a man and a woman were sitting over two glasses of beer, saying to them, 'My name is John Kennedy and I'm running for President.' The man turned his head toward Kennedy, looked him over slowly and said, 'President of what?'"[13]

It was in Wisconsin that Kennedy and his people first recognized the vote-getting appeal of Jackie Kennedy. Her glamour and beauty seemed to stun the people of Wisconsin. Even Humphrey admired what he called her "fragile beauty [that] beguiled and entranced men and women and children in an almost mystical way."[14] "[S]he worked hard in Wisconsin," wrote Ken O'Donnell, "not only in March and April . . . but on weekends in January and February when the rough winter weather was at its worst." The candidate and his wife would often work different sides of the same street in small Wisconsin towns. Jack "kept his eye on her," O'Donnell recalled, "and often muttered to one of us, 'Jackie's drawing more people than I am, as usual.'"[15]

Humphrey's little campaign, however, could not keep up with the well-funded Kennedy juggernaut. Humphrey recalled the difficulty: "Muriel and I and our 'plain folks' entourage were no match for the glamour of Jackie Kennedy and the other Kennedy women, for Peter Lawford and Sargent Shriver, for Frank Sinatra singing their commercial, 'High Hopes.' Jack Kennedy brought family and Hollywood to Wisconsin. The people loved it and the press ate it up. While we worked to get a couple of dozen folks to coffee parties in a farm home in . . . Sheboygan or Wausau or Eau Claire, the Kennedys, with engraved invitations, were packing ballrooms in Milwaukee or Superior or Green Bay. Mink never wore so well, cloth coats so poorly."[16]

Kennedy zipped around the state in his private plane, the *Caroline*, while Humphrey chugged along in, what he called, his "old, slow, and cold rented bus" outfitted with an army cot in the back so the candidate could cat nap. "Once, as we started in the darkness of the rural countryside," Humphrey recalled the agony, "I heard a plane overhead. On my cot, bundled in layers of uncomfortable clothes, both chilled and sweaty, I yelled, 'Come down here, Jack, and play fair.'"[17]

It was in Wisconsin that religion—Kennedy's religion—first became a significant political issue. Certainly, Kennedy's Catholicism had been discussed before the Wisconsin primary, but it was in Wisconsin that for the first time the issue was used by a candidate opposing him; and for the first time Kennedy had to defend his faith to voters who might harbor beliefs on the nature of religion and the state. Certainly, it was a legitimate issue, and there were voters who refused to vote for Kennedy because he was Catholic. But it also became an issue, at least in part, because of the nature of the campaign. Humphrey and Kennedy did not confront each other in Wisconsin. They did not attack each other, and they really did not even address each other or the other's opinions. At the same time, the Republicans had already chosen Nixon by default. For the press, the 1960 campaign offered very little to report. There were no confrontations, hardly even a difference of opinion among the candidates. With such a dearth of political stories in a campaign season to report, political reporters like Arthur Krock and W. H. Lawrence of the *New York Times* were probably screaming for anything to write about. Consequently, they took the religious issue about as far as it would go. The issue did exist. In fact, Humphrey's choice of West Virginia as the second battleground state was a definite attempt to make the most of the issue. But in Wisconsin and West Virginia, with little else to write and talk about, the press turned religion into a big issue. In the final analysis, there is no evidence that it was decisive in the primaries—and as it turned out, it was barely an issue in the general election. In fact, it may well have been more of an issue for the press than for the voters.

The Kennedy campaign in Wisconsin was run brilliantly. It gained momentum, held it, and then built on it. As Humphrey recalled later, "The Kennedys had orchestrated a symphony of victory, and everyone seemed to want a chair in the orchestra."[18] But the campaign left a bad taste in Humphrey's mouth. The Kennedys spread rumors that Teamster president Jimmy Hoffa was funding Humphrey's campaign. And someone sent an anonymous mass mailing of anti-Catholic, Protestant fundamentalist literature to Catholic households throughout the state. "Underneath the beautiful exterior [of the Kennedys] there was an element of ruthlessness and toughness that I had trouble either accepting or forgetting," Humphrey wrote.[19] But on the other side of the line, Ted Sorensen recalled later, "vicious falsehoods were whispered about Kennedy's father, Kennedy's religion and Kennedy's personal life."[20] And at one point, Humphrey, speaking to a Milwaukee Jewish audience, compared Kennedy's well-oiled campaign to Nazi Germany, "one of the best-organized societies of our time."[21]

When the Wisconsin snow finally melted, Kennedy had won a substantial victory. He pulled above 56 percent of the vote, winning six out of ten districts. But the win had some glitches. The districts he won were predominantly Catholic, while the four districts that Humphrey won were predominantly Protestant—including Madison, the heartland of Wisconsin liberalism. The question remained: could Kennedy command broad backing in a national election? Was he a vote getter on a national scale? The numbers showed that Kennedy (at least in Wisconsin) was only a candidate whose religion made a difference. And that was not enough. When Kennedy saw the returns, realizing that it was his religion—and really only his religion—that showed up in the voter turnout, he grumbled, "damn religious thing."[22] When his sister Eunice asked, "what does it all mean," Kennedy replied, "It means that we've got to go to West Virginia in the morning and do it all over again."[23] He had to show that he could win votes—and votes beyond just Catholic votes.

It was generally assumed that the Wisconsin primary eliminated Humphrey from the nomination. If he could not win in a neighboring state that was much like his own with a large percentage of farmers and liberals, his mainstay, then he was really unlikely to win anywhere. But Humphrey believed he could beat Kennedy in West Virginia, a state that was 96 percent Protestant and with an unspoken reputation of being largely bigoted and anti-Catholic. Also, with Jack out ahead of the pack, it was clear that the stop-Kennedy movement was at least trying to coalesce around Humphrey for the moment—and that it would likely culminate at the convention. Any anti-Kennedy push would probably come from two groups within the party: from the Left, possibly under the leadership of Stevenson and Eleanor Roosevelt; or from party regulars, possibly led by the nation's labor leaders in conjunction with Lyndon Johnson, Stuart Symington, and Sam Rayburn.

Kennedy was running his campaign outside of the Democratic Party structure, at least in part because he did not need party money. Humphrey was a Democratic Party insider and close to both of those groups. Even a modest run in West Virginia, a strong showing, might thrust Humphrey to the top of a stop-Kennedy movement with the potential of running over Kennedy at the convention. Humphrey would, then, be the natural convention choice.

In his memoirs, Humphrey only referred to "offers of help from other candidates," but the press certainly saw him at the head of a stop-Kennedy movement, and running in West Virginia seemed more about keeping that hope alive than winning. West Virginia's senator, Robert Byrd, an active supporter of Johnson, made no secret of the fact that he was endorsing Humphrey in hopes of stopping Kennedy. "If you are for Adlai Stevenson, Senator Stuart Symington, Senator Johnson or John Doe, you better remember that this primary . . . may be your last chance." And it was clear that he meant "your last chance" to stop Kennedy. Kennedy complained in the press about the organization against him. "West Virginia became such a blatantly open effort on the part of all the other contenders to stop Kennedy," wrote Ken O'Donnell, "that Jack's aroused Irish temper made him eager to plunge into it."[24]

The analysis is always that Humphrey challenged Kennedy to battle in West Virginia, and from that it became a battleground. In fact, the Kennedy people had scoped out West Virginia as early as the summer of 1958 when Kennedy sent pollster Lou Harris there to gauge public opinion. By January, the Kennedys had placed some of their best people in the state to get the organization rolling. A local politico named Bob McDonough ran the organization, known as "West Virginians for Kennedy." He knew his way around the state's awkward politics and proved to be an effective organizer and advisor. In May 1959, a year before the primary, Sorensen and Bob Wallace were on the ground in the state, and by December 1959 they had organized forty counties.[25] The question must be asked, then, why did the Kennedy organization make such detailed preparations in a small state, with a nonbinding primary? The answer must be that they successfully anticipated Humphrey—that they knew Humphrey would pick Wisconsin (the state closest to—and the most like—his own) and then he would choose West

Virginia (a poverty-stricken state with few Catholics, a New Deal heritage, and a large labor vote). Theodore White, quoting what he calls "one of the Kennedy early planning papers" wrote that the Kennedy family intended that "the trap could be baited for Humphrey to enter." When Humphrey took the bait, White continued, "the Kennedys jubilantly followed suit and closed the trap around him."[26]

For Kennedy, West Virginia was important because Wisconsin had left some questions unanswered, while raising some new questions about his ability to win votes. Wisconsin was about 30 percent Catholic and just about all Catholics voted for him, no matter what their political affiliation. For anyone trying to determine if Kennedy would be a vote getter in the general election against Nixon, this bloc voting eschewed the numbers. If Kennedy only aroused the Catholics in the nation, then he would do poorly in the national election.[27] At the same time, it was the conventional wisdom that Catholic bloc voting might well cause an anti-Catholic backlash. No one knew whether or not that was true in the spring of 1960. But all of those questions needed to be flushed out before the convention. In fact, the West Virginia primary was really necessary to Kennedy's nomination. In later years, Kennedy operatives realized that it was West Virginia that really won the nomination for Kennedy.[28] Had Humphrey dropped out in Wisconsin, Kennedy would have faced no opposition in West Virginia, and any victory there would have proved little; and there would, of course, been much less national exposure.

Humphrey was right when he wrote that West Virginia "was made for my politics and not for Jack Kennedy's." It was a low-income state with a strong labor movement, and that translated into strong liberal appeal. It was also 97 percent Protestant, and of that number the vast majority was religious fundamentalists who generally had no use for Catholics. Humphrey saw all this as placing him in a good position.[29] But, in fact, it was exactly what Kennedy needed to convince party regulars that he was the candidate who could pull votes from a broad constituency. For that very reason, Bobby insisted that they use West Virginia "to meet the religious issue head on."[30] Jack needed to show that he was not "The Catholic Candidate," and that as a Catholic, he would not provoke any significant anti-Catholic bias—even in West Virginia. In fact, for those party members who were gauging the situation, it was clear that if there was no significant anti-Catholic vote that emerged against Kennedy in West Virginia, then there would be none in the general election. By confronting a Protestant in a Protestant state, Kennedy showed that he was, in fact, a strong vote getter, a winner of more than just Catholic votes. It could truly sew up his nomination.

So Kennedy jumped into West Virginia, trying to show that he could win votes in a state that was not Catholic. And Humphrey entered the race (most likely) to show that he could lead a stop-Kennedy movement of party regulars and grab the nomination in July. Humphrey may also have been thinking about the vice-presidential nomination. Considering how he prac-tically groveled for the number two spot with Johnson in 1964, he may well have had that thought in 1960 on the Kennedy ticket. Humphrey would have been a natural choice, particularly in light of the perception in the spring of 1960 that Kennedy was a conservative Democrat with little liberal support and weak in the Midwest and with labor leaders—Humphrey's strengths. Humphrey's major detriment, of course, was that he was disliked intently in the South. Immediately after the West Virginia primary, Kennedy began looking at possible running mates, and among the several candidates suggested in the mix, Humphrey was listed and categorized in a memo by campaign advisors to Kennedy as: "Helps with Negroes and farmers—his pri-maries' attacks on JFK may be used by the Republicans anyway."[31] But be-yond that, Kennedy seems never to have considered the possibility of Humphrey as a running mate, and Humphrey never mentioned in his mem-oirs or in later interviews any such desires to be on the ticket with Kennedy.

When the Kennedy group arrived in Charleston the day after the Wis-consin vote, they were hit by two setbacks. First, the United Mine Workers, by far the largest union in the state, had thrown in with Humphrey.[32] And second, a Harris poll showing Kennedy with a 70 percent lead in the state had been taken before most West Virginians were aware that Kennedy was Catholic. These were minor problems, but they seemed to push Kennedy harder. He was hardly the underdog in the election, and the pundits knew and reported that he would win easily, but the new conditions seemed to raise a greater challenge.[33]

As it turned out, the West Virginia victory was perhaps the most impor-tant aspect of John Kennedy's nomination, but as the campaign began there, the Kennedys came to the conclusion that a contentious run against Humphrey in West Virginia was really not necessary. Why cut at each other when the final outcome was predetermined? So, Kennedy operatives ap-proached several of Humphrey's advisors and close associates with the argu-ment that the party could only suffer from a Humphrey-Kennedy confronta-tion in West Virginia. Humphrey, however, rejected the overtures. In fact, as Theodore White reported, these propositions made the candidate mad, caus-ing "the combat wrath [to be] aroused in Humphrey."[34]

At the same time, Humphrey's insistence on engaging the challenge made the Kennedys furious. As they saw it, they had won Wisconsin fair and square—and Humphrey, clearly defeated, refused to accept his defeat. He had no real chance of winning the nomination for himself; he could only apply his efforts to deny the nomination to Kennedy in the name of the stop-Kennedy noncandidates, particularly Johnson and Symington, two candidates who refused to get dirty in the trenches of primary politics. So it was, then, with little recourse, that the two candidates went head on in West Virginia. Humphrey limped along with almost no money and very little organization. The Kennedys, in response, grabbed the gauntlet and flooded into West Virginia, saturating the state with money, people, and the Kennedy family vigor; as many as fifty Kennedy family members and friends descended on the state to help in the campaign.[35]

The Kennedy women may have done the most good—at least at the grass-roots level. They rang doorbells, made phone calls, appeared on television, and gave speeches. In past Kennedy campaigns, much of this was organized by the very political Rose Kennedy, the family matriarch. But because she had been designated a "Papal Countess," by the Vatican, she was advised to remain in Hyannis. Jackie, then, took the lead. In the early stages of pregnancy, she tramped the state visiting miners' wives, shaking hands on the streets, passing out bumper stickers, and in one case, she spent time chatting with railroad workers during their lunch break. Ken O'Donnell recalled Jackie's resolve in one incident. While traveling through the hollows and hills of the state, Jackie spotted a group of women across a brook. "[T]he only way to speak to them was to walk across a plank about 10 feet long and 6 inches wide. She removed her shoes and walked across the sagging plank to chat with the women." Four "Kennedy women," Polly Fitzgerald, Pat Twohig, Helen Keys, and Eunice Ford set up "teas" throughout West Virginia. These "teas" had been an enormously successful campaign strategy in Kennedy's 1952 campaign against Henry Cabot Lodge in Massachusetts, and these women, by 1960, were, Dave Powers recalled, "experts in their fields." But in West Virginia, the "teas" were closer to hot dog roasts and barbecues.[36]

Humphrey entered West Virginia both broke and exhausted. He spent most of his time trying to raise the money necessary just to keep his campaign going. Deeply in debt from the Wisconsin run, Humphrey tried to tap into just about every public and private resource he knew. Much of his Wisconsin money had come from big labor, but in West Virginia (with the significant exception of John L. Lewis and the United Mine Workers) the labor leaders had left him—and taken their money with them. Stevenson supporters had done a lot to keep Humphrey propped up in Wisconsin. But Kennedy worked to see that that source of money to Humphrey dried up as well. Working through Connecticut governor Abraham Ribicoff, Kennedy sent a message to those Stevenson-Humphrey supporters that if the money to Humphrey did not end, Stevenson would not be considered for Secretary of State in a Kennedy administration. The money to Humphrey stopped.[37]

Humphrey toured the state in his sad bus, with "Over the Hump with Humphrey" painted on the side, and occasionally blaring "Give Me That Old Time Religion," from loudspeakers in a pathetic attempt to awaken anti-Catholic sentiment. As the candidate's financial problems became more and more public, television stations began demanding payment in advance and in cash. In one such incident, Theodore White reported, Humphrey lost his temper. "'Pay it,' Humphrey snarled. 'Pay it! I don't care how. . . .'" Then Humphrey pulled out his personal checkbook and wrote the check himself. "Mrs. Humphrey watched him do so," White continued, "with dark, sad eyes, and one had the feeling that the check was money from the family grocery fund—or the money earmarked to pay for the wedding of their daughter who was to be married the week following the primary." At the same time, White estimated that Kennedy spent $34,000 on television ads alone.[38]

Kennedy's surprise in West Virginia was Franklin Roosevelt, Jr. Certainly, the name alone was enough to evoke the memory of the great man himself—who had carried West Virginia in four presidential elections and who many West Virginians believed had given them significant opportunities during the Great Depression. And for West Virginia's mineworkers, it was, of course, the New Deal Wagner Act that had allowed them to organize unions and to earn a living wage for the first time in history. Franklin, Jr., had been working in the Washington areas as an importer of foreign cars and was eager to get back into politics. One of his best lines was to raise his hand to the crowds and hold his first two fingers close together and say: "My daddy and Jack's daddy were just like that." For anyone in the Kennedy camp (including John) who knew the stormy wartime relationship between FDR and Joseph Kennedy, that statement was difficult to swallow. But it worked for the West Virginians who seemed to accept it without question.[39] Possibly to make the best use of the Roosevelt image, Kennedy's people had thousands of vote-for-Kennedy letters, signed by FDR, Jr., shipped to Hyde Park, post-marked there, and then mailed back to voters in West Virginia.[40]

Possibly Roosevelt's most important contribution was a supposedly off-hand remark that questioned Humphrey's contribution in the war. Roosevelt had served on a destroyer in the Pacific, and Kennedy, of course, served on a Navy PT boat. "He's a good Democrat," Roosevelt said of Humphrey, "but I don't know where he was in World War II." Kennedy immediately apologized, and Sorensen and others in the Kennedy camp insisted that the statement was unplanned.[41] But Bobby apparently pushed Roosevelt to make the statement, and several other times Kennedy was introduced on television as "the only veteran in the West Virginia primary." West Virginia had a high percentage of veterans who only needed to be reminded once that Kennedy had fought in the war and Humphrey did not. Kennedy's open and seemingly sincere apologies could not remove the fact.[42]

The Kennedy plan was to use Franklin, Jr. to display support from the Roosevelt family, but Eleanor and her oldest son had been on divergent political paths for some time. In 1948, Franklin (along with his younger brother Elliot) had colluded with a group who tried to draft Eisenhower to run as a Democrat. He demurred, and Eleanor criticized her sons' efforts.[43] And here, in the spring of 1960, she was a long way from getting behind Kennedy.

On May 5, Humphrey and Kennedy debated in Charleston. Kennedy had avoided a debate in Wisconsin, but in West Virginia it was important for him to confront the "Catholic question" head on, and at that moment a stop-Kennedy movement seemed to be growing behind Humphrey, and Kennedy needed to show that he was the better candidate. For Humphrey it was a welcomed opportunity to be seen throughout the state with little-or-no cost to his economically strapped campaign.

Almost nothing emerged from the debates that differentiated the candidates on any significant issues. In fact, they spent most of the hour agreeing with each other. But Humphrey, in his memoirs some thirty years later, said bluntly, "I debated Jack Kennedy in Charleston and he won."[44] Kennedy was, by then, much more interested in attacking the failings of the Eisenhower administration—and, of course, Nixon by default. At some point prior to the debate, Kennedy had stowed under the table the average supply of surplus food available to the poor in West Virginia. Much to everyone's surprise—including Humphrey's—Kennedy pulled out several cans of beans, some powdered milk, and other cans. He attacked the Eisenhower administration for not making available enough surplus commodity goods to the poor of West Virginia. He promised that when he became president all that would change. He also revealed that the unbelievable poverty and misery in West Virginia had opened his eyes, and that as president he would remedy the situation. "If I am elected," Kennedy said, "West Virginia will have done it, and I'll do everything I can for the interests of this state"[45] Even Humphrey wrote that "It was dramatic and effective."[46]

Kennedy wisely met the Catholic issue head on in West Virginia. As he became more familiar with the state and its people, he was convinced that West Virginians did not hate Catholics, but they feared that a Catholic president might somehow threaten their independence and freedom. He responded by looking West Virginia straight in the eye and confronting the issue as openly as possible. In Wheeling, much to the surprise of several of his advisors who had hoped he would skirt the issue, Kennedy responded to a question about the "Catholic issue," by saying "I am a Catholic, but the fact that I was born a Catholic—does that mean that I can't be President of the United States? I'm able to serve in Congress and my brother was able to give his life, but we can't be President?" The crowd reacted positively, and from then on *he* brought up the issue first, confronting it at every turn. "Is anyone going to tell me that I lost this primary forty-two years ago when I was baptized?" he asked a crowd in Fairmont. Over and over, he told crowds, "I will not allow any pope or church to dictate to the President of the United States. There is no conflict between my religion and the obligations of office. . . . I refuse to believe that the people of this state are bigots, guided in this most important choice by prejudice."[47]

The question that was pitched to Kennedy the most was whether he would accede to the wishes of the church. Norman Vincent Peale, Billy Graham, and other Protestant leaders openly questioned this point, asking whether Kennedy's first loyalty was to the church or the nation. In Charleston, Peale addressed the question of Kennedy's political independence by asking Kennedy if he was as "free as any other Americans to give his first loyalty to the United States."[48] Kennedy responded often to such criticisms, insisting that he believed strongly in the separation of church and state. I do not, he said, "take orders from any Pope, any Cardinal, any Bishop or any priest—not that they would give me orders." At one point he even insisted that "The American Catholic Church is devoted to the separation of church and state."[49]

On the night before the West Virginia election, Kennedy appeared on a statewide television broadcast to make it as clear as possible that his loyalty to the church was secondary to his loyalty to the nation and that he believed in the separation of church and state. In a staged question-and-answer session on a television sound stage with Franklin, Jr. acting as the commentator, Kennedy answered questions about his religion. In a response that Theodore White called "the finest TV broadcast I have ever heard any political candidate make," Kennedy looked straight into the camera, mustering every last ounce of sincerity, and "spoke from the gut," as White recalled, to the people of West Virginia:

> So when any man stands on the steps of the Capitol and takes the oath of office of President, he is swearing to support the separation of church and state; he puts one hand on the Bible and raises the other hand to God as he takes the oath. And if he breaks his oath, he is not only committing a crime against the Constitution, for which the Congress can impeach him—and should impeach him—but he is committing a sin against God.

Kennedy then raised his hand from an imaginary Bible, "as if lifting it to God," White recalled, and then said softly, "A sin against God, for he has sworn on the Bible." As White saw it, "over and over again there was the handsome, open-faced candidate on the TV screen, showing himself, proving that a Catholic wears no horns."[50]

In several speeches, he wisely tied his religion to his military record. "Nobody asked me if I was a Catholic when I joined the United States Navy," he told a crowd in Morgantown.

By making these points over and over, Kennedy, by Election Day, had successfully neutralized the Catholic issue. Most assuredly, there were large numbers of West Virginians who voted against him because of his religion. At the same time, however, by directly confronting the issue, Kennedy successfully removed the horns of Catholicism and made it acceptable to vote for a Catholic. Others voted for him because, by God, they would not be bigots.

Election Day, May 10, was wet and drizzly. Early that day, Kennedy flew back to Washington to await the returns at his home in Georgetown. He had come to believe that he would do badly and he wanted to sulk alone. Bobby Kennedy and Ken O'Donnell agreed. They had concluded that the Catholic issue was such an unknown factor in the voting that Kennedy could easily lose the election, and the entire campaign would end that evening.[51] But by about 10 p.m., it was clear that Kennedy had scored a big victory. Jack had taken Jackie to a movie. They returned at 11:30, and Jack immediately reboarded the *Caroline* for a flight back to Charleston. At 1:00 a.m., Humphrey's concession telegram arrived at Kennedy headquarters. With the candidate still en route, Bobby made his way to Humphrey's headquarters. Holding back tears, Humphrey conceded and then withdrew from the campaign.

In his victory speech, Kennedy told his supporters that "The religious issue has been buried here in the soil of West Virginia. I will not forget the people of West Virginia, nor will I forget what I have seen or learned here."[52]

The most important aspect of Kennedy's Wisconsin and West Virginia wins was that Kennedy showed party doubters that he could win votes, that he was a viable candidate, and not just a wealthy playboy who wanted to be president. The primaries also placed the candidate before the nation, giving him much needed exposure. Following the conventions, when the campaign began against Nixon, the nation knew John Kennedy. It would take the debates in the fall to prove to many Americans that Kennedy was Nixon's equal in that arena, but the news coverage of the primary campaigns gave most Americans at least a good look at the candidate.

Kennedy also used the two campaigns to weaken the Catholic issue. In fact, by the spring of 1960 he had forced a shift in the manner in which that issue was perceived. Before the primaries, Kennedy's religion was unquestionably a detriment to his candidacy. Following the primaries, it had become apparent that if Kennedy did not win the nomination, that Catholics in the Democratic Party would consider it a personal affront to their religion. And with many Catholics (particularly suburban Catholics) moving into the Republican Party, a number of Democratic Party leaders had come to the conclusion that a Catholic candidate would be more of a help than a hindrance.

Kennedy's primary victories also changed the nature of American politics—although it was not apparent until later in the decade. Kennedy was the first presidential candidate to win the nomination directly as a result of his primary victories. Prior to 1960, primaries were generally symbolic, Truman's "eyewash." After 1960, primaries became the road to the nomination, a necessary part of the campaign process. Kennedy clearly saw that, but it is just as important that Lyndon Johnson did not and refused to enter the primaries. In the future of American politics, no serious candidate (unless he had no rivals for the nomination) could avoid entering the primaries. A strong record in Washington was no longer enough.

Johnson, in fact, almost certainly missed his greatest opportunity by not entering the primary in West Virginia, a state whose voters would certainly have found him an attractive candidate. West Virginia had a southern perspective and its abject poverty made it a sure winner for someone like Johnson who had roots in the South and in the New Deal, and whose down home campaign style had always appealed to rural Texans. Had Johnson joined the battle in West Virginia and won, he almost certainly would have pushed Kennedy out of the picture.

There were, of course, other primaries, but none with the significance of Wisconsin and West Virginia. The Oregon primary on May 20 carried a bit of interparty drama. Stevenson's campaign was still an unanswered question. Oregon was a strong Stevenson state, and there was great speculation that he would enter the race there and go from a nostalgic reminder of campaigns past to a legitimate candidate for the 1960 nomination. The prospect clearly frightened the Kennedy campaign, and in hopes of forcing Stevenson to withdraw, Kennedy promised to appoint Stevenson secretary of state in a Kennedy administration in return for his support. Stevenson refused, apparently still harboring hopes that the convention would come to him for a third time. Kennedy never again made the offer, he won the Oregon primary, and Stevenson never became secretary of state.[53]

CHAPTER FIVE

~

Waiting for Nixon

From the early days of 1960, it was common knowledge that Nixon would be the Republican nominee. With the exception of the slightest of challenges from New York governor Nelson Rockefeller, Nixon stood alone, the heir apparent to whatever legacy Eisenhower would leave behind. Twice, once in 1952 and again in 1956, Eisenhower had considered replacing Nixon with a moderate, but Nixon persevered in both cases and kept his place on the ticket. Now, in 1960, with nearly no opposition, Nixon could rest, build his war chest, and watch from the sidelines as the Democrats spilled each other's blood, energy, and resources in their nominating process. But that strategy did not necessarily work in Nixon's favor.

One problem was that Nixon had to keep his party members, workers, voters, and most of all the press interested in his campaign—which was, in fact, no campaign at all. With no one challenging him for the nomination, he simply made no news. If he had been engaged in a primary fight for the nomination, of course the press would have covered every moment of his campaign, recording his every word. His face, his ideas, his every utterance would have been before the nation. But through the spring and summer of 1960, Nixon had difficulty getting any press. At the same time, every move the Democrats made was covered in every newspaper in the country, giving all the Democratic candidates important exposure and priceless publicity. Eisenhower, and any other Republican watching the campaigns, worried about Nixon's isolation. In April, Ohio senator John Bricker pushed Nixon to get out onto the campaign trail, to make some noise that would draw press coverage. But Nixon responded that he needed to stay fresh until the last month before the election. Speeches given now, he reasoned, would "be pretty well forgotten."[1] It was a strategy that made some sense, but it kept him out of the news while it allowed Kennedy, mostly unknown outside of New England, to build up his image through the spring and summer.

Another problem that Nixon faced was that he was stuck in a kind of political purgatory. As vice president, he represented the Eisenhower administration; it was part of his job to support and defend the administration's policies. But he was also a candidate, running for office on his own. He had to show that he had his own ideas, that he was independent and not just a mimic of Eisenhower. Eisenhower seemed to understand this—at least to a degree. He stayed clear of much of the campaign, his brother Milton argued, "at least in part to allow Nixon to show himself as a leader on his own and not merely as a shadow of (or a man riding on the coattails of) President Eisenhower."[2] That may have been true, but despite that, just about every time Nixon said anything that varied from the Eisenhower script, the president made it clear that he thought Nixon was ungrateful and trying to dismantle his policies. Part of this problem came from Eisenhower's own insecurity. He had begun to realize that whoever was elected in 1960 would almost surely take down much that he had built. Eisenhower had wanted to achieve two primary goals as president: peace and prosperity—goals that he believed went hand in hand. By prosperity, he meant a balanced budget that would build business confidence. To balance the budget he would have to keep spending low, and that meant keeping military spending as low as possible without jeopardizing national security. As the 1960 campaign began to play out, just about every candidate on both sides of the political spectrum wanted to appear strong on defense and argued hard for more military spending. In addition, the Republicans were pining for a big tax cut, and the Democrats were clearly willing to take the budget as far out of balance as necessary to serve their social agenda and push the economy upward. The Eisenhower years, they all seemed to be arguing, were the stationary years, the age of no growth and no progression while the Soviets had made big jumps in several areas. The candidates and the leadership in both parties were calling for the nation to move forward again. For Ike, all this was anathema. He had come to the conclusion that just about everyone running in the campaign, including Nixon, was set on undoing his vision—and would thus be the cause of the nation's problems as the next decade approached. He also seemed to feel that no one running, including Nixon, had the character and the guts to step into the arena with Khrushchev and the Soviets.

Nixon was caught in the middle of all this. If he voiced his own opinions, it appeared that he opposed the administration and its policies, and that made Eisenhower mad. And Nixon, of course, needed Eisenhower's endorsement and assistance in the campaign. If the president decided to sit out the campaign and not endorse Nixon, it would appear that he opposed the vice president's candidacy, and the political burden of that would be unbearably difficult to carry through the campaign. On the other hand, if Nixon simply parroted the Eisenhower vision, he looked unimaginative and incapable. Without a great deal of charisma or personal appeal, Nixon might find himself with very little to offer voters in November.[3]

Then there was always the question as to whether Ike and Dick got along. Did the president want to hand over the reigns of power to his vice president? Did he think Nixon could carry the burden of the presidency? In 1952, and then probably again in 1956, Eisenhower would likely have been delighted if Nixon had bowed out of the campaign. In both of those campaigns, Nixon continued to be associated with the GOP Right, the Red Scare, and McCarthyism. That was, of course, why Eisenhower chose Nixon in the first place as his running mate—to placate the Right and keep that wing of the party in line. By 1960 things had changed. Nixon had managed successfully to reinvent himself as an Eisenhower moderate, and that certainly went a long way toward acquiring the president's support as the 1960 campaign approached. But even though Nixon had embraced Modern Republicanism, Eisenhower was still not satisfied that Nixon could do the job. Stephen Ambrose, who wrote biographies of both men, pared the point down to two sentences: "Ike liked Dick well enough, but then Ike liked almost everybody. Eisenhower the President regarded Nixon the potential successor as unready."[4] Generally, Eisenhower thought Nixon was immature and inexperienced. At the same time, he did think that Nixon was far superior to anyone else on the campaign trail in 1960. He thought Johnson lacked "the depth of mind [and] the breadth of vision to carry great responsibility," and he saw Kennedy as "incompetent," vowing that he would "do almost anything to avoid turning my chair and country over to Kennedy." And he considered Rockefeller both egomaniacal and brainless.[5] With his approval ratings dropping below 50 percent and the campaigns shaping up to oppose his own policies, Eisenhower began to see the 1960 campaign as a referendum on his presidency. He was so upset by these prospects that he probably would have run again had the Constitution allowed it.

Eisenhower responded to all this by trying to get others in the Republican Party interested in running—while reserving his endorsement. He seemed to be saying that his hand of approval was available to the right person. At a press conference he was asked if he would, in fact, endorse Nixon. The president refused, asserting "that there are a number of Republicans, eminent men, big men, that could fulfill the requirements of the position. . . ." He added that Nixon understood how he felt on this point. Then he inserted a sort of left-handed compliment to Nixon that must have made the vice president cringe: "I am not dissatisfied with the individual that looks like he will get it."[6] Eisenhower even tried to convince Deputy Secretary of Defense Robert Anderson and NATO commander Al Gruenther to run and considered a number of other possibilities from Treasury Secretary George Humphrey to Henry Cabot Lodge. But no one, as *Newsweek* pointed out, "would be quixotic enough to try and win the nomination over Nixon."[7]

While Eisenhower evaded the issue, Nixon did everything he could, including adopting a new persona, to win the president's approval—and his endorsement. The "New Nixon" was an Eisenhower Republican and a Middle Roader, although he spurned those titles knowing what they meant to the party's right wing.[8] And the strategy worked extremely well. He managed to embrace the popular Eisenhower Center without alienating the Right. The shift was apparent to the press as early as January 1960. Following a speech in Florida, *Newsweek* reported the change: His tone was "leaning over backward moderation. . . . It was hard to believe that this was the Nixon who used to be known for his 'instinct for the jugular,' whose no-holds barred campaigns since 1946 had earned him the hatred of Democrats from Harry Truman and Sam Rayburn right on down." Nixon went out of his way to praise his Democratic rivals; he even called Truman a strong president and said he had "real respect" for Kennedy.[9] Eisenhower was apparently willing to accept the sea change in his vice president. When Democrats tried to brand Nixon an Old Guard Republican and a "reactionary," Ike responded, calling Nixon a "liberal Eisenhower Republican."[10] In a campaign biography written by Nixon's friend, Earl Mazo, the candidate is depicted as a student of the Eisenhower philosophy: "It is wrong," Nixon is quoted, "for the Republican party to become a far-right party as it is for it to become a radical party. As a matter of principle . . . it must never put itself in the position of dividing Americans into classes. To take the far-right viewpoint would destroy it as a national party. . . . The middle," he concluded, "usually prevails in the United States because extremists have one thing in common: they push too hard and drive reasonable, fair-minded people away."[11] It would be a while before the GOP Right would come to trust this New Nixon, but in 1960 Nixon's new character worked to unite the party.

The 1958 midterm election was a portent for the future of Republicans. The election was a disaster. With the nation in a fairly strong recession, voters let the administration know of their dissatisfaction. In the Senate, Democrats increased their majority to thirteen seats, and won forty-seven additional seats in the House. Of the twenty-one gubernatorial races up for grabs, they took thirteen and thus controlled thirty-four of the forty-eight governorships. Party heavyweight John Bricker of Ohio lost; so did Knowland in California. But there were two bright spots. In Arizona, Barry Goldwater had won a Senate seat by a respectable margin and almost immediately became a darling of the Republican Right. Now that Taft was dead and Knowland was out of the Senate, Goldwater walked into a void and filled it almost immediately. In New York, Nelson Rockefeller defeated Averell Harriman for governor there as the state replaced one rich man with one who was fantastically rich. Rockefeller immediately became a fresh face among a sea of the defeated. He called himself a Republican liberal, and like so many before him who had occupied the New York governor's mansion from Theodore Roosevelt to Tom Dewey, he irritated his party's Right Wing. The explanation for the policies of New York's liberal Republicans (and other urban northeastern Republicans) has always been that—in order to get elected—these candidates had to be liberal enough to understand the needs of the urban poor, urban ethnic groups, and organized labor. For the Republicans, these two men, Goldwater on the Right and Rockefeller on the Left, had begun to represent the severe ideological split in the party that would open up following the 1960 election. The fight would continue until the Right would finally emerge victorious in the 1980s.

⌐

As the pragmatic Nixon shifted his weight away from the right and toward the political middle in order to absorb the successes of Eisenhower's Modern Republicanism, he ran afoul of Goldwater, the new darling of the Right. Possibly seeking to shore up his right flank just as Goldwater and his people began to grow more rebellious within the party, Nixon sought a relationship with Ronald Reagan, one of the new and up-and-coming leaders on the Right. In the summer of 1959, Nixon began a cordial correspondence with Reagan. By that time, the sun had mostly set on Reagan's movie career, and he had become a spokesperson for General Electric, the sponsor of a television program he hosted. Reagan was still a Democrat, the political party of his father. He had voted for Roosevelt and in 1950 had worked for Helen Gahagan Douglas's campaign against Nixon. In 1952 he began his transition to political conservatism by casting his first Republican vote for the Eisen-hower-Nixon ticket that year. In 1960, Reagan was still a registered Demo-crat, and in that election he would be a vocal member of an organization called "Democrats for Nixon." Two years later, Reagan would change his reg-istration to Republican and work tirelessly for Nixon's California gubernato-rial campaign.[12]

By the late 1950s, Nixon may have seen that Reagan had a future in politics as a leader of the Right, possibly an important figure in the future of California politics. For whatever reason, Nixon had become an avid Reagan watcher. Rea-gan, during this period in his life, was making a name for himself among con-servatives traveling the nation, delivering to business groups what his advisors called "The Speech," a well-constructed discourse on the virtues of free market capitalism—and by implication, the evils of communism. Over time, he had honed the speech, learned to deliver it effectively, and won the approval of a growing conservative constituency throughout the nation.

On June 18, Nixon wrote to Reagan: "Speeches such as yours should do much to cause some solid thinking about the inherent dangers in [the Dem-ocratic party's] philosophy with the final result being a nationwide demand for reform." A few days later, on June 27, Reagan responded with a charac-teristic letter in longhand: "During the last year particularly," he wrote, "I have been amazed at the reaction to this talk. Audiences are actually mili-tant in the expression that 'something must be done.' . . . I am convinced there is a ground swell of economic conservatism building up which could re-verse the entire tide of present day 'statism.' As a matter of fact," he con-cluded, "we seem to be in one of those rare moments when the American people . . . are ready to say 'enough.'" Nixon, then, responded with a short note in early July, again complimenting Reagan's speech and his "ability of putting complicated technical ideas into words everyone can understand."[13]

The Nixon-Reagan relationship was complex. Although the two men were roughly the same age, Reagan was a political generation behind Nixon and admired him as something of a political mentor. Reagan greatly admired both Nixon-the-politician and Nixon-the anticommunist and always under-stood Nixon to be a strong conservative even though they occasionally dis-agreed. Both were Californians and both were self-made men, a point that was at least important to Reagan in his appreciation of Nixon. (That John Kennedy was not a self-made man grated on the souls of both men.) At the same time, Reagan saw Nixon as crude and ill-mannered, and much too po-litically pragmatic—that is, too willing to go to the dark side of liberalism in exchange for votes. Neither counted the other as a friend.[14]

⌒

In the summer of 1959, Nixon scored a political coup that changed the direction of the campaign, brought him strong poll numbers, shored up his relationship with the Right, and—most importantly—showed him as a leader. In late July, Eisenhower sent Nixon to Moscow. On July 23, in a nearly comic confrontation with Soviet Premier Nikita Khrushchev in the kitchen of a model American home display at Sokolniki Park in Moscow, Nixon held his own with the Russian Bear as the two men jabbed fingers at each other and argued over which nation produced the best televisions and rockets. This had followed a minor exchange at a television studio just before the two men walked into the kitchen, and that exchange was recorded and shown on U.S. television. The Kitchen Debate itself was covered in U.S. newspapers with photos of Nixon and Khrushchev, clearly arguing, and with transcripts of the event. In each case, Nixon was fully engaged with Khrushchev and was giving at least as much as Khrushchev was giving. This was valuable press. The incident cleared the doubt that many American voters had of Nixon's ability to stand up to the Soviets. There he was, if there was ever any doubt, with his finger in Khrushchev's face.[15]

Nixon's trip to Moscow and the Kitchen Debate had no significant diplomatic consequences. As Stephen Ambrose points out, Khrushchev did not even mention Nixon's visit in his memoirs, and the event was quickly overshadowed by Khrushchev's own visit to the United States in mid-September. But when Nixon returned to Washington, his poll numbers jumped, by Nixon's own recollection, by five to six points. Before the trip, Gallup polls showed Kennedy at 61 percent, with Nixon dragging at 39 percent. After the trip, the gap closed to 52 percent for Kennedy and 48 percent for Nixon.[16]

When Nixon returned from Moscow, he renewed his correspondence with Reagan. For Reagan, the Nixon-Khrushchev confrontation was a seminal event, and it may reflect how conservatives saw Nixon as an effective anticommunist, despite his shift to the moderate center. In September, Reagan wrote Nixon another handwritten letter in which he made three points about U.S.-Soviet relations and how the United States should deal with the Soviet Union. "'[C]o-existence,'" he said, "means 'don't do anything while I steal your horse.'" Then he added, "'Communism or Marxism' is the only system with aggression advocated as an essential part of its dogma." And in his final point, Reagan wrote: "'Communism' is dedicated to imposing its 'way and belief' on all the world."[17] Apparently the two men agreed.

The Kitchen Debate was important because it went a long way toward keeping the Republican Right in line, while allowing Nixon to continue his pragmatic shift toward Ike's middle road. It also placed Nixon in the public eye and showed him as a candidate who could stand up to communism.

⌣

Officially, Nixon was unopposed in his quest for the nomination—and ultimately Ike's blessing. But all the questioning of Nixon's abilities and the president's obvious ambivalence toward his vice president brought Nelson Rockefeller into the mix. Almost immediately after his 1958 victory over Harriman, he began running for president. In fact, within days of his election he told Nixon that almost certainly "his friends" would try to run him for president in 1960; and as early as February 1959, a few New Hampshire Republicans were pushing Rockefeller to enter that state's primary just a year away in March 1960.[18] In December 1959, Rockefeller headed out on an exploratory campaign trip to Texas, Oklahoma, and Florida obviously intent on testing the waters outside the Northeast. But his efforts attracted very little press coverage or interest. Possibly more importantly, Rockefeller believed he was treated badly by state party officials who already had their man in Nixon. He returned to New York convinced that the party had closed its doors on his candidacy in favor of Nixon, and he clearly resented it. Additional animosities began to grow between Rockefeller and Nixon when Nixon's political organization in New York apparently spurned Rockefeller. Rockefeller responded by criticizing the administration's policies, particularly in the area of defense and education, forcing Nixon to rise to the defense of the administration when he was trying to make his own way and separate himself from Eisenhower.[19]

Rockefeller never entered any primaries against Nixon, and he never officially announced that he would run for the nomination. But through 1959, he employed some seventy people to research the possibility of stripping Nixon of the nomination. In December his advisors presented their findings; he did not have a chance against the vice president. He responded by dropping out of the race that he had never entered.[20] But Rockefeller would not go away, and he remained a thorn in Nixon's side throughout the campaign.

Just after he quit the race, Rockefeller produced a nine-point program for saving the nation. It was, in fact, a scathing indictment of the policies of the Eisenhower administration and the "leading Republican candidate" for their failure "to make clear where this Party is heading." "We cannot, as a nation or a party," the manifesto continued, "proceed to march to meet the future with a banner aloft whose only emblem is a question mark." That statement, along with Rockefeller's nine-point plan itself, infuriated Eisenhower.[21] It appeared that Rockefeller was still on the hunt for the nomination.

Although polls showed that Rockefeller had no real chance of challenging the vice president, Nixon insisted on keeping a close eye on the New York governor. He hired a young Seattle attorney, John Ehrlichman, to shadow every Rockefeller move, and he had a staff member, Herb Klein, look into all aspects of Rockefeller's business involvements. Nixon was particularly interested that Rockefeller might have violated election laws (that did not allow donations of more than $5,000) by making use of an airplane registered with the Rockefeller Foundation, an independent organization.[22] Nixon was running a quiet campaign, but behind the scenes he was covering all his bases.

Then in June, Rockefeller suddenly decided to move back into the campaign. Early that month he delivered a scathing attack on the administration, called for a $3.5 billion increase in the Pentagon budget to answer what was being called "the missile gap," and criticized Nixon for refusing to take a stand on any of the administration's policies. Also, he had conducted a series of polls that showed that he would do better against the Democrats than Nixon by pulling votes from independents and moderate Democrats. He tried to use these polls to build support, but because they were conducted by his own pollsters the press refused to take them seriously. Then he made a big news splash when, during a press conference, he refused to endorse Nixon and said that he was willing to make himself available for a draft at the convention.[23]

Rockefeller seemed to have burned his bridges with the president, but he realized that since Eisenhower had not endorsed Nixon, that an Eisenhower endorsement (and thus the nomination) was still up for grabs. On June 11, he put in a call to the president and asked if he should make a run. Eisenhower took the opportunity to bore in on Rockefeller, complaining that the governor's criticisms of his administration were unwarranted, and that, particularly, Rockefeller's call for greater defense spending was alarmist and unnecessary. Then he told Rockefeller that it would be nearly impossible to take the nomination away from Nixon. The president's best advice was for the governor to wait until 1964; if Nixon lost in November, he would have a good chance then. Rockefeller did not ask directly for an endorsement, and Eisenhower did not offer.[24]

Nixon was trying to walk the fine line between the two increasingly antagonistic wings of his party: The Left and Rockefeller; and the newly invigorated Right now led by Barry Goldwater. What would become, in the 1964 campaign, a clapping thunder from the Right was just beginning to rise in 1960. A small Goldwater for president boomlet began to gain momentum in the spring and early summer of 1960 when some Goldwater supporters convinced the Arizona senator that Nixon was not a true Republican. By the end of July 1959, Americans for Goldwater had mobilized in some thirty states. In March 1960, Goldwater spoke to a crowd of Republicans in South Carolina and, to his own surprise, roused them to pledge their thirteen national convention delegates to him for president. Goldwater was a realist and certainly had no illusions of taking the nomination from Nixon, but he would allow himself to be nominated at the convention where he would use the opportunity to appeal to the party's conservative wing.[25]

Nixon clearly saw himself as the key figure standing between these two groups with the direct obligation of uniting them and bringing the party together. But for Nixon in 1960 the decisive threat to his nomination was from the Rockefeller Left and he set out to pacify that wing of the party. Part of his plan was to try and coax Rockefeller to join the ticket. In May, Nixon seemed to be testing the waters for choosing Rockefeller as his running mate, but Rockefeller made several definitive statements that he would not be willing to run in the number two spot.[26] Nixon continued to push Rockefeller to join the ticket, and Rockefeller continued to spurn the offers.

As the Republicans headed off to their convention in Chicago, Nixon worried that Kennedy and the Democrats had monopolized the publicity, but he saw them as badly divided. He was also encouraged that polls showed him running roughly even with Kennedy.[27] He believed he had done a good job of walking the line between the two wings of his own party, between Rockefeller on the Left and Goldwater on the Right. And with Eisenhower's good graces, he expected to go to Chicago, unite the party, and head out onto the campaign trail. So far, the road of the heir apparent had been reasonably smooth.

CHAPTER SIX

~

The Conventions

When the Democrats arrived in Los Angeles in early July, it was clear the winds of change were in the air. The Kennedy machine marked a changing of the guard, and their youth stood out like a light among the party's old pols. The nominee's four chief lieutenants, the most visible of the group, included Bobby Kennedy, age thirty-four; Ken O'Donnell, thirty-six; Pierre Salinger, thirty-five; and Lawrence O'Brien, the elder statesman at forty-three. The Jim Farleys and the Tommy Corcorans, the power brokers from a political generation now past, seemed to founder in the sea of youth and vigor. The most apparent symbol of this change was that Harry Truman, the perennial representative of the last generation if there ever was one, was conspicuous by his absence from the proceedings.[1] Stevenson fell in as a member of the older generation. One of his closest allies wrote to him as the convention began. "It is hard to watch the younger generation take over and that seems about to happen here."[2]

The question was immediate. Was this the beginning of an era for the Democrats—leading to a new way of thinking, of new ideas spurred on by the new faces in the crowd? There were new people to be sure, and their youth was almost startling; but for any new ideas, for the most part, there was little that was new in the Kennedy vision. Kennedy had developed his foreign policy philosophy from the staid lessons from World War II and had not strayed too far from those ideas. For a domestic philosophy, he looked to the lessons of the Great Depression and the New Deal. None of that was much different from the way Truman and the elder generation saw the world and the nation

71

in 1960. Kennedy did bring to his party, and later to the nation, a new hope for the future—that revolved mostly around his youth and perceived vigor—and a new belief in the need for public service to the nation. But the basic foundations of Kennedy's philosophy were steeped in the events of the prewar and wartime generation. Nevertheless, for the convention-goers in Los Angeles in July 1960, the air seemed filled with the smell of youth and a new future for the party that contrasted abruptly with old politics of the past. They felt they were bearing witness to the ideas of one generation giving way to another.

Kennedy's people arrived on Saturday July 9, five days before the balloting was to begin. By all accounts, their bandwagon was on a roll and they seemed just about to wrap up the nomination. They carried with them a certain 600, 161 short of what they needed to win. Lyndon Johnson controlled between 450 and 500 delegates. Symington had between 100 and 150, and Stevenson controlled only about 50 delegates. A total of 52 votes were pledged to favorite sons: George Docking of Kansas and Hershel Loveless of Iowa. And there were five states that were unknown—up for grabs. Pennsylvania and California, with 81 delegate votes each; New Jersey with 41; Minnesota with 31; and Illinois with 69. Kennedy had a chance to capture just about every one of those votes. So, it seemed he would easily pull together the votes he needed to win the nomination on the first ballot.

Just before Kennedy arrived in Los Angeles, a growing conflict with Harry Truman finally came to a head. Truman had been making statements that Kennedy family money had bought the nomination for John and that the convention had been prearranged for a Kennedy victory. Truman had also made it clear that he disliked father Joe Kennedy and his influence on his son. "It's not the pope that worries me," Truman said, "it's the pop."[3] In May, Truman had announced his support for Stuart Symington, but it seemed common knowledge that he hoped his support for Symington would keep the doors open for Johnson, the man Truman most admired and hoped would win the nomination. At a televised press conference on July 2, Truman said that Kennedy was too young, and "not quite ready" to be president. Then he charged again that Kennedy's nomination had been prearranged. He said he would like to see an open convention and suggested that several other candidates might be better suited for the job, particularly Johnson, Symington, or Chester Bowles.[4]

Kennedy immediately demanded equal time and replied to Truman's statements two days later. He said that Truman's idea of an open convention was one "that studies all the candidates, reviews their records, and then takes his advice." Kennedy then argued that his sixteen years in the House and the

Senate gave him more experience in public office than any president in the twentieth century, and that included Woodrow Wilson, Franklin Roosevelt, *and* Harry Truman. He added that he was older than Washington when he took command of the Continental Army, older than Jefferson when he wrote the Declaration of Independence, and older than Christopher Columbus when he discovered America.[5]

Following the convention, Kennedy made a requisite pilgrimage to Independence, Missouri to visit the old warhorse. He realized the value of Truman's image as an iconic man of the people, and he understood his worth in the coming campaign. The two reconciled (perhaps more because of Truman's hatred of Nixon than for his approval of Kennedy), and Truman finally got on board and campaigned for Kennedy.[6]

⁓

By the time the convention opened its doors in Los Angeles, a stop-Kennedy movement was well underway. And the man of the hour was Stevenson. He continued to insist that he was not interested in the nomination, but such statements really did not resonate much with his supporters; he had said the same sort of thing in 1952 and then again in 1956. He had, in fact, made a career of being coy and reticent, playing the old political game of, "I won't run, but if my party wants me I will accept the nomination." Then on July 8, Stevenson was interviewed on CBS and said fairly bluntly that he would accept a draft, although he considered it unlikely. That same day, he told Anthony Lewis of the *New York Times* that he would accept a draft and do "my utmost to win."[7] With that then, Stevenson supporters flocked to Los Angeles to draft their man—really for a third time since 1952. And they expected him to hear their call, rise to the occasion, and lead them to the nomination. In one way or another it had happened in 1952 and then again in 1956. Why not in 1960?

The draft-Stevenson plan was simple. Keep the undecided delegates and those tied up by favorite sons from going over to Kennedy. That would force a second ballot in which most of the delegations would be released from their first ballot obligations. The assumption was that Kennedy's influence would weaken on a second ballot and Stevenson would begin to pull in delegate votes and finally ride to victory. This strategy was supported by Johnson, Symington, and others who opposed Kennedy because an open second ballot meant the same opportunity for them as it did for Stevenson.[8]

For Kennedy, of course, the objective was to derail this strategy by pulling in enough delegates to win the nomination on the first ballot. And for the Kennedy people, all this planning and posturing in an attempt to derail the

Kennedy machine was futile. "All of us in the Kennedy contingent," Ken O'Donnell recalled, "were amused by the speculation that [Kennedy] might lose if there had to be a second ballot. We knew that we could get at least one hundred more votes on a second ballot than we figured to get on the first ballot."[9]

Johnson officially jumped into the race (and onto the stop-Kennedy bandwagon) on July 5. *Time* wrote that he "galloped into the race later than any serious presidential hopeful on record." In his announcement, he took a jab at Kennedy. "Those who have engaged in active campaigns since January have missed hundreds of votes [in the Senate]. This I could not do. . . . Someone has to tend the store." Then he predicted he would win on the third ballot.[10] Johnson probably believed he could take the South away from Kennedy on a second ballot, sweep the West, and with that base of support, win the nomination as a compromise candidate. He also may have believed that if Stevenson was successful in stopping Kennedy (and then it finally became apparent that Kennedy could not win the nomination), that a disgruntled Kennedy would throw his support Johnson's way before he would surrender to Stevenson, the spoiler.[11]

Johnson had just succeeded in pushing through the Senate the 1960 Civil Rights Act. The bill was another characteristically Johnson compromise. It focused on voting rights but included an ineffectual provision for court registration of black voters. It seemed to satisfy all sides at the moment: white southerners, civil rights advocates, the Eisenhower administration; even the *New York Times* praised it, expecting that it would lead to Johnson's candidacy. Like the 1957 Civil Rights Act, another Johnson-endorsed bill, the 1960 bill was considered an additional step forward (albeit a small one) toward an end to segregation and race discrimination.[12]

But Johnson really had no chance to win the nomination in 1960. Despite his attempts to extricate himself from the stigma of being a southerner and to remake his political self as a national politician, he was still stuck with the old southern image in the minds of most northern politicians and most northern voters—and most of the delegates in Los Angeles. As Kennedy told his advisors just as Johnson announced that he would run. "Do you think that [Chicago mayor] Dick Daley or [Pennsylvania congressman] Bill Green and [New York congressman] Charlie Buckley or [Michigan governor] Mennen Williams would ever accept Johnson? They know he would never get them any votes in the North in a fight against Nixon."[13] Johnson had the most delegate votes besides Kennedy, but his chances of even pulling an upset were really very slim.

On Monday evening, July 11, the convention began at the Los Angeles sports arena. By that time, two of the most important undecided delegations had broken from the stop-Kennedy movement. On Saturday, Pennsylvania governor David Lawrence released his delegates and 64 of the 81 declared for Kennedy. Then on Sunday evening, Chicago mayor Richard Daley released his Illinois delegates. Fifty-nine declared for Kennedy; two declared for Stevenson. This was by far the most important break on the stop-Kennedy strategy because it left Stevenson without a base of support, without his home state to hold as an anchor. If Stevenson ever had a chance to win the nomination, it most likely flittered away here. Then on Monday, the Pennsylvania delegation caucused and gave Kennedy 64 votes. It put Kennedy well over 700.[14]

For the rank-and-file Stevenson supporters, the road to the nomination had just begun. Buoyed by Stevenson's preconvention promise to do his "utmost to win" if nominated, his supporters (perhaps as many as ten thousand) met the noncandidate at the airport on Sunday evening when his plane landed; then the next day, thousands more flooded into the parking lots surrounding the arena. It was, Theodore White recalled, "more than a demonstration. It was an explosion." Stevenson supporters chanted "We want Stevenson, We Want Stevenson." The delegates had to run a gauntlet of Stevenson supporters just to enter the arena. Then on the second night, the throng doubled in size. By Wednesday morning the overburdened Los Angeles police force began calling in reinforcements.[15]

It should be no surprise that a demonstration of such magnitude outside would influence the proceedings inside. By Tuesday afternoon there were rumors that the California delegation was about to revolt and go over to Stevenson despite Governor Pat Brown's insistence that they hold the line and not commit. More rumors circulated that North Dakota, Alabama, Kansas, and even New York were swaying. Old friends were pushing Stevenson to act, to lead, to give the word. On Monday afternoon, Eleanor Roosevelt was scheduled to hold a press conference at the Biltmore Hotel, the nerve center for the convention. Stevenson was to introduce her. The delegates seemed to hold their breath. This, they thought, would be his announcement, his call to arms. It was not. Several in attendance recalled that Mrs. Roosevelt was clearly distressed, hoping herself that Stevenson would rise to the occasion.[16] The next afternoon, Stevenson accepted an invitation to speak to the Minnesota delegation, but again he said nothing about his candidacy—and did not even ask for the support of the delegates. That evening, Tuesday, Stevenson decided he would go to the arena. The word got out, and he was met by a crowd of some seven thousand. When he entered the arena, the demonstration "was spontaneous, not contrived," as one observer recalled. "The galleries went mad," Arthur Schlesinger wrote. Stevenson was delighted by a group of enormously pregnant women carrying signs that read, STEVENSON IS THE MAN.[17] He was finally coaxed to speak. As he made his way to the podium, it was clear to his supporters that this was it, the moment their leader would take command. Instead, he told a bad joke. "After going back and forth through the Biltmore today," he told his followers, "I know who's going to be the nominee of this convention—the last man to survive." The audience went silent. As one of his closest friends recalled, "[W]e had worked hard for [him] . . . but then he went up on the platform and [threw] it out the window. He could have swept that Convention. I could have murdered him. . . . He should have told us he wouldn't fight." Others around Stevenson accused him of not having the stomach to make the fight.[18] Many of Stevenson's supporters were idealists, even romantics. To them, their man had a chance, if only he had picked up the gauntlet and led the faithful. But Stevenson knew better. He did not control nearly enough delegates to make a reasonable stand against Kennedy. In fact, any pragmatic politician could see that his career was over. Although the demonstrations, ovations, and outpouring of support for Stevenson in Los Angeles had not been intended as a farewell gesture, most likely that's how Stevenson took it. He did not intend to lead. He did not intend to stop Kennedy. He simply intended to step aside.

On Tuesday evening, California had split about even. The Kennedy machine tallied its votes. "I don't want generalities or guesses," Bobby told his lieutenants. "I want to hear only the votes we are guaranteed on the first ballot." While Stevenson's supporters were ripping the roof off the arena, Kennedy's people were coldly calculating strategy and collecting delegates. It was, of course, the name of the game. Bobby's body count was 740, just 21 short of the magic number.[19]

By this time, Kennedy had become increasingly frustrated with Stevenson's unwillingness to step aside. Although it seemed clear that Stevenson was not really pushing any stop-Kennedy movement, his reluctance to withdraw his name from contention and the very vocal draft-Stevenson movement was having much the same effect. The earlier offer of secretary of state had failed to garner Stevenson's support, and by now, certainly, that offer was off the table. In one last attempt to get Stevenson on board, Kennedy asked Stevenson to place his name in nomination, as Jack had done for Stevenson in 1956. But again, Stevenson demurred, insisting that he would remain "neutral."[20]

The next morning, due mostly to saturation rumors, the vast majority of the delegates, along with the throngs of Stevenson supporters inside and outside the arena, were under the impression that Stevenson was in the ring—that he was running. On that day, Wednesday, Stevenson's supporters began smuggling themselves into the arena, using either counterfeit credentials or running an elaborate scheme of slipping groups of credential cards from the delegates inside to nondelegate supporters outside. By the time Stevenson was nominated, the arena was packed with his supporters from the floor to the galleries.

That evening, the nomination speeches began: Sam Rayburn nominated Johnson. With Stevenson still "neutral," Kennedy chose Minnesota Governor Orville Freeman to deliver his nominating speech. That was followed by Eugene McCarthy's nomination of Stevenson. McCarthy had just won election to the Senate from Minnesota and was considered one of the party's new lights. His speech, Theodore White recalled, was "the height of drama." "Do not reject this man," McCarthy called to the faithful. "Do not leave this prophet without honor in his own party." That was followed by such a riotous demonstration that Florida governor Leroy Collins, the permanent chair, ordered the lights turned off in the arena in an attempt to bring some order out of the uproar. This, Schlesinger recalled of the Stevenson surge, "was the last burst of defiance."[21]

The balloting began on Wednesday evening. Kennedy was tucked away in a hideout apartment watching the count on television with his advisors. Just as the tallying began, a fuse blew out the apartment, and the television sets went dark. Kennedy ran downstairs to a neighbor's apartment where he watched the returns with the pajama-clad family. As each state announced their vote, Kennedy's numbers moved closer to 760, the number needed to clinch the nomination. Finally, with the vote from Wisconsin, the tally reached 748. A television camera caught Ted Kennedy working the Wyoming delegation. According to Ken O'Donnell, Ted looked up at the TV camera and smiled. "This could be it," Kennedy told his advisors. And it was. Wyoming's 15 votes put him over the top.[22]

At first glance, all the ingredients had been in place for a dramatic and typical, old-time Democratic Party convention fight. But in fact when the smoke cleared, it was apparent that the Kennedy steamroller had really been unstoppable from the start. Stevenson's time in the sun had passed, and Johnson arrived with too little, too late. In the days following the convention, *Time* reported on the reality of the events. "Despite Lyndon Johnson's belated drive, despite the boisterous demonstrations for Adlai Stevenson, the efficient, machinelike Kennedy team had the nomination won before the first gavel." Had it not been for the eruption for Stevenson, the nomination choice would have been fairly mundane. In the same article, *Time* recorded that "the convention oratory seem[ed] superfluous and the floor demonstrations archaic."[23]

It was true. By 1960 the nation's political parties were beginning to move away from the raucous floor fights and smoke-filled rooms of the first half of the century and toward the less boisterous political coronations that dominated most of the second half of the century. The steamroller affect, the momentum generated by months of primary campaigns, television ads, and publicity in the press carried candidates to the conventions with the decisions generally already made. There would be exceptions, but for the most part, beginning in 1960, the purpose and significance of the American political convention was changing.

The next order of business was for Kennedy to choose a running mate. For many of Kennedy's closest advisors and supporters, the obvious choice was Lyndon Johnson. Kennedy had thrown out other names throughout the year, if for no other reason than to keep his decision close so that, if necessary, he could use it as a bargaining chip at the convention. He often spoke of Missouri senator Stuart Symington. A protégé of Harry Truman, Symington was popular with labor and strong in the Midwest, but Kennedy was being counseled that he had to win Texas in November. Texas had gone for Eisenhower in both 1952 and 1956; Johnson could deliver it and probably much of the South as well. In a closely held strategy memo issued to Kennedy's men immediately after the candidate's nomination, one point is clear. "Senator Kennedy was nominated . . . with fewer Southern votes than any Presidential candidate in the history of the Democratic Party."[24] Kennedy simply could not afford to turn away from the South.

The problem for Kennedy and the Democrats was, of course, race—a problem the party had grappled with for a century. The Platform Committee, under the leadership of Chester Bowles, a strong Kennedy supporter and a liberal, had pounded out a platform that *Time* described as "a far-out liberal manifesto containing a tough civil rights plank that enraged the South."[25] The civil rights plank was a seven-point document that covered just about every aspect of civil rights: the right to vote, the abolition of literacy tests, an end to discriminatory practices in federal housing, the establishment of a permanent Fair Employment Practices Commission, and a permanent Commission on Civil Rights.[26] Delegates from ten southern states immediately responded with a minority report that called for, among other things, the authority of the individual states to regulate education. The southerners also complained that it was their states (and no others) that had gone to the

Democratic candidate in 1952 and again in 1956, and now their demands were being pushed aside and they, as a bloc within the party, were being vilified. It was a strong argument, but Bowles expected to hold the South despite the civil rights planks in the platform, and the southerners avoided all talk of bolting the convention because Johnson appeared to be the leading contender for the vice presidential nomination. Although there is no evidence of any deals made, it seems clear that by choosing Johnson as his running mate, Kennedy was able to keep the strong civil rights plank in the platform and thus win black votes, while holding most of the South in line.

Everything pointed to Johnson for vice president—except that the Kennedy family and the candidate's campaign lieutenants simply did not like the Texas senator, and the feelings were generally mutual. Kennedy's people considered Johnson an uneducated hick and had taken to calling him "Colonel Cornpone." Johnson in turn had referred to Kennedy as "that little scrawny fellow with rickets," who "looked like a spavined hunchback." He often called him a "playboy" and a "lightweight." In the month prior to the convention, Johnson questioned Kennedy's McCarthy connections, questioned his health, and even revived Eleanor Roosevelt's statement that he "understands what courage is, and admires it but has not quite the independence to have it."[27]

Immediately following Kennedy's nomination in Los Angeles, lists of possible running mates began to surface among Kennedy's people. Johnson headed several of these lists, but Kennedy, at that time, did not think Johnson would give up his Senate leadership position to accept the offer. At the same time, several political heavyweights had been urging Kennedy to choose Johnson, particularly columnist Joseph Alsop, *Washington Post* publisher Phil Graham, Chicago mayor Richard Daley, New York's Carmine DiSapio, and party warhorse Tommy Corcoran.[28]

On Wednesday night, July 13, Corcoran, Massachusetts congressman "Tip" O'Neill, and others tried to pressure Johnson into accepting the nomination if Kennedy offered it. Johnson replied that he would do it, but only if Sam Rayburn would agree. Historian Robert Dallek has argued that Johnson and Rayburn had already decided that if Kennedy made the offer Johnson would accept it, but they wanted it to appear that Johnson had accepted it reluctantly.[29]

Earlier that day, Kennedy (apparently under the assumption that Johnson would not accept the number-two position) had offered the vice presidential nomination to Symington. After some discussion with his family (who advised him against it) Symington accepted the offer. Rumors spread to the floor of the convention, and the Los Angeles press picked up the story.[30] But by the next morning, everything had changed.

On Thursday morning, Kennedy had become convinced that Johnson would, in fact, accept the offer, and at about 9:00 a.m. he visited Johnson's room at the Biltmore and asked him to be his running mate. It is often assumed that Kennedy made the offer under an assumption that Johnson would not take it, that he wanted to be offered the nomination as a sort of political courtesy. According to Johnson's own recollections, he turned Kennedy down flat. But according to Bobby Kennedy's account, Jack returned to his room and announced that Johnson had, in fact, accepted the offer. According to Bobby, Johnson's unexpected acceptance set the Kennedy crowd into a tizzy. "Oh, my God!" Bobby was to have said, "Now what do we do?"[31] All this seems fairly incredible. Kennedy would not have visited Johnson unless he knew Johnson would accept; and by late Thursday (and probably well before that) Johnson had been convinced to accept the offer.[32] What is clear, despite Johnson's diary entry to the contrary, is that when Kennedy returned to his suite after visiting Johnson, an offer had been made and accepted.

The real problems for the ticket began when the choice was leaked to the public, and the liberals, as *Time* reported, "began raging with indignation." And that may have caused the Kennedys to balk, momentarily, at the decision. The list of unhappy Democrats was long. Liberals, particularly those who had supported Stevenson, were barely containable, and many left the convention in protest or disgust; labor leaders like Walter Reuther and Arthur Goldberg were livid; Symington felt betrayed and the Midwesterners who supported him were upset as well. Arthur Schlesinger told *Newsweek*, "I felt sick. . . ." *Time* reported in absurd, flowery language that "many liberals had the feeling that they had been whipsawed by a Univac in a button-down collar."[33] Perhaps most importantly, Kennedy's loyal lieutenants rebelled immediately. Ken O'Donnell, who was Kennedy's liaison to labor, said "I felt that we had been double-crossed." He later wrote that he "was so furious" that he "could hardly talk," and he told Kennedy that it was the worse mistake he had ever made.[34] By 11:00 labor leaders, unaware that an offer had been made and accepted, had gotten word that Kennedy was considering Johnson as a running mate. They filed into Kennedy's suite and objected strenuously. Jack Conway told Kennedy, "don't do it. Because if you offer it to him, he'll take it. We've come a long way. . . . If you do this, you're going to fuck everything up."[35] The Kennedy brothers began to doubt their decision. They made the obvious argument that a Kennedy-Johnson ticket was a winner, that Roosevelt had chosen Texan John Nance Garner in 1932, and Stevenson had chosen John Sparkman from Alabama twenty years later. Kennedy argued that with Johnson out of the Senate, Mike Mansfield, a man he could trust and control, would be majority leader. These were all good arguments, and within hours most Democrats would see their wisdom. But here, just minutes after accepting Johnson as his running mate, John Kennedy (and Robert) may have gotten cold feet. The common story is that Bobby (either on his own or at his brother's direction) visited Johnson at least three times during the afternoon and tried to convince him to back out of the offer and accept the chairmanship of the Democratic National Committee.[36] Parts of that may be true, but most likely the story was concocted to satisfy liberals that as a result of some strange set of events, Johnson somehow grabbed the vice presidential spot when it really had not been offered. According to Arthur Krock of the *New York Times*, who was in Johnson's room at the time of Bobby's visits, the discussions were mostly directed at making sure that Johnson would support a fight against the liberals on the floor if it came to that.[37]

The choice of Johnson for running mate was the right decision, and even the liberals came around by the end of the day. Any practical politician could see the wisdom of it. Kennedy and Johnson were, in fact, almost a caricature of what a political ticket should be. Although Johnson was only a few years older than Kennedy, he looked much older and represented the past generation of politicians, the old New Dealers, while Kennedy represented youth and the future. Kennedy was from the Northeast and was strong in the industrial states, popular with labor, ethnic groups, and, of course, Catholics. Johnson just about covered the rest of the nation, the South, the West, large parts of the Midwest, farmers, and he could carry Texas. Kennedy attracted liberal intellectuals like Schlesinger, Galbraith, Niebuhr, and finally Stevenson. Johnson knew how to appeal to the grassroots, the average American, the farmer in the field, the southern landowner. Whatever Johnson was, Kennedy was not; and whatever Kennedy was, Johnson was not. It truly was the perfect ticket.

～

In his acceptance speech, before some eighty thousand people at the Los Angeles Coliseum and before millions on television, Kennedy talked of a "New Frontier." It is not, he said, "a set of promises; it is a set of challenges. It sums up not what I intend to offer to the American people, but what I intend to ask of them." On religion, he promised to reject "any kind of religious pressure or obligation that might directly or indirectly interfere with my conduct of the Presidency in the national interest. . . ." On foreign policy, he warned the nation: "The old era is ending. The old ways will not do. . . . The world has been close to war before—but now man, who has survived all previous threats to his existence, has taken into his mortal hands the power to exterminate the entire species some seven times over. . . . It is time," he added, "for a new generation of leadership—new men to cope with new problems and new opportunities. . . . We stand today on the edge of a New Frontier—the frontier of the 1960s—a frontier of unknown opportunities and perils—a frontier of unfulfilled hopes and threats." Then, to the disappointment of many in attendance, Kennedy stepped back from his theme of hope and the future of the nation and attacked his opponent. Nixon, Kennedy told his audience, was no Eisenhower: "For just as historians tell us that Richard I was not fit to fill the shoes of Henry II, and that Richard Cromwell was not fit to wear the mantle of his uncle, they might add in future years that Richard Nixon did not measure up to the footsteps of Dwight D. Eisenhower." The reaction was an indication of how many Americans had come to see Kennedy—as a symbol for the nation's future instead of just another politician. *Time* called this portion of the speech a "daisy cutter," and insisted it had "misfired because Jack Kennedy's campaign had seemed to show promise of something vastly better."[38] Could Kennedy run a high-minded campaign and still attack Nixon?

For most Democrats, the events of mid-July 1960 sounded the rise of a new generation in the party and the end of the era of the New Dealers. Arthur Schlesinger later wrote, "One watched the changing of the guard with a mixture of nostalgia and hope."[39] Kennedy certainly felt comfortable in that position, and he played it well during the campaign and after the election. He would be a strong candidate—and Nixon knew it. Nixon wrote to journalist George Sokolsky just after Kennedy's nomination: "This means that the election will be a close, hard-fought one. There have been press reports to the effect that I thought Kennedy would be the easiest to beat. Nothing could be further from the truth. . . . In any event, it will not be a dull campaign."[40]

⌢

Immediately following the Democratic convention, Ronald Reagan sent Nixon one of his celebrated handwritten notes—his thoughts on the convention. The Democrats, Reagan wrote with a full dose of sarcasm, "could pick up some campaign money by selling their collection of [speeches] as, 'talk suitable for any patriotic occasion with platitudes and generalities guaranteed.' . . . Unfortunately," he added, Kennedy "is a powerful speaker with an appeal to the emotions. He leaves little doubt that his idea of the 'challenging new world' is one in which the Federal Gov't will grow bigger and do more and of course spend more." Then he added what Nixon may have seen as a warning as he prepared to attend the Republican convention in Chicago and face the growing conservative movement in his party. "I know there must be some short sighted people in the Republican Party who will advise that the Republicans should try to 'out liberal' [Kennedy]. To my opinion this would be fatal."[41]

The Republicans met at the huge International Amphitheatre in Chicago, a facility built near the old Chicago stockyards. No one expected many fireworks. There was no doubt that Nixon was the heir apparent. He had control of some one thousand of the six hundred-plus delegates needed to win the nomination without having done much of anything to win their support. Perhaps the only anticipation was that Barry Goldwater had won control of the South Carolina delegation and therefore would be nominated and have his time at the podium. Many expected him to rouse the conservative faithful. He would not disappoint them.

Nixon's only real problem was the irascible Rockefeller. The New York governor had no realistic chance of taking the nomination away from Nixon, and everyone knew that. Most thought he would do little more than have himself nominated, make a speech designed to set up his political future, and then step aside in the spirit of party unity. That was generally the proper course of events. But Rockefeller had enough support among the moderates in the party to force Nixon to commit to issues that could damage his position with others in the party—either Eisenhower and his supporters, or the party's right wing. That clearly worried Nixon. Then, if Rockefeller chose to turn all this into a scuffle, it could produce a floor fight over the platform that might damage Nixon's campaign and reopen old wounds that could hurt the party in the future. Perhaps more importantly, if Nixon failed to appease Rockefeller, and the result was that Rocky responded by refusing to aid Nixon's campaign, Nixon might lose all chance of winning New York's all-important forty-five electoral votes in the general election. At a national governors' conference at Glacier National Park in Montana, Rockefeller was asked by other Republican governors to sign a pledge supporting Nixon's candidacy. He refused, and the rebuff was leaked to the press.[42] Nixon knew he would have to give something to Rockefeller.

At the same time, Rockefeller knew exactly where he stood in all this; he believed he could deliver his state (as it turned out he could not), and, of course, he knew that Nixon needed New York to beat Kennedy. He had significant leverage and he intended to use it. Nixon's problem was even more acute now that Kennedy, with Johnson on the ticket, would have a good chance of taking Texas and much of the rest of the South. New York was even more important.

Nixon had other problems. Several foreign policy events in Eisenhower's second term damaged the Eisenhower presidency, and by association, Nixon's candidacy. The question of what was being called "the missile gap" affected the campaign the most. This was the simple argument that the Soviets had advanced beyond the United States in its development of high tech nuclear weaponry—specifically in the development of missiles (ICBMS) that might soon have the ability to reach U.S. targets. A missile gap with the Soviets did not exist, information that was in the president's hands because of top secret U-2 reconnaissance overflights of Soviet air space. Nevertheless, a series of events in the three years leading up to the campaign and the election turned the "missile gap" into a political football, allowing both liberals and conservatives in the Republican Party to attack the administration's policies—and then giving the Democrats a powerful issue against Nixon in the general campaign. In October 1957, the Soviets amazed the world by launching *Sputnik*, the first artificial earth satellite. This was little more than a propaganda victory for the Soviets until the United States tried to follow with their own launch that ended in a humiliating failure. Americans had always taken pride in their technological superiority. Now, clearly, they were in second place.

In the political arena, this was a reason to criticize the administration for allowing the Soviets to get the upper hand in a highly strategic area. Democrats had been charging for years that the Eisenhower administration had not been spending enough on national defense. Senator Symington insisted that Eisenhower call Congress into special session to deal with the problem, and Adlai Stevenson accused the president of "unilateral disarmament at the expense of our national security." Kennedy insisted that "the deterrent ratio during 1960–1964 will in all likelihood be weighted against us."[43] As the convention approached, it was Rockefeller, however, who would make the most noise on the issue, insisting that the next Republican nominee—presumably Nixon—take on this issue and promise advances in nuclear weapons systems. That placed Nixon in a dilemma because to call for significant advances in military spending was a direct criticism of Eisenhower and his administration.

In mid-September Khrushchev visited the United States, and it appeared that Eisenhower would leave office as a peacemaker. The two leaders met at Camp David in the Maryland mountains and agreed to meet again in Paris in May 1960. It was not a great diplomatic advancement, but it clearly eased world tensions. But the worldwide sigh of relief did not last long. On May 1, the Soviets shot down a U-2 high-altitude reconnaissance aircraft, and that touched off a storm that impacted the campaign. Khrushchev refused to meet Eisenhower in Paris unless he agreed to discontinue the overflights. When Ike refused, the conference was called off, and Khrushchev withdrew an invitation for Eisenhower to visit the U.S.S.R. the next year. This gave more ammunition to the Democrats, who gained some traction by accusing the president of handling the situation badly.

Although Eisenhower was hurt by the collapse of the Paris summit, the entire U-2 incident may have actually helped the Republicans. It made the president appear to be standing up to the Russians while protecting the nation from a Pearl Harbor-like attack by authorizing the U-2 overflights. The incident made the Soviets appear even more intransigent and difficult to deal with. Nixon was able to argue that he, more than the Democrats, could confront the Soviets, and the incident highlighted Kennedy's youth and inexperience in foreign affairs.

The administration may have avoided severe damage over the U-2 incident, but in June, Eisenhower suffered the most humiliating diplomatic setback of his entire presidency when massive anti-American riots in Japan forced the Japanese prime minister to cancel the president's scheduled visit. The Democrats jumped on the event, claiming that Eisenhower's complacency had caused the United States to lose influence abroad.

Then in January 1959 Fidel Castro took control of Cuba, just ninety miles from American shores, and began a slow drift into the Soviet orbit. By July 1960, Khrushchev was denouncing the Monroe Doctrine as a dead document, and Soviet influence in Cuba had begun to take on a frighteningly military appearance. It looked as though international relations were further deteriorating when a civil war broke out in the Congo, and it appeared to many observers that communism was the catalyst. Then, just as the Republicans took their seats in Chicago, the Soviets shot down another surveillance plane.

These events were in the headlines and in the minds of the Republican delegates as they took their seats at their convention in Chicago. Nixon did not need to worry about the outcome, but there were figures on the Left and the Right who saw the administration's foreign policy as weak, underfunded, and running in second place. Rockefeller, among others, hoped to pull Nixon away from the policies of the Eisenhower administration and into a new era of military buildup and confrontation. Nixon was stuck in the middle.

In mid-July the Republican Platform Committee began meeting and pulling together the ideas of various party members and factions. As had been the case at the last few conventions, the committee was dominated by the party's right wing. Chaired by Charles Percy of Illinois, it went about its arduous business of balancing ideas and demands, including soliciting from Rockefeller his ideas for the platform. Rockefeller responded in true Rockefeller fashion by submitting an entire platform that spelled out his demands for the party and the party's future. He called for "a second-strike nuclear retaliatory power capable of surviving" a first strike; and a "capacity for limited warfare that can deter or check local aggression." His platform submission also called for the construction of more bombers, more Polaris submarines with nuclear launch capabilities, more missiles, and a more effective civil defense program. He also wanted federally subsidized health insurance for the elderly, funded through a boost in the Social Security tax.[44] The Platform Committee then set out to try and satisfy Rockefeller's demands. Kentucky senator Thurston Morton, Percy, and others on the committee fully expected Rockefeller to accept Nixon's offer to be his running mate, so the committee tried hard to meet as many of Rockefeller's demands as possible. At the same time, of course, the president's people and the party's right wing had to be satisfied as well. Finally, on Friday, July 22, after the committee had been meeting for a few days, Rockefeller announced, from his executive chambers in Albany, that the committee had not satisfied him, saying that the direction of the platform is "seriously lacking in strength and specifics."[45]

This was an obvious threat of open civil war within the party and on the floor of the convention. Nixon would have to contain the problem. As he wrote in *Six Crises*, "under present circumstances he would not come to me—I had to go to him." After some intermediary haggling through their mutual friend, Herbert Brownell, it was finally decided that the two would meet at Rockefeller's Fifth Avenue penthouse apartment. Nixon flew to New York from Washington that Friday evening, July 22. The two had a cordial dinner, and then Nixon, as he recalled it in his memoir, "got down to brass tacks."[46] He tried almost desperately to convince Rockefeller to accept the number two spot on the ticket. Nixon promised to give the vice presidency greater significance—more than even Eisenhower had. Rockefeller again said no. Nixon pushed the point for two hours, until finally agreeing that he would respect Rockefeller's decision and no longer belay the point.[47] He later admitted that he needed the balance on the ticket that Rockefeller would provide, but that he was relieved that Rockefeller had turned down the offer. "Rockefeller's independent temperament would have made him a much more difficult running mate for me to deal with than Johnson would be for Kennedy."[48]

Then for eight hours, until 3:30 the next morning, the two pounded out the party platform, often on the telephone with Percy in Chicago. The result was a fourteen-point accord. It called for greater military defense with the clear implication for greater defense spending; medical care for the aged, although it did not specify how that benefit would be funded; federal intervention to stimulate the economy; a strong civil rights plank, including support for the sit-in movement then sweeping across the South; and an agreement to repeal right-to-work. It seemed cordial and workable, but it was definitely more Rockefeller than Nixon. At 3:30 Saturday morning, a tired Nixon left New York and flew back to Washington. Rockefeller phoned the decisions in to Percy in Chicago, then he released the document to the press. Nixon slept until noon.[49]

The Republicans in Chicago awakened the next morning to the news. Those who approved of the agreement called it "The Treaty of Fifth Avenue," a compromise for moderation.[50] Conservatives, however, were stunned. They began calling the agreement "The Surrender of Fifth Avenue." It "stung them," *Newsweek* reported, "like a wet towel in the face." To them it appeared that Rockefeller had summoned Nixon to his lair and then forced him to accept his terms. They said Nixon had done little more than "take dictation." Goldwater was furious. He called Nixon a "two-fisted four-square liar," and he persisted in calling the agreement the "Munich of the Republican Party."[51] Ronald Reagan, who had been supportive of the vice president, fired off a telegram to Nixon that pretended to speak for Goldwater. "Goldwate[r] . . . cannot support a ticket if it includes Rockefeller."[52] The Texas delegation went so far as to release their delegates from their commitment to Nixon.[53] Nixon may have shored up his Left, but he managed to alienate his Right. The event set the stage for the Republican Party for at least the next twenty years. Nixon would never again be trusted by the Republican Right, and the "Rockefeller wing" of the party would be their nemesis.

Perhaps it was the Platform Committee itself that was the most frustrated. "No words of pain, outrage and fury can describe the reaction of the Republican Platform Committee," Theodore White wrote.[54] The 103 members of the committee, mostly conservatives, had labored for days to put together a platform that, they thought, balanced Eisenhower, Rockefeller, and Nixon. They produced a document, only to have it brushed aside by the new Nixon-Rockefeller compromise. But more importantly, it appeared to be the normal pattern of things within the party. Since the war, the Republican Right would work to bring its influence to bear—often in the Platform Committee or in the nomination of their candidate—only to have some mysterious Eastern conspiracy drop in from on high to frustrate the effort, to push them aside in favor of the Establishment moderates. With no candidate to support in 1960 and no other party to support but the Republicans, all this was becoming a bitter pill for the Right to swallow.

Then, to make all things worse, Rockefeller showed up at a rally in Chicago, waved a copy of the agreement over his head, and yelled, "If you don't think this represents my views, you're crazy." The Right cringed.[55]

When Nixon arrived on Monday morning, July 25, just three days before the convention began, he was immediately attacked from all sides. But

Nixon saw the agreement with Rockefeller as healing a deep wound in the party; and, he believed, he had guaranteed Rockefeller's support in the campaign. The next day he called a press conference. He tried to explain that he agreed with everything that came from the meeting, and that the two men had not, in fact, agreed on everything, citing their difference of opinion on how to fund medical care for the aged. "I need Rockefeller," he said, but "I am calling the shots."[56]

It looked like Nixon would stick to his guns, but when the president, vacationing at Newport, got wind of the agreement, he weighed in—and it was clear that he was furious. He saw Nixon's willingness to go along with Rockefeller's demands for greater defense spending as a criticism of his policies. A harried Nixon called the president to discuss the issue. Eisenhower's secretary, Ann Whitman, summarized the conversation. "Nixon said the members of the Platform Committee were mad because they don't want to appear to be giving in to Rockefeller and because . . . Rockefeller made [the] statement himself and the way he made it." Goldwater, Nixon said, "was personally stimulated by what has happened." Eisenhower responded. "Some of the members [of the Platform Committee] felt that [in the agreement with Rockefeller] there was implied and indirect criticism of the Administration." The president then, according to Whitman's summation of the conversation, "threatened indirectly no enthusiasm for [the] campaign if [the] platform criticized [the] Administration. . . ." And in another conversation, the president said: By doing this "you are saying that you and I haven't done a proper job." Nixon was boxed in again. "What we are trying to do," he told the president, "is to find some ground on which this fellow [Rockefeller] can be with us and not against us."[57] By Saturday afternoon, Eisenhower's people had rallied their forces and were in full revolt against the Nixon-Rockefeller agreement. At the same time, the now-spurned Platform Committee had decided to publish and distribute their original platform. The party was headed for a floor fight over the platform—the last thing Nixon wanted.

Nixon then had his aides cobble together a vague statement to be included in the platform that would, supposedly, satisfy everyone. "The United States can and must provide whatever is necessary to insure its own security. . . . To provide more would be wasteful. To provide less would be catastrophic." Percy called Eisenhower and offered him $100 for every word in the platform he disliked.[58] Everyone, it seemed, was satisfied with the vagueness of the statement. Everyone except Goldwater. Like many other Republicans, Goldwater was calling for a stronger national defense. Consequently, he hated the first Nixon compromise with Rockefeller; and he hated the second compromise with Eisenhower.

This event might have threatened to send the Republican Party down a divisive path, but it was almost certainly the right thing for Nixon to do. In fact, he surrendered very little—if anything. The substance of the fourteen-point agreement violated none of Nixon's basic principles or policies. Like many other leading figures at the time, he believed that the nation under Eisenhower had been strong, but the Soviets had been allowed to step forward in most areas of defense; it was time for the United States to expand in that area. He may have made a mistake by thinking that if he issued a joint statement with Rockefeller that he would be able to make that assertion without incurring the wrath of the president. But nevertheless, he probably had not compromised very much on that issue. Everyone in the party knew that Rockefeller had to be appeased in some manner. The Manhattan agreement allowed Nixon to say to his detractors (from Eisenhower to Goldwater) that this is the price we must pay for Rockefeller's support. It might be uncomfortable for everyone involved, but it was necessary to bring the party together and avoid a floor fight.[59]

At the same time, he may have alienated the Right, but in 1960 that group was not yet the power within the party it would become. The threat to Nixon was from Rockefeller and the Left. He had to deal with that group. If in the process he alienated Goldwater and a few vocal western conservatives, it was not a dear price to pay. In fact, by compromising with Rockefeller and bringing him into his campaign, Nixon believed he stood a good chance of carrying New York. And he might also take Pennsylvania and his own California, states with strong moderate Republican bases.

The only real mistake that Nixon made was allowing Rockefeller to release the compromise document to the party Platform Committee and then to the press. That, of course, made it appear that Nixon had just signed on. Nixon also allowed the document to be written in Rockefeller's language—language that Republicans were familiar with because of Rockefeller's June pronouncement that had included many of the same demands.

In the long run, this event had a huge impact on the Republican Party. It drove a wedge between the Rockefeller moderates and growing Goldwater conservatives. All this would play out in 1964. In that campaign, Nixon would refuse to run, Eisenhower would not endorse a candidate, and Goldwater would beat Rockefeller in several brutally divisive primaries and take the nomination. By the end of the 1964 convention, the Rockefeller moderates had been drummed out of the party and there was so much animosity that the wounds would not heal for years. Just a week following the Nixon-Rockefeller compromise, *Time* wrote that "it changed the course of the Republican Party for the 1960s, and perhaps beyond."[60]

Goldwater had intended to withdraw his name from nomination and re-lease his delegates (from South Carolina) before the convention. But fol-lowing the Nixon-Rockefeller pact, Goldwater decided, "that can wait."[61] He accepted the offer to address the convention (in withdrawing his name from nomination), and conservatives seemed to know that he was going to stir things up. He began his speech by calling for party unity, but he immediately turned to admonishing his fellow conservatives. "We must remember," his voice raised, "that Republicans have not been losing elections because of more Democrat votes . . . we have been losing elections because conserva-tives often fail to vote. . . . Let's grow up conservatives," he yelled. "Let's—if we want to take this party back—and I think we can someday—let's get to work."[62] For many conservatives that was a call to arms, the beginning of the modern conservative movement—the beginning of the modern American political system.

⌒

Nixon's difficulties with the Right would only be made worse by his choice of a running mate. He had won the nomination even before he set foot in-side the Chicago Amphitheatre, so he had no reason to go through the usual convention process of floating names of possible running mates in exchange for delegate votes. Thus, he quickly narrowed the choice down to two men: Thurston Morton from Kentucky and Henry Cabot Lodge, Jr. from Massa-chusetts.

Immediately, Eisenhower (who refused to come to Chicago and work on Nixon's behalf but clearly wanted to influence just about every decision) made it clear that he wanted Lodge. It was Lodge who had handled Eisen-hower's 1952 noncampaign while the general continued his duties as the head of NATO. Lodge was Ike's ambassador to the United Nations, and he was considered a strong foreign affairs figure. He was also seen regularly on the evening news bantering, negotiating, and arguing with the world's heads of state.[63] When Khrushchev visited the United States in the late summer of 1959, Lodge was assigned to be at the Soviet Premier's side at all times. Per-haps more importantly, neither Kennedy nor Johnson had any significant for-eign affairs experience, and Nixon hoped to make that a campaign issue. There were, however, downsides to Lodge. He was not a very dynamic figure. During the campaign, he would not light fires under crowds of voters. And there was one other nagging point. It was Kennedy who had defeated Lodge for his Senate seat in 1952.[64]

Morton was the southern candidate. He was a senator from Kentucky, the GOP chairman, and a past assistant secretary of state. He was genial, well-liked, and a forceful speaker. But when Kennedy chose Johnson, it became less important for Nixon to chose a southerner; Morton's popularity in the South was no match for Johnson. Also, it would be necessary for Morton to resign his Senate seat to run, which would allow Kentucky's Democratic governor to name a Democrat to that seat, a seat that Republicans could ill afford to lose.[65]

At the Sheraton Room at the Blackstone Hotel in Chicago, Nixon pulled together some thirty-five of the Republican leadership—conservatives were not invited. They met just three floors below the notorious "smoke-filled room" in which the hapless Warren Harding had been chosen by party bigwigs in 1920. After several hours of discussion, cigars, and Scotch, it seemed to come down to a statement by Tom Dewey. "It all simmers down to this," Dewey said, "If we want to send the delegates home happy, we ought to agree on Morton. . . . But if we want to make the *people* happy, it should be Lodge. . . . [H]e would put the emphasis on foreign policy, where it should be."[66] Dewey prevailed.

There was a rumor among the party's right wing that at the "Surrender of Fifth Avenue," Rockefeller turned down the offer to run with Nixon but insisted that Nixon choose a Northeastern moderate. When Nixon announced that Lodge would be his running mate, the wedge cut deeper. Lodge was Eastern Establishment (not unlike Rockefeller), a moderate, and an internationalist. He was also a Boston Brahmin. For conservatives like Goldwater, Lodge was a long way from acceptable.

The parties had chosen. Both men knew that the campaign would be hard-fought and the outcome would, most likely, be close. *Time* looked forward to reporting the events. "[A] Nixon v. Kennedy match could be one of the most fascinating and intellectual campaigns in U.S. history."[67]

CHAPTER SEVEN

~

Campaign One

Most postconvention polls showed Nixon with about a six-point lead over Kennedy. The polls also showed that despite Kennedy's exposure in the primary elections, Nixon was still much better known and generally considered the more experienced candidate. The polls also showed that Kennedy was still having trouble shaking his reputation as a wealthy, inexperienced young man who would very much like to be president.[1] At the same time, the Democrats seemed to be losing some of their footing. The South, traditionally Democratic for some eight decades, was now uncertain because of the party's stand on civil rights and Kennedy's religion. The rest of the nation was generally split. Another problem for Kennedy was the big Democratic strongholds of New York, New Jersey, Michigan, Illinois, and Pennsylvania. They had all fallen to the Republicans in the last two presidential elections; and although they remained Democratic at the state and local levels, a majority of the voters had grown accustomed to voting for a Republican presidential candidate. Pulling these two regions back into the Democratic Party would be crucial to Kennedy's campaign.

Nixon headed into his campaign with the significant advantage of having the executive branch of government and the president in his corner. Eisenhower had reigned over eight years of general peace and prosperity; he was an immensely popular figure and had proven to be an amazing vote getter. If Nixon used Eisenhower correctly in the campaign, it would be a tremendous advantage. At the same time, Eisenhower's moderation had blurred many of the old defining lines between the two parties. Because of Eisenhower's policies and popularity, large numbers of Democrats had crossed over to vote for him in both 1952 and 1956. That did not exactly pull the Republicans out of their long-time minority party status, but it certainly opened the doors for Nixon to capitalize on the trend. Nixon understood that, and he moved in that direction by reinventing himself as an Eisenhower moderate. But to bring this trend to fruition, Nixon would have to use Ike, to push the big man himself into the arena. Nixon would need Eisenhower on the stump.

An important advantage for Kennedy was that he showed significant strength in the polls (although he was behind), yet he was still not well-known nationwide. As many as 60 percent of the electorate admitted that they had, thus far, not paid much attention to the campaign. All that, of course, would change before November. As the nation became more and more involved in the campaign, and as Kennedy received more and more exposure in the press, his numbers, already strong, would surely improve.

Perhaps the most unique aspect of the Kennedy campaign was the candidate's strong organization. The Kennedy organization was, in fact, the first truly modern campaign organization. Before 1960, presidential campaign organizations were generally small and run by the candidate and supported by a few advisors and fund-raisers. The campaigns themselves only lasted a couple of months, at most. The candidate traveled the nation by train, dragging the print press along behind, speaking several times a day from the platform of the rear car. Truman had perfected the "whistle-stop" campaign in 1948, but it was nothing new, even then. It was well-tested and well-worn, but by 1960 the strategy had passed its day.

Instead of a whistle-stop tour, Kennedy and his people used all the modern tools of the day: air travel and television, particularly. The organization incorporated advance men, a brain trust of advisors, and a cluster of pollsters to keep his campaign in touch with voting trends clear down to the precinct level. Communication was key; the Kennedy people always arranged for giant telephone banks at their campaign headquarters to keep in touch with those on the ground, or on the floor of the convention, those with their fingers on the pulse of the voters. Other talented people around Kennedy were experts at generating huge, friendly crowds for the candidate's appearances, and then getting the events on the evening news.

The workings of the inner circle of the Kennedy organization ran particularly smoothly. Kennedy had decided early on that he would not be his own campaign manager. He left that to his brother Bobby, his brother-in-law Stephen Smith, and the other "Kennedy men" who scheduled events, raised money, organized, and planned. The candidate concentrated on public and television appearances, getting his ideas across to the American people, and creating a public image for himself. The plan worked well. It kept Kennedy in the news, his face on television, and it kept him from worrying about the intricacies of the campaign.

But Kennedy's focus on a tightly run, even exclusive, organization irritated some Democrats who were left out of the loop. Stevenson wrote to Eleanor Roosevelt, complaining that Kennedy's "interest and concentration seemed to be on organization and not ideas. . . ."[2] And Arthur Schlesinger argued that there was more to a campaign than organization: "Organization has an important role to play," he wrote to Kennedy, "but to suppose that organization . . . will win New York and California is nonsense."[3]

Kennedy's broad message was simple: The age of Eisenhower had been devoid of new ideas; the nation had stagnated and the administration had done little more than maintain the status quo and govern through crisis management. From that came the Kennedy catch phrase, "let's get American moving again," and the much-touted Kennedy image of "vigor" and activity. It was an effective strategy, mostly because it hurt Nixon. As much as Nixon wanted to close the book on the past and embrace the future, he found himself playing defense, defending the policies of the Eisenhower administration against the intangibles of what the future might hold. Not surprisingly, many voters began to see Nixon as a representative of the past, while Kennedy personified the nation's future.

Kennedy's basic campaign strategy was simple. Perhaps in response to Nixon's campaign promise to visit every state, Kennedy set out to visit as many states as humanly possible—forty-five out of fifty, as it turned out. He focused on twenty-four swing states but then focused even further near the end of the campaign on the seven largest states.

Most of the South was left to Johnson who whistle-stopped through the region touting himself as the grandson of a Confederate soldier and insisting that religion should not be an issue in the campaign. He also refused to back down on civil rights. Johnson was particularly useful in getting most of the southern political leadership in line behind the Kennedy campaign. The South's governors and congressmen were less than enthusiastic about Kennedy, but Johnson insisted that a Kennedy-Johnson victory would mean a great deal for the future of the South in legislation, patronage, and public funds.[4]

Nixon's campaign organization was different. While Kennedy was the organization man to a fault, Nixon's campaign centered around the candidate—to the point, in fact, that Nixon micromanaged just about every detail of his entire campaign. He had all the right people around him, but his nature was to trust no one and to consult no one; he generally kept his own decisions, and no one had his ear. For eight years, Nixon had worked under the thumb of Eisenhower and the senior figures inside the Republican Party. Now, in 1960, he was in control of his own campaign and his own destiny. In his mind he needed no one to keep him on course. He planned most of his own itineraries, wrote large parts of his speeches, and even planned the routes his cars would take through cities. Any decisions that he did not make directly could only be carried out with his final approval.

Nixon's nature was to work alone—and he was a lonely man. Stephen Ambrose has, in fact, called him the loneliest man in America—and so different from Eisenhower who cultivated friends and friendships his entire life. Eisenhower respected those around him and often sought out advice from close friends and those he respected in making some of his biggest decisions.[5] In early September, Eisenhower visited Nixon at Walter Reed Hospital while Nixon was recovering from an illness. When the president returned to the White House, he mentioned to Ann Whitman, "as he has several times," Whitman recorded in her diary, "the fact that the Vice-President has very few personal friends."[6]

The campaign strategies of the two candidates were almost opposite. Whereas the Kennedy campaign staff had planned their candidate's campaign to take up every minute of his time from early August through Election Day, Nixon kept his options open. In fact, the word most used by Theodore White and others to describe Nixon's campaign was "flexibility." Nixon believed in the ebb and flow of a campaign, that there would be times to hit certain states and certain issues, and it would only become apparent at that moment; and when that moment came, Nixon wanted the flexibility to pounce. Kennedy, in contrast, was fully scheduled in advance, and he hit the campaign trail running flat out with almost no room for flexibility or adjustment. In fact, Kennedy only allowed for two open dates on his calendar between the convention and the election.

Another part of Nixon's flexible plan was a sort of Jekyll and Hyde approach. He would begin the campaign as "the New Nixon," the Eisenhower moderate, to "erase the Herblock image first," he said. (Herblock was the pen name of *Washington Post* political cartoonist Herbert Block who drew an unflattering, pugnacious Nixon with a heavy beard, ski nose, and sagging jowls.) In early October, he planned to turn up the pace of his arguments, and then finally in the last two or three weeks of the campaign, the Old Nixon would emerge from the dark and he would explode with a barrage of attacks against Kennedy in a series of television ads and presentations.[7] In contrast, Kennedy paced himself, with no discernable spurts or wanes, focusing on certain states, regions, and voting blocs as his predetermined plan dictated. He would only make adjustments in the manner in which he addressed certain issues as they came and went in the campaign discussions and debates.

For Nixon, all this sounded viable, but he got too wrapped up in his commitment to visit all the states. As he maneuvered and adjusted his plans through September and October to meet certain demands from various states, he found himself in the last week of the campaign flying off to Alaska to meet his obligation there and campaign for that state's nearly insignificant three electoral votes, while Kennedy followed his advance schedule for the last week of the campaign into Illinois, New Jersey, and New York. In addition, the Old Nixon's explosive preelection attack on Kennedy never materialized.

Nixon's campaign strategy also called for the organizing of Nixon-Lodge Volunteer Clubs in each state. In 1952 Eisenhower had set up Citizens for Eisenhower groups with great success. Local party officials often groaned at being pushed aside by these citizen groups (in both 1952 and in 1960), but Nixon realized that he needed support from Independents and Democrats to win the election. He understood well that if he won every Republican vote in the country, he would still lose the election by ten percentage points; and he had learned from Eisenhower's 1952 campaign that many Independents and Democrats (particularly in the nation's suburbs) were more comfortable joining a local volunteer political club than joining the Republican Party.[8]

～

Following the convention, Kennedy flew off to Hyannis Port for some rest and relaxation. Jackie was five months pregnant, and Jack promised to spend a week with her and Caroline before he jumped back into the campaign; but after only two days he plunged into a series of planning meetings, and then he quickly headed back out to the campaign trail to shore up his political flanks. The convention had left some loose ends, and almost immediately after the convention he headed off on three pilgrimages, in the name of party unity, to visit the party's spiritual guides: Stevenson, Truman, and Eleanor Roosevelt. Without their support (and the support of those who followed their lead) Kennedy would have a difficult time winning in November.

The unifying force for all three of these political heavyweights was their intense dislike of Nixon, and Kennedy definitely played on that point. Stevenson, Truman, and Eleanor Roosevelt might well have thrown their support to just about anyone to keep Nixon out of the White House.

Immediately after the convention Arthur Schlesinger, who never quite got over the Johnson decision in Los Angeles, wrote to Kennedy several times through August insisting that the candidate make a number of overtures to party liberals. "Putting Lyndon on the ticket had its advantages," Schlesinger wrote, but "it also exacted its price. It interrupted the emotional momentum of your drive." The liberals, he added, "were set back and put off a bit. . . . [T]hey are not at the moment committed heart and soul to the Kennedy-Johnson campaign." He then suggested that Kennedy meet with Stevenson to bring the liberals back into the fold. "Adlai Stevenson," Schlesinger continued, "can bring you more electoral votes than Lyndon Johnson seems likely to."[9] At the end of July, Kennedy invited Stevenson to Hyannis Port. He wanted Stevenson's endorsement and support in order to keep the liberals in line. Stevenson wanted to be secretary of state. Kennedy got what he wanted; Stevenson did not.

Throughout his political life, Stevenson had quietly pined to be secretary of state—perhaps more than he wanted to be president. But Kennedy had never seriously considered him for the post, at least in part because Stevenson refused to withdraw his name from contention during the primaries and because he allowed himself to get caught up in the draft campaign at the convention. All that gave a great deal of credence to a stop-Kennedy movement that hung over Kennedy's head through most of the campaign year. Kennedy also did not like the idea of answering to the liberal wing of his party through Stevenson as his secretary of state. And lastly, Stevenson represented the Democratic Party of the past, and the huge losses of the fifties, and Kennedy was preparing to give the party a new image (beyond simply the keeper of the New Deal flame) whose candidate's youth and vigor was the door to the nation's future. Thus for several reasons, Stevenson did not fit into that plan—just as Johnson also did not fit in. But Kennedy needed Johnson. He did not need Stevenson, and he did not want him as close as secretary of state.

The meeting took place on Sunday, July 31st in Hyannis Port, and there, Stevenson wrote a friend, "followed five hours in the bosom—or the shark's teeth—of the Kennedy family ashore and afloat. Even the Black Prince [Robert Kennedy] and his wife were there. . . ." Stevenson agreed to campaign for Kennedy, but, he added, "there was no hint of post election plans re Sec. State, etc. and I said nothing."[10] Following the meeting, the two men held a joint press conference, and Kennedy promised to take Stevenson's advice in the future.[11] To the press, this was an official endorsement, but it took Stevenson another two months before he finally got around to an open endorsement. In late September he sent out a "Dear Friend" note to his supporters thanking them for their support and then, finally, endorsing Kennedy.[12]

The postconvention odyssey to get the party icons in line continued. On August 14, Kennedy traveled to Hyde Park to meet with Eleanor Roosevelt. During the convention, she had thrown her considerable weight behind the draft-Stevenson movement. But now, Kennedy hoped, she would fall in line, close ranks, and unite for the good of the party. Kennedy did not expect a contentious meeting with Mrs. Roosevelt (she was generally not a contentious person), but he did expect that she would have a price for her support—most likely Stevenson's appointment as secretary of state, something that Kennedy had no intention of offering. To a friend, he called the meeting "the raft at Tilsit," referring to the meeting on a raft in the middle of the Neman River between Tsar Alexander I and Napoleon I resulting in the 1807 Treaty of Tilsit and the Russian-French alliance.[13] Somewhat surprisingly, Mrs. Roosevelt made no demands, insisting instead that that all presidents should have the freedom to choose their own cabinets and that she had no intention of interfering, and thus had no price for her endorsement. Following the meeting, Kennedy delivered a speech that focused on the expansion of the New Deal and New Deal-type programs, particularly medical care for the aged, and an expansion of Social Security benefits.[14]

Mrs. Roosevelt sent her account of the meeting to several of her friends and then a copy to Kennedy. She advised the candidate that in order to bring Stevenson's people into the campaign, he should assure Adlai's supporters that the two men would work together, that they "would appear on the same platform," showing "that there was close cooperation." Kennedy agreed that he would "try to do this. Now, I have no promises from [Kennedy]," she added, "but I have the distinct feeling that he is planning to work closely with Adlai. I also had the feeling that here was a man who could learn. . . . I think he has a mind that is open to new ideas." Then she concluded, "I think I am not mistaken in feeling that he would make a good President if elected."[15] A few days later, Kennedy thanked Mrs. Roosevelt for the meeting and her support, and then promised that he would work closely with Stevenson.[16] He did not.

Kennedy then headed off to deal with Truman. It was no secret that Truman held in the palm of his hand a sector of the Democratic Party that was the most alienated by Kennedy: the plain people, the average American, rural people, farmers, the unsophisticated, often factory workers in the Midwest, and southerners. If nothing else, they were Democrats who were put off by Harvard degrees, Boston accents, and daddy's money. Kennedy could not afford to appear to look down on plain people. He needed Truman.

Truman had endorsed Symington early in the campaign, and just before the convention he had lashed out at Kennedy, insisting that he was too young and too inexperienced to deal with complicated world affairs. His comments were of no real significance (Kennedy nearly had the nomination in hand at that point), and it did little more than make Kennedy and most other Democrats mad. But Truman was the consummate politician, and when the smoke cleared in Los Angeles, he was ready to close ranks and campaign—as he always had. And of course he would do anything to beat Nixon. To Dean Acheson, Truman wrote one of his many letters that he would not send. "You and I are stuck," he wrote, "with the necessity of taking the worst of the two evils or none at all. So—I'm taking the *immature* Democrat as the best [sic] of the two. Nixon is impossible," he added. "So, there we are."[17]

The Kennedy-Truman meeting was arranged by Clark Clifford, one of Truman's closest advisors during his years in office. In a letter to Kennedy, Clifford explained Truman's appeal: "He continues to have a great deal of popularity among the rank and file of Democratic voters. They will turn out by the thousands to hear him speak and he can reach more Democratic voters than anyone else in the party except you." Kennedy decided that he would open the pathways first by sending Johnson to talk to Truman.[18] That strategy worked, and finally "After some grumbling," Clifford recalled, Truman agreed to meet with Kennedy. They met at the Truman Library in Independence on August 20. Truman greeted Kennedy at the door of his office, grabbed the candidate under the arm and said "Come right on in here, young man. I want to talk to you." Forty minutes later, they emerged with an announcement that Truman would campaign for Kennedy. Asked what made him change his mind, Truman responded, that he had decided to support Kennedy "When the Democratic National Convention decided to nominate him for President. That is all the answer you need." It would be his last campaign. He whistle-stopped through nine states and gave thirteen speeches.[19]

Kennedy's successes with the giants of his party did a great deal to heal party wounds and appeal to several groups that were less than enthusiastic about his candidacy. But even though Stevenson and Eleanor Roosevelt had come over to him, he still had difficulty appealing to the liberals who, immediately following the convention, seemed agreeable but uninspired. A good example was the Americans for Democratic Action (ADA), the self-appointed keepers of the postwar liberal flame. The ADA no longer carried the clout it did in the late 1940s, but to many old school liberals the ADA was still the leading light of American liberalism. And as the 1960 election approached the ADA, collectively, was not particularly excited by Kennedy. Its executive secretary, James Loeb, openly refused to support Kennedy, voicing often that he believed Kennedy to be a cold and ruthless politician, a conservative who had modified his stance to win all-important liberal votes.

Following the convention, the ADA board met to decide if they would en-dorse Kennedy or simply endorse the party platform and ignore the candi-date. Those who prevailed argued that the ADA should support the ticket, that Kennedy deserved and needed liberal support against Nixon. Most of the state ADA chapters finally went along, agreeing reluctantly to accept a candidate who had agreed to stand on a strong liberal party platform. Others were willing to accept Kennedy as simply the candidate who could keep Nixon out of Washington—the "lesser of two evils."[20]

Kennedy had more success with the liberals of the ADA type later in his campaign when he began listening to Schlesinger and others that the reti-cent liberals would be more receptive if he would talk about new ideas and convey the hope of a new generation and the nation's future. Schlesinger constantly pushed this point with Kennedy, but in one instance the advice came from Henry Kissinger, then a young Harvard professor who had been advising Nelson Rockefeller's campaign. In late August, Schlesinger and Kissinger met for lunch, and Kissinger's ideas had impressed Schlesinger. He wrote to Kennedy: "I had lunch today with Henry Kissinger," Schlesinger be-gan, "who hardly qualifies as a bleeding heart. He said to me, 'We need some-one who will take a big jump—not just improve on existing trends but pro-duce a new frame of mind, a new national atmosphere. If Kennedy debates with Nixon on who can best manage the status quo, he is lost. The issue is not one technical program or another. The issue is a new epoch. If we get a new epoch and a new spirit, the technical programs will take care of them-selves.'"[21] It is not clear if Kennedy consciously embraced this advice, but in mid-September he spoke to the Liberal Party in New York where he called for a "new and better world." "We have the capacity," he said, "we have the resources—we have the courage and the vision. But we need leadership." Then he called for a new liberalism. "Only liberalism can repair our national purpose and liberate our national energies." We must, he said, "move ahead in the liberal spirit of daring and doing."[22] This seemed to mark an important turning point in Kennedy's campaign, perhaps for the remainder of his life. From mid-September on he focused his speeches on the themes of new ideas, a new future for the nation, hope, and new leadership.

⌒

While Kennedy pulled his party together and found his voice, Nixon nearly worked himself to death in the campaign, while grappling with the problem of Eisenhower's support and endorsement.

In his acceptance speech, Nixon announced that he would visit all fifty states. It sounded like a good idea at the time, and in his memoir *Six Crises* he explained that Kennedy would almost certainly sew up the Northeast industrial states, so he would visit (and thus he hoped) win the electoral votes of the small states. "To balance our anticipated losses there, we needed every Western, Southern, and Midwestern state we could possibly win."[23] But it was almost an insurmountable task. It was also unreasonable. While Nixon stumped Delaware, Kennedy made eight speeches in New York City. Perhaps realizing that it was a popular promise but unrealistic, Nixon, immediately after the convention, set out to hit those states that were of little significance (Hawaii, and several New England states that were solidly Republican) so that he could concentrate on the important states in the last two months of the campaign.

In his memoirs, Nixon wrote that the election "would be decided by which candidate was able to put on the most intensive campaign."[24] Oddly, he did not mention ideas, or image, or organization—only intensity. His campaign, even in the immediate days following the convention, was grueling, driving the candidate to near physical exhaustion. From July to November, everyone around him implored him to relax, rest, and ease up on his brutal schedule. His first campaign trip covered twelve thousand miles in just four days. Then he made two swings into the South in less than two weeks. He often spoke at eight or ten venues in one day.[25] He was constantly tired, and it showed—in a campaign where image would be a deciding factor, where the candidates would appear on television often and needed to look fresh and alive. Nixon always seemed pale, thin, and gray.

Nixon's real ringer in the campaign was Eisenhower. The president's numbers had begun to sink in the polls a bit, but he was still an immensely popular figure. Even if a voter did not like his policies, Ike was still the leader of the European victory, the grandfatherly character with the big smile, the middle-of-the-roader who brought a general peace to the world and ended most of the contention in Washington. His appearance for Nixon on the stump would be invaluable. But Nixon never really made use of the president. Either that, or Eisenhower did not want to be used.

Eisenhower had two excuses for not getting into the campaign on Nixon's behalf. He told Nixon often that he wanted him to establish his own identity as a new leader in the party and that if he took an active part in the campaign, it would overshadow Nixon's own efforts. Nixon may have agreed. Eisenhower also wanted to maintain his image as president of all the American people, and not a partisan figure. He often cited Truman who fought partisan battles and got down in to the gutters of politics while in the White House and after. Eisenhower wanted none of that. From the very beginnings of his political career in the late 1940s, he considered himself above politics and the political process. And although he could get into political scraps (and he did campaign effectively for himself in 1952 and 1956), he hated and avoided it whenever possible. In 1960 he wanted to leave office as a beloved national and international leader. The last thing he wanted to do was campaign for Nixon. He did concede to Nixon that in the last week of the campaign he would stump for his vice president, and, if necessary go on the attack against the Democrats. Nixon must certainly have worried that that would be too little too late.

At the same time, Nixon may have thought that Eisenhower would not be able to stay out of the campaign even if he wanted. Ike disliked Kennedy, and he distrusted Johnson. And he was incensed by their call to "get America moving again" and their argument that a "missile gap" existed with the Soviets. Jerry Persons, one of Eisenhower's aides, insisted that the president would soon "get his dander up," as he told Nixon, and would go after the Democrats to protect the legacy of his administration. However, his hatred for politics was apparently stronger than his hatred for the Democrats because he never really got into the campaign.[26]

He did offer Nixon advice. He told Nixon that it would be a mistake to debate Kennedy, noting that he was much better known than Kennedy and was therefore perceived as more experienced. A televised debate, the president argued, could only give Kennedy more exposure and hurt Nixon's campaign. He also told Nixon that in any debate Kennedy would be on the attack and that Nixon would be forced to defend every policy of the Eisenhower administration.[27] Nixon knew all that, but he chose not to take the president's advice.

The president not only did not help Nixon, in one important case he seemed to intentionally hurt Nixon's campaign, causing many observers to wonder if the president actually wanted Nixon to win. In a press conference on August 10, Eisenhower was asked if he would give Nixon more responsibilities now that he was a candidate for president. Eisenhower replied that he alone made the decisions, indicating that Nixon had never been included in the White House decision-making processes. Pressed again, a reporter asked the president if he felt Nixon had appeased Rockefeller in the days before the convention. "Well," Eisenhower replied, "I don't think he feels that he was appeasing [Rockefeller]," making it clear that he thought Nixon had appeased Rockefeller but that he failed to realize it. Charles Bartlett, a columnist and close Kennedy friend, then asked if there were any significant differences between the president and Nixon on the question of nuclear testing. Eisenhower responded that "I can't recall what he has ever said specifically about nuclear . . . testing."[28] Nixon-the-appeaser, it seemed, had been on the outside looking in during the big White House decisions. On August 25, on the *Tonight* show with Jack Paar, Nixon attempted to cover himself by trying to explain what Eisenhower meant—which was, of course, correct—that in the end, "only the President of the United States can make the great decisions affecting the country."[29] Nevertheless, Eisenhower was making it difficult for Nixon to claim that Kennedy lacked the experience to be president.

From there, however, things only got worse. Two weeks later, at another press conference, the press corps decided to push the president a little harder on Nixon's role in his administration. The irascible Sarah McClendon asked Eisenhower to name some of the "big decisions that Mr. Nixon has participated in." The president snapped back: "I don't see why people can't understand this: No one can make a decision except me." Minutes later, Charles Mohr of *Time* pressed the point a step further. The vice president, he said, "almost wants to claim that he has had a great deal of practice at being President." Eisenhower again responded that the decisions were his own, that he received counsel, including Nixon's, but that in the final analysis only he made the decisions. Eisenhower was becoming irritated, but Mohr refused to leave the point. "I just wonder," he continued, "if you could give us an example of a major idea [of Nixon's] that you adopted?" "If you give me a week," the president responded, "I might think of one. I don't remember." That was the end of the discussion.[30]

Eisenhower immediately called Nixon to tell him what he had done and to apologize before the story hit the wire services. At the same time, he told Ann Whitman that all this was Nixon's fault. If, in 1956, he had accepted the president's offer to become secretary of defense he would, by now, have a track record he could run on.[31] The Democrats, of course, saw this as an opportunity to defuse the issue that was damaging Kennedy the most: that Nixon was experienced and Kennedy was not. They also insisted that it was evidence that Eisenhower was not enthusiastic about Nixon's candidacy. Almost immediately, Truman went on the attack: "[T]he president," he said, "could not even remember any important recommendations of Mr. Nixon's which had been accepted during the whole time he has been vice-president."[32] Nixon tried to contain the damage by asking Eisenhower if he could have some credit for dealing with the events that were bubbling up in Cuba. The president refused.[33]

∾

One significant aspect of Nixon's strategy was to continue Eisenhower's inroads into the South. In 1952, despite advice that campaigning in the South was a waste of time, Eisenhower insisted that he would simply not give up on that section of the country. He campaigned there, and he broke the Solid South by taking Texas, Virginia, Florida, and Tennessee, along with the border states of Oklahoma, Truman's Missouri, and Maryland. In 1956 he gave back Missouri, but he won the other southern states he took in 1956 plus Louisiana, Kentucky, and West Virginia. The South was naturally conservative; it really always had been. As African-American voters, particularly those in the North, began their slow drift into the Democratic Party in response to the Democrats' support of civil rights issues, white southerners began to see their destiny with the Republicans and the Republican Party's stronger stance on states' rights. All this was an extremely slow process, but Eisenhower had tapped into it, and Nixon hoped to make further inroads into the South in 1960.

Nixon had another problem. It was in the late 1950s that many of the Old World colonies of Asia and Africa were winning their independence, and the cold war was coming to the steps of each of these new nations. Khrushchev, Nixon's personal nemesis, had turned America's racism into an international human rights issue. Most of the inhabitants of these new nations had dark skin, and the Soviets were able to point to the treatment of blacks in the United States as a reason for these emerging nations to come under Soviet influence, or at least declare neutrality outside the American sphere of influence. By 1960, as African nations were gaining independence in rapid succession, this issue began to worry members of both parties, but particularly anticommunist Republicans like Nixon. In the 1950s, racism in the South could be tolerated by the Republicans, but when it became a cold war issue in 1960, the entire situation changed. Losing the cold war could not be the price of maintaining an archaic southern system of segregation.

Nixon made several trips into the South, and he often discussed this issue while connecting it to civil rights and human rights. "In every speech I made in the Southern states," he wrote in his memoirs, "I touched on the civil rights issue—not because I wanted to lecture the people of the South on what I knew was a difficult problem for them, but because I had always believed it to be the responsibility of a political leader to tell the people exactly where he stands on issues, even when those stands may be unpopular, and to use his influence, wherever possible, to further causes in which he deeply believes."[34] But Nixon always added a small caveat, a point that the southern audiences understood to mean that a Nixon administration would not interfere with southern segregation, particularly in the schools. It would be into the mid-1960s when George Wallace and others would make extensive use of code words and phrases to convince white voters that they had their interests in mind. But in 1960, as he headed into the South looking for conservative white votes, Nixon made certain that white southerners knew he would keep his hands off the southern system. That did not mean that he approved of the system. In fact, he opposed segregation at least in part because the Soviets had been so successful in exploiting it. But he needed the votes.

In Greensboro, North Carolina, Nixon told his audience that he had a unique understanding of their difficult problem, meaning the race issue, because of the three years he had spent in their midst at Duke University Law School. He talked little about civil rights but spoke extensively about the Democrats' threats to use federal authority to enforce civil rights. Then he connected that to state education: "But let us never forget that in American education we always want to preserve freedom, and one of the essences of freedom in this country is local and State control of the educational system. . . ."[35] That was enough to satisfy any white southerner in 1960 that Nixon and the Republicans would keep their hands off the southern system of segregated education.

The Greensboro speech was Nixon's first major speech since the convention. He made a quick trip to Detroit, and then back to the South. On August 26 he spoke in Birmingham and then later that day in Atlanta. Both speeches drew large crowds. And in both cases, Nixon hit hard at the issue of states' rights versus federal authority.

Nixon did a great deal to increase the stock of the Republicans in the South. In the election, he held Florida, Tennessee, Kentucky, and Virginia, and he nearly won Texas and South Carolina. He pulled strong support in the Bible Belt and the New South urban areas as well. Four years later, the South would do a flip-flop. The Deep South states of South Carolina, Georgia, Alabama, Mississippi, and Louisiana would vote Republican, while the rest of the South and border states would vote Democratic.

⁓

Despite all of Nixon's problems, ranging from his difficulty with the press corps to Eisenhower's lukewarm support and his own antisocial nature, one of his biggest problems in the campaign turned out to be physical. On August 17, while in Greensboro, he cracked his knee on the door of his car. A week later, back in Washington, the knee began to ache and swell. The next day the White House doctor removed some fluid from the knee. It was infected. Nixon spent the next two weeks in excruciating pain at Walter Reed Hospital. He had to cancel his campaign just as it had picked up valuable momentum from the convention. He also had to cancel several trips he had planned, and it looked as though he would not be able to fulfill his promise of visiting all fifty states.[36] While Nixon, frustrated and in pain, languished in the hospital, Kennedy drew big crowds in just about every corner of the country.

At just the moment when Nixon was about as helpless as he could be in dealing with volatile issues, Dr. Norman Vincent Peale, possibly the nation's most prominent Protestant minister of the time and head of an organization called the National Conference of Citizens for Religious Freedom, signed a statement questioning whether a Catholic president could effectively disassociate himself from the power of his church and thus be under great pressure "to bring American foreign policy into line with Vatican objectives."[37] When I read that, Nixon later wrote in his memoirs, "I knew we were in for real trouble."[38] The outcry against Peale was overwhelming, to the point that several newspapers around the nation cancelled his syndicated column. Nixon concluded that Peale must have simply signed the statement by mistake. He then went on *Meet the Press* to insist that he wanted religion out of the campaign, and that he would never mention the issue. Kennedy refused to respond to the statement in a press conference.[39]

The religious issue had been played out for about all it was worth in the spring and in the primaries, and whatever anti-Catholic votes that remained would automatically go to Nixon. But it was also becoming apparent that there was a growing national backlash against anti-Catholic bias (or perceived anti-Catholic bias), and that many Protestant moderates were moving into the Kennedy camp either to prove their religious tolerance and progressive attitude toward the issue or because of their disgust with all the anti-Catholic bias and prejudice—and probably both. Either way, Nixon had nothing to gain by scraping up the religious issue again. In a letter to Claire Booth Luce, he wrote: "[T]he effect may well be to drive a small percentage of Catholic voters who are still on our side to vote for Kennedy out of protest."[40] And in fact that may have happened.

Just as Peale's statement hit the newspapers, Kennedy was invited by a group of Protestant ministers in Houston to defend the right of a Catholic to be president. Kennedy was warned not to go. Sam Rayburn told him "They're mostly Republicans, and they're out to get you." Bobby counseled against it and so did most of Kennedy's campaign staff. But Johnson urged him to go.[41] The candidate took his running mate's advice and decided that, again, he would confront the issue head on.

On September 12, Kennedy and Johnson traveled first to El Paso, then Lubbock, and on to San Antonio. Both men were to speak that afternoon at the Alamo; they were met by a fairly hostile crowd carrying signs that read, "We Want the Bible and the Constitution," and "We Don't Want the Kremlin or the Vatican." Johnson gave what he called his "little ole war hero speech," insisting that no one asked Kennedy's religion during his time on PT-109. Kennedy spoke, telling the crowd of Texans that "side by side with Bowie and Crockett died MCafferty and Bailey and Corey, but no one knows whether they were Catholics or not. For there was no religious test at the Alamo." It seemed to humble the crowd, but most of the signs stayed up.[42]

That evening in Houston, the program called for Kennedy to speak, followed by a question-and-answer session. The ballroom at the Rice Hotel was crowded and peppered with newsmen from around the country to see quite possibly the most significant campaign event between the conventions and the debates. It was televised. Robert Strauss, the Kennedy advance man for the event, said later that he picked the "meanest, nastiest-looking" ministers that he could find in the room to put in the front row where the television cameras would direct their coverage.[43]

Kennedy began his speech by arguing that there are real issues in the campaign, and that religion should not be one of them. He insisted that no Catholic prelate should tell a president what to do any more than a "Protestant minister [should] tell his parishioners for whom to vote." "I believe in an America," he said, "where the separation of church and state is absolute . . . and where no man is denied public office merely because his religion differs from the President who might appoint him or the people who might elect him."[44] It was a strong speech; Ken O'Donnell thought it was "probably the best speech [Kennedy] ever delivered in his lifetime. . . ."[45] The question-and-answer session that followed contained none of the fireworks or embarrassing questions that Rayburn and others expected. O'Donnell recalled that "Kennedy handled each [question] as quickly and calmly as a major-league shortstop handles an easy grounder. . . ."[46] Kennedy again deflected the religious issue and made it work for him.

As the two candidates headed into the debates, their poll numbers now ran generally about even. Kennedy stood ready to benefit the most from that situation because the debates would place him before even more Americans, and he believed he would be able to show that he belonged in the arena with Nixon, that he was not too young and too inexperienced to be president. Nixon, on the other hand, believed that his superior debating abilities would allow him to defeat Kennedy, possibly even destroy his candidacy in front of millions of Americans. It would be the first time in history that the American people would be able to see their candidates, together, debating the issues before them. It would be the beginning of a new era in politics, truly the origins of the modern era of American presidential elections.

~

CHAPTER EIGHT

The Great Debates

By September 12, Nixon was back on his feet and back on the campaign trail. His aides had suggested that the hospital stay was an adequate excuse to renege on his pledge to visit all fifty states, but Nixon insisted on keeping the pledge. Kennedy had caught up in the polls during Nixon's hospitalization, and the Republican candidate wanted to explode out of the gate and make up lost ground. On the first day of his renewed campaign, he spoke in Baltimore, Indianapolis, Dallas, and San Francisco. From there he went to the Northwest—to Oregon, Washington, and Idaho. Besides the grueling speaking schedule, Nixon found himself engulfed in paperwork, work that most other candidates would have assigned to a staff member, such as questionnaires from various news agencies. But not Nixon. "I felt it was my clear responsibility to review each answer in detail because they had asked for my views, not those of my staff." The result was that, after being sick for some two weeks, "I had to work literally night and day to catch up on this backlog and still keep current on the very important speeches that had to be made daily." After only three days, Nixon woke up in St. Louis with a bad case of the flu, a raging fever, and chills. Instead of resting, he pushed his doctor to pump him full of aspirin, antibiotics, "and other assorted pills," and he met his speaking engagements the next day. "I don't know when I have ever felt so weak," he wrote in his first memoir, *Six Crises*.[1]

Nixon continued pushing himself, intent on campaigning in every state, insistent on micromanaging his campaign. He lost weight. His face became

Figure 8.1.   Kennedy and Nixon meet following their second debate. AP Images

drawn. By the time the two candidates met in Chicago for their first debate, Nixon looked awful.

～

It was the four televised debates, and the first debate in particular, that became the decisive events in the 1960 campaign, perhaps one of the most significant political events of the twentieth century. The debates have, in fact, taken on almost mythical proportions as a singular event that both decided an election and changed the course of the nation—while at the same time changing the nature of political campaigns for the future. Theodore White called the debates a revolution in American politics. As many as seventy million Americans watched the first debate— nearly two-thirds of the nation's adult population, the largest audience for any political event in history. The average adult saw at least three of the debates, while more than half of all adults watched all four.[2] The debates led to increased interest in the presidential campaign and a record turnout at the polls. They also led to Kennedy's victory in November. Surveys showed that the debates enabled

Kennedy to win over independent voters by a margin of more than two to one.[3] It was the first debate, however, that drew the most interest.

Kennedy's primary disadvantage in the campaign was that he was perceived as too young and too inexperienced to be president. His religion, his background, his father's influence, his health did not come close to the issue of his youth and inexperience. Nixon, although nearly the same age as Kennedy, had been in the public eye for at least eight years, and most Americans saw him as experienced, sitting next to the president for two terms. For Kennedy, nothing could defuse that issue more than to debate Nixon and show the nation that he deserved to be president—that, if elected, he could serve. James Reston wrote in the *New York Times* just two days following the first debate: "Kennedy stands to gain from these confrontations. . . . So long as he remains alone before the TV cameras . . . he stands out like a youthful Harvard don at a boilermaker's picnic."[4]

Nixon, on the other hand, believed that he was a master of television. In the 1952 campaign, Eisenhower was about to drop Nixon from the ticket because of some alleged financial improprieties. In his celebrated "Checkers Speech," Nixon took to the airways and appealed to the nation. His speech was so effective that Eisenhower decided to keep Nixon on the ticket. From

Figure 8.2.   Kennedy and Nixon struggle to make points in their last debate, October 21, 1960. AP Images

then on, Nixon was convinced that he had great television appeal. Just before the 1960 campaign began, Nixon told Earl Mazo, "I think I am a pretty fair judge of political television. . . . Above everything else, a candidate to be effective on television must know what he is talking about, believe deeply in the rightness of his cause, and speak naturally and sincerely just as if he were carrying on a conversation with two or three people in a typical American home which he had happened to visit."[5]

Nixon also thought he was something of a master debater, and like many Americans he thought Kennedy was inexperienced, naïve, and possibly incapable of holding the floor effectively in a debate. He thought, in fact, that using his TV experience and his debating skills he might sucker punch Kennedy and knock him out of the race by showing the nation that the young Kennedy was sorely inexperienced in handling and understanding world affairs.

Nixon never really considered not debating Kennedy, even though Eisenhower argued against the debates, insisting that Nixon would be placed in the awkward position of defending the administration's record against Kennedy's attacks.[6] Nixon was well aware of Kennedy's advantage. "I knew from long experience," Nixon later recalled, "that in debate, the man who can attack has a built-in advantage that is very hard to overcome."[7] In 1946 Nixon, in his first run for Congress, had debated the incumbent Jerry Voorhis and later recalled the advantage of being on the offensive. No matter what the odds or what the advantage to Kennedy, Nixon realized that he could not turn down the challenge. In *Six Crises* he explained his decision: "I felt it was absolutely essential that I not only agree to debate but enthusiastically welcome the opportunity. Had I refused the challenge, I would have opened myself to the charge that I was afraid to defend the Administration's and my own record."[8]

It was, of course, television's enormous impact that changed American politics—for better or worse. Television had been covering politics and political events since at least 1948 when both networks broadcast the political conventions. Very few Americans then owned televisions and few watched the events, but it was clear very early on that television would be covering national politics. In 1950, of the forty million American families, only 11 percent owned TVs. Ten years later, at the time of the Kennedy-Nixon debates, that number had jumped to 88 percent.[9] The obvious impact of this development on American culture was enormous. Image, physical appearance, and presence before the camera became as important as issues, endorsements, and political events. Television changed American politics, making the 1960 presidential campaign the first modern campaign.

The debates were made possible only because Congress agreed to lift the equal time rule. That ruling had held that all candidates must be given equal time if any one candidate is given free coverage on television. In a following interpretation by the Federal Communications Commission, it was determined that free time must not only be given to the candidates of the two major parties, but to all candidates running for that office. In 1960, there were fourteen peripheral candidates running for president, including nominees from the Vegetarian Party, the Beat Consensus Party, and the National States' Rights Party. Not surprisingly, the Democrats and Republicans refused to debate under those circumstances, and voters began to clamor for a rule change to allow for debates. In response, Congress, in the spring of 1960, agreed to suspend the equal time rule for that campaign year allowing for the debates by the candidates of the two major parties.[10] By the beginning of August, both Kennedy and Nixon had agreed to the debates. The first was set for September 26 in Chicago.

Most of the exact conditions and circumstances for the debates were pounded out in early September. Although the format for each debate was different, it was decided that four newsmen would ask questions, the candidates would not have use of notes, opening statements would be eight minutes, and responses would be two and one-half minutes. Nixon's people wanted only one debate, under the assumption that any time on television with the vice president would help the lesser-known Kennedy. Kennedy's people wanted five debates, under the same assumption. J. Leonard Reinsch, Kennedy's man in the negotiations, told Theodore White, "Every time we get those two fellows on the screen side by side, we're going to gain, and he's going to lose." The compromise was four debates. The first was to focus on domestic issues; it would be held in Chicago and produced by CBS. The second was scheduled for October 7 in Washington and be produced by NBC. ABC would produce the third debate on October 13 and the fourth on October 21. The last debate was to focus on foreign policy.[11]

Each candidate prepared for the event differently. Don Hewitt, who produced the first debate for CBS, recalled that Kennedy took that debate more seriously than Nixon.[12] In his memoirs, Nixon admitted that he wished he had set aside more time to prepare for the debates. "But it was too late to do anything about the situation now, except to . . . lighten the schedule somewhat before each of the next three debates so that I could have more time for studying the issues and also for some needed rest after a hard week of campaigning."[13] Kennedy took pains to meet with Hewitt before the event to grill the producer on how it would all work. "He asked all the right questions," Hewitt recalled. "Kennedy knew just how important it [would] be to his campaign, and he didn't want to leave anything to chance."

Nixon, on the other hand, Hewitt added, "treated it as just another campaign appearance."[14] He arrived in Chicago late the night before the debates. The next morning he insisted on speaking to a convention of the Carpenters Union, which left him only five hours to prepare for the debate. Nixon was still tired, and he had managed to lose another five pounds since he had left the hospital. He worked by himself, behind closed doors. However, he later recalled, "By the time I had completed my boning and was ready to take off for the television station, I felt that I was as thoroughly prepared for this appearance as I had ever been in my political life. . . ."[15]

While Nixon studied alone, Kennedy brought in a team of brain trusters to help him prepare. The Kennedy entourage occupied the two top floors of the Ambassador East Hotel. The candidate's debate coaches, known to themselves as "the issue team," stayed at another hotel nearby where they worked around the clock preparing about fifteen pages of boiled down copy that were then transferred to question and answer note cards for Kennedy to study. Kennedy spent most of his time studying with three men: The always-close Ted Sorensen; Richard Goodwin, who White described as "an elongated elfin man with a capacity for fact and reasoning that had made him Number One man only two years before at the Harvard Law School," and Mike Feldman, a law professor on leave from the University of Pennsylvania.[16] Kennedy studied through the day, revising, rewriting, working through the material. Goodwin recalled the atmosphere: "[T]here was no outward sign of tension, no reference to the import of the occasion, to disturb our subdued concentration on the particulars. We might as well have been preparing for a press conference in Albuquerque. . . ."[17] According to Sorensen, Kennedy "had, in a sense, been preparing for this moment for years, in hundreds of rapid-fire question-and-answer sessions with newsmen, college audiences, TV panels and others."[18]

In the afternoon, Kennedy spoke to the same Carpenters Union that Nixon had addressed in the morning. A three-hour nap was followed by another review session and dinner. Kennedy then headed off to the CBS affiliate to meet Nixon, who arrived first. Herb Klein, Nixon's press advisor, was with the candidate on the drive to the studio. When Nixon got out of his car, Klein watched as he cracked his sore knee on the side of the door. Klein recalled that Nixon, in obvious excruciating pain, lost all color in his face; but he recovered quickly.[19] Nixon headed to the reception room where he bantered with photographers and talked with CBS executives. After a few minutes, Hewitt recalled, Kennedy arrived and the entire scene changed. Nixon "and I were standing there talking when Jack Kennedy arrived. He looked like a young Adonis." Kennedy was tall, thin, tanned, and wearing a well-tailored dark suit. The photographers immediately abandoned Nixon and rushed to Kennedy as if a movie star had just descended. Hewitt thought that the episode destroyed Nixon's confidence.[20]

Hewitt introduced the two men: "I assume you two guys know each other," he said, and sent them off to private offices to wait for the debate to begin. But before they left, and in the presence of both, Hewitt asked if either wanted makeup. Kennedy, who was well tanned from his open-air campaigning in California, declined.[21] Nixon also declined, but Hewitt noted that he badly needed makeup "to cover a sallow complexion and a growth of beard. . . . I think," Hewitt added, that Nixon "thought it wouldn't be good for his image if the public knew he was made-up and Kennedy wasn't. Then," Hewitt continued, Nixon's advisors "did a dumb thing. Instead of [using] one of television's best makeup artists" who had come to makeup the candidates for the program, "Nixon's guys smeared him with a slapdash layer of something called 'shavestick' that looked . . . terrible." Hewitt and others at CBS tried to convince Nixon's handlers that their man looked washed out, but the advice was ignored.[22] The two men exchanged nervous smiles as they waited for the debate to begin.

Kennedy spoke first, beginning with a message that was focused more on foreign affairs than on domestic issues—the evening's topic by agreement. He argued that U.S. domestic policy "involves directly our struggle with Mr. Khrushchev for survival." If our nation is secure at home, he added, "if we meet our obligations, if we are moving ahead, then I think freedom will be secure around the world. If we fail, then freedom fails." He continued in an obvious attempt to put Nixon on the defensive by pointing out problems on the national domestic front, in each case pushing his point that he believed the nation could do better. He spoke of the weaknesses in the industrial sector, the increasing number of Americans in poverty and requiring more federal assistance, the need for better education in the face of Soviet successes, and problems in attaining civil rights for African-Americans and other minority groups. "If a Negro baby is born . . . in some of our cities," Kennedy said, "he has about one-half as much chance to get through high school as a white baby. He has one-third as much chance to get through college as a white student. He has about a third as much chance to be a professional man, and about half as much chance to own a house." Kennedy went on to counter Nixon's claim that a Democratic administration would drastically increase the size of the federal government. "[T]here are those who say that we want to turn everything over to the Government. I don't at all." But, he added, individuals, states, and the federal government all have responsibilities that need to be met.[23]

Nixon's first statement was to agree with Kennedy: "[T]he things that Senator Kennedy has said, many of us can agree with." He agreed that domestic issues have an important bearing on foreign affairs, and that the United States was in competition with the communist world. "I subscribe completely to the spirit that Senator Kennedy has expressed tonight, the spirit that the United States should move ahead." Some observers argued afterward that it sounded weak to begin by agreeing.[24] But then he asked, "Where then do we disagree?" He insisted that the nation was not, as Kennedy had implied, standing still. The economy, he argued, was strong, now that the 1958 recession had ended. He said that the government under Eisenhower had built schools, hydroelectric facilities, and hospitals—more in each case than the Truman administration. The gross national product had increased by 19 percent in the Eisenhower administration, while inflation decreased and the average national income had gone up by 15 percent. He insisted then that his domestic programs would cost less than those proposed by Kennedy, arguing further that his plan would achieve the same results. Then he concluded: "Let us understand throughout this campaign that his motives and mine are sincere. I know what it means to be poor. I know what it means to see people who are unemployed. I know Senator Kennedy feels as deeply about these problems as I do, but our disagreement is not about the goals for America but only about the means to reach those goals."[25]

This point had become one of the primary focuses of Nixon's campaign. It was, however, an old Republican campaign argument that went back to the 1930s and 1940s—that the Republicans could achieve the same goals that the Democrats proposed, only with less expense and more efficiency. Conservatives in the party hated this argument, insisting that a truly conservative platform would bring a Republican victory. Four years later, in the 1964 campaign, Goldwater and others on the Right would insist that Nixon lost in 1960 because he took this "me-too" path.

A question and answer period followed. The first question to Kennedy was a simple, "why do you think people should vote for you rather than the Vice President?" He went through a series of points, arguing that he was the descendant of Wilson, Roosevelt, and Truman and the Democratic Party that had sustained the programs that they proposed. He added that the Republicans had opposed those programs, including federal aid to education, medical care for the aged, the Tennessee Valley Authority, and the development of the nation's natural resources. Then he concluded: "The question before us is this: Which point of view and which party do we want to lead the United States?" It was a forceful statement that placed Kennedy in the company of the Democratic Party leadership and Nixon among the obstructionists of popular programs. Nixon was asked to respond. Forfeiting the point, he said simply, "I have no comment."[26]

Nixon was then pushed on the question of Eisenhower's support. He was then asked to explain the president's "give me a week" response to the question about Nixon's influence on White House decisions. Nixon explained that the answer was "probably a fastidious remark," and then added that it would be improper for the president to comment on how he reaches decisions. "The President has asked for my advice, I have given it; sometimes my advice has been taken, sometimes it has not. I do not say that I have made the decisions, and I would say that no President should ever allow anybody else to make the major decisions. The President only makes the decisions." It seemed a good response to a difficult problem for Nixon.

Nixon then returned to the charge that Kennedy's programs would be expensive, increase the tax burden, and take the budget out of balance. In what the *New York Times* called "one of the evening's few shows of incipient heat," Kennedy replied "wholly wrong. Wholly in error."[27] As long as the economy was vibrant, he argued, his proposed programs, particularly medical care for the aged and federal funding for school construction, could be initiated within a balanced budget and without raising taxes. "My view is that you can do these programs . . . within a balanced budget if our economy is moving ahead."[28]

Kennedy continued, attacking Republicans for opposing Democratic Party social programs, including an increase in the minimum wage, federal aid to education, and medical care for the aged. "In my judgment," he underscored his point, "a vigorous Democratic President, supported by a Democratic majority in the House and Senate, can win support for these programs. . . ." Nixon responded that there was, at that moment, a majority of Democrats in both houses of Congress, and if they were unable to get their programs passed it was because they had failed to rally their party's support for the bills. He then added that the bills had failed because the American people, voicing through their elected representatives in Washington, had opposed them. "[T]hey were," he said, "too extreme." The alternative Republican proposals "are not extreme, because they will accomplish the end without too great a cost in dollars or in freedom. . . ." Kennedy insisted that they were not extreme, but in fact, moderate, and the Republicans should support them.[29]

As the two candidates bantered back and forth it was apparent—to television watchers only—that there was a distinct difference in their styles. Nixon had embarked on a college debating technique in which he rebutted and refuted in what appeared to be an attempt to score points with judges.

He looked for inconsistencies and errors in Kennedy's arguments, then argued each individually. He addressed his answers to the newsmen who asked the questions or directly to Kennedy. Viewers said the next day that they felt Nixon was talking down to them.[30] Kennedy's demeanor was different—and again, this was only apparent to those watching the debate on television. He spoke to the audience—to the American people. In addition, his answers did not dwell on the minutiae of politics or on specific bills passed or not passed. He seemed to be offering a vision for the future, a new direction for the nation.

For the ten or so questions that followed, the candidates each had an opportunity to discuss farm subsidies, communist subversion at home, taxes, and education. In each case, Kennedy talked about what the nation could become under a better administration, while the vice president, as Theodore White described the situation, "scored excellently against [Kennedy], yet forgetful of the need to score on the mind of the nation he hoped to lead."[31] Nixon also suffered a great deal from constantly being forced by Kennedy to defend the administration's policies.

When all was said and done, however, the first debate came down to image. Those who listened to the debate on radio considered the debate a dead heat, according to one poll, with both candidates giving about what they had received. (And to read the transcripts of the debates today gives the same impression.) But to those who watched the event on television—and that was the vast majority who tuned into the debate—Kennedy was a clear winner. "The contrast of the two faces was astounding," White recalled. Nixon "was tense, almost frightened, at turns glowering and, occasionally, haggard-looking to the point of sickness." White continued with the line that is perhaps the most famous from the debates: "Probably no picture in American politics tells a better story of crisis and episode than that famous shot of the camera on the Vice-President as he half slouched, his "Lazy Shave" powder faintly streaked with sweat, his eyes exaggerated hollows of blackness, his jaw, jowls, and face drooping with strain."[32] Chicago mayor Richard Daley said, "My God! They've embalmed him before he even died."[33] The New York Times reported in a secondary headline, "Most Viewers Call Kennedy the 'Winner'—Many Say Nixon Looked Unwell."[34] The Wall Street Journal added, "We would personally award the edge to Mr. Kennedy." Nixon, the Journal concluded, "looked very tired. . . ."[35]

The next three debates did not quite hold the drama of the first. They were, however, important. Just before the second debate, held in Washington on October 7, it became clear that image had won over substance in the first debate when Nixon's people insisted that the thermostat in the building of the NBC affiliate be turned down to 64 degrees to end, as the *New York Times* reported, Nixon's "heavy perspiration problems that contributed to his generally unsatisfactory appearance on television last week." After some jostling, it was finally agreed that the thermostat would be set at 70 degrees. And Nixon showed up wearing professionally applied makeup. He did not, the *New York Times* recorded further, "have the thin emaciated appearance" of the week before.[36]

The second debate was watched by fewer viewers than the first. The *New York Times* surveyed the largest northern and northeastern cities, and only 45 percent watched the second debate compared to 53 percent for the first debate.[37] Those numbers must have surprised Nixon, who had been convinced by his advisors that the numbers of those watching would increase dramatically from the first to the last as the public's interests rose. His advisors were partly correct; the last debate was watched by more people than any of the others.[38]

Nixon saw the need to confront Kennedy and be more aggressive in the second debate. The next morning, the *New York Times* reported that his first debate demeanor "was criticized as too agreeable toward Mr. Kennedy's politics. . . ." He "was consciously more aggressive tonight."[39] But nevertheless Nixon was forced to remain on the defensive through most of the debate. Kennedy accused the Eisenhower administration of losing Cuba to communism and allowing a hostile force to gain a foothold just ninety miles off the coast of Florida. Nixon countered that Cuba was not lost to communism and that the problems there would be solved. The discussion then turned to civil rights. Nixon argued that the problems of civil rights in the South could be resolved through a stronger economy that would foster lower unemployment for southern blacks. He also said that the federal government should "give assistance" to school districts that agreed to integrate. Kennedy attacked Nixon for not supporting fair employment practices or racial equality in the schools, and he attacked the Eisenhower administration for failing to give its support to the *Brown* decision. Nixon offered little in response.

Kennedy, however, provoked a sharp response from Nixon when he tried several times to associate Nixon with, what he argued, were the failings of the Eisenhower administration. Nixon shot back: "I think Senator Kennedy should make up his mind with regard to my responsibility. In our first debate he indicated that I had not had experience or at least had not participated significantly in the making of decisions. I am glad to hear tonight that he does suggest that I have had some experience." The two went on to discuss foreign affairs in Asia, concluding with the sharpest clash so far over the defense of Quemoy and Matsu, the two small islands controlled by Taiwan in the straits between Mainland China and Taiwan. Kennedy insisted that the United States had not promised to defend the islands. Nixon responded that "this is the same kind of woolly thinking that led to disaster for America in Korea." "I hope," Nixon added, "that Senator Kennedy will change his mind if he should be elected."[40]

By the end of the second debate, the question of image over issues was already clear to anyone who had watched the events. "To what extent substantive points of debate affect a huge viewing audience like tonight's is a moot point," the *Times* reported. "[A]ll were intensely interested in the battle of 'images.'"[41] Perhaps the most important point is that Kennedy clearly realized it before Nixon.

The third debate, held a week later on October 13, was something of a curiosity for the time, with Kennedy on camera from New York and Nixon in Los Angeles. Bill Shadel of ABC described the candidates as "joined for tonight's discussion by a network of electronic facilities which permits each candidate to see and hear the other."[42] This is usually considered Nixon's best performance. He was both forceful and at ease, and he noticeably made the point of addressing the cameras—to the American people. Perhaps Nixon was more comfortable not having to share the set with Kennedy and his charisma. The *New York Times*, however, described both men as "robust and combative."[43]

The two again tangled over Quemoy and Matsu. In the intervening week, Kennedy had said that Nixon was "trigger happy" over the two islands. Nixon responded in the debate with a sharp, "I resent that comment." Kennedy evaded questions on other topics to make his point that the United States had not signed any treaty to defend the two islands, and that they were insignificant and not worth American lives. Nixon continued to argue that Quemoy and Matsu were the equivalent of "the tragic experience leading to World War II," and insisted that "to turn over these islands, he is only encouraging the aggressors, the Communist Chinese, and the Soviet aggressors, to press the United States, to press us to the point where war would be inevitable." Kennedy responded: "I don't think it's possible for Mr. Nixon to state the record in distortion of the facts with more precision than he just did." Kennedy went on to cite General Matthew Ridgway and others who opposed going to war over Quemoy and Matsu.

Kennedy continued discussing foreign affairs by calling for talks with the Soviets to achieve nuclear arms reductions, and he accused the Eisenhower administration of avoiding the issue. Nixon responded: "When Mr. Kennedy suggests that we haven't been making an effort [at nuclear disarmament] he simply doesn't know what he's talking about." In the ending minutes of the debate, Nixon dragged the topic back to Quemoy and Matsu. "I can think of nothing that will be a greater blow to the prestige of the United States among the free nations of Asia than for us to take Senator Kennedy's . . . advice . . . and to say in advance we will surrender an area to the Communists."[44] The tone of Nixon's comments was that he was deeply disturbed by Kennedy's position on that point, but he may well have felt that he had found an issue that worked for him in the atmosphere of the debate.

The fourth debate was one debate too many. Theodore White called it "dreary." The *New York Times* called it "comparatively tepid," and "probably the tamest" of the series.[45] The candidates mostly rehashed old topics and restated their positions on the primary issues. Kennedy's opening statement was a striking appeal. He hit hard at America's strength relative to the Soviets. It was not, he said, increasing. "We are going to have to do better," he continued. "Mr. Nixon talks about our being the strongest country in the world. I think we are today, but we were far stronger relative to the Communists five years ago." Then he added that under current conditions he did not believe that the United States would be stronger than the Soviets by mid-decade. Nixon, in his opening statement, talked about growing the economy and keeping the nation's military strong.[46]

It was in this last debate that the two candidates finally got around to the escalating events in Cuba and how they might handle the situation there. It was an interesting portent for the future. Kennedy stated flatly that he would train anti-Castro Cubans to overthrow Castro. Nixon, who was at that time privy to anti-Castro Cubans being trained in Honduras for just such a mission, argued that to engage in such activity was counter to the U.N. Charter and would cause the United States to lose all prestige throughout Latin America. He went on to argue that an economic quarantine of the island was the best way to contain Cuba. Kennedy disagreed, arguing that a quarantine would fail.[47]

Kennedy, apparently feeling vulnerable on Quemoy and Matsu, brought the issue up again, arguing that he would defend the islands as part of a larger defense of Taiwan. That, he said, was the Eisenhower administration's policy and he had supported it since 1955. Nixon only responded by pointing out that the Korean War began, as many believed at the time, because Truman's Secretary of State Dean Acheson, in a speech before the National Press Club in 1950, said that the U.S. defense perimeter in Asia did not include Korea. The point was clear that if the United States did not state its resolve in Quemoy and Matsu, the communists would take advantage of the situation and occupy the islands.

In one heated exchange, Nixon implied that it was Kennedy's responsibility as a citizen to be correct in his criticisms. Kennedy shot back, "I really don't need Mr. Nixon to tell me about what my responsibilities are as a citizen." And then in the only instance when one of the candidates addressed the other directly, Kennedy added, "What I downgrade, Mr. Nixon, is the leadership the country's getting, not the country." From that, the last debate languished, as the candidates made one last stab at hitting all the issues they had discussed throughout the campaign. As the last word, the moderator, Quincy Howe from ABC, said, "as members of a new political generation, Vice President Nixon and Senator Kennedy have used new means of communication to pioneer a new type of political debate."[48] It was recognition that the 1960 campaign was the first truly modern presidential campaign.

⌒

If it is possible to identify winners and losers in the debates, by all accounts Kennedy was the clear winner of the first debate. Here, image was the decisive factor, and Nixon simply failed to match up. Most important, however, was Kennedy's ability to introduce himself to most of the American people for the first time and to show that he was a capable and deserving candidate. That in itself was worth more to the Kennedy campaign than any statement on any issue by either candidate. In the second debate, Nixon seemed to recover from his lack of preparedness in the first go-around. He was less willing to agree with Kennedy, and he was on the terra firma of foreign affairs. The second debate should probably be marked as a draw, although James Reston of the *New York Times* called it a Nixon victory.[49]

Nixon was at his best in the third debate. He spoke to the cameras, and thus to the American people; and without Kennedy in the room, he seemed more confident, less intimidated, and he made his points effectively. Although the American audience had probably grown tired of the Quemoy and Matsu issue, Nixon was able to drive that issue home, making the point clear that Kennedy was willing to give up those little islands to communism to avoid a larger conflict. To many Americans, that was blatant appeasement, one of the dirtiest words in American foreign policy. Nixon refused to use that word, but there were certainly large numbers of Americans who cringed at the thought of giving away *any* land to the communists—and who believed that World War II had begun because England and other European nations chose to appease Hitler rather than confront him. The point probably hurt Kennedy by putting him on the defensive in the debates for the first time, and it allowed his critics to label him soft on communism—the last thing he wanted at the height of the cold war. It was a simple fact that Kennedy had to present a strong stance against communism or he would lose the election. Nixon was the clear winner of the third debate.

The fourth debate was probably a narrow victory for Kennedy. It was the least interesting of the four, generally a rehashing of the others. But Kennedy was able to pull together a reasonable response to the Quemoy and Matsu issue by showing that his stance was actually the official opinion of the Eisenhower administration. His big advantage in the fourth debate was his opening statement which pounded home one of his most successful campaign points: that the United States is a great nation, but, as he stated with some force directly into the cameras, "I think we're going to have to do better." It was very effective, a complement to his often-stated, "Let's get America moving again." Nixon, who spoke first, said little that he had not said before.[50]

Overall, there is little question that Kennedy won the debates. When the debates began in late September, Nixon was perceived as the frontrunner in the campaign, with Kennedy trailing—although the numbers were close. A Gallup Poll showed Nixon ahead by 47 to 46 percent with 7 percent undecided. Following the debates in late October, Kennedy not only led in the Gallup Poll (51 to 45 percent with 4 percent undecided), he was now a known commodity, a legitimate candidate in the minds of the American people.[51] He had also shown that he was Nixon's equal, that he was more than just an attractive figure, and that he deserved to be in the arena with Nixon. In short, he showed that he was qualified to be president of the United States.

Kennedy's performance in the debates also allowed him to unify his party, to solidify Democratic Party support behind him. Those in the wings (party leaders and voters alike) who had reservations about his abilities, his experience, his character, were brought into line in large numbers. Kennedy finally became what a party candidate needs to be in an election, a central figure for the party loyal to rally around.

One gauge of Kennedy's success was the increase in the size of the crowds that greeted him during and following the debates. Theodore White called it "a quantum leap" in numbers, and he attributed the increase to the debates. White noted that Kennedy's crowds had been growing in number throughout the campaign. But now, he wrote, with the debates underway, "overnight, they seethed with enthusiasm and multiplied in numbers, as if the sight of him, in their homes on the video box, had given him a 'star quality' reserved only for television and movie idols."[52]

Although Nixon was criticized often for simply agreeing with Kennedy, in fact, the two candidates had disagreed on just about every issue, but generally the disagreements were ones of degree. They disagreed on housing. Kennedy had advocated two million public housing units per year. Nixon said that he was willing to consider spending more money on housing than the Eisenhower administration, but he refused to commit to a number. On education, Kennedy wanted direct federal money to augment teachers' salaries. Nixon wanted to give money to the states to build schools. On medical care for the aged, Kennedy wanted to finance a program through Social Security. Nixon wanted to give federal support to private insurance companies to pay for the program. At various times, Nixon pointed out that he and Kennedy did not differ on the goals of these programs; the two candidates only differed on the means of achieving them.

For many Republican conservatives, Nixon's willingness to disagree only by degree was particularly annoying; and it led others to argue that there was really very little difference between the two men. Eric Sevareid, in a column early in the campaign, wrote "The 'managerial revolution' has come to American politics and Kennedy and Nixon are its first completely packaged products." These two men, he wrote, were little more than tidy, buttoned-down junior executives on the make, and the choice was between "the lesser of two evils."[53] That was a bit harsh. In fact, the two men differed on every broad point: Although their goals may have been similar, Kennedy wanted to achieve them through direct federal funding and regulation. Nixon wanted to achieve many of the same goals through the authority of the states or through private enterprise. It was a basic Democrat-Republican distinction. But Sevareid and others saw that the two candidates differed little on the broad matters of principle, on their vision for the nation, and certainly on how they approached the cold war.

Both candidates also believed that the nation had the ability and the will to solve all its problems, bring an end to racial discrimination, improve the economy, end poverty, and confront and defeat communism without sparking a third world war. Considering with hindsight the difficulties the nation would have to endure in the upcoming decade, the outlook of these two men seems almost Pollyannaish. This might simply have been the nature of politicians who must reflect an optimistic view of the future as part of a vision— or a perceived vision. But it may also reflect a basic belief of the era in the perfectibility of mankind, the idea, pervasive in the sixties, that with the right opportunities everyone can achieve high goals in society. Certainly, this attitude was grounded in America's successes against the adversity and challenges in the three prior decades when the United States achieved heroic victories over the Great Depression, the Nazis, and the Japanese and halted communist aggression in Korea.[54] By 1960 the challenge to the American way of life from Soviet communism had not only brought all Americans to believe strongly in their system, but also to believe in the ability of the nation to solve its problems and even the problems of the world.

⁓

There was some call for a fifth debate, but Nixon demurred, and Kennedy followed suit. Walter Lippmann, writing in the *Washington Post*, said, "So far I have not met anyone who heard the fourth debate and is yearning for a fifth."[55] The great debates ended.

Just prior to Kennedy's death in November 1963, he apparently agreed with Barry Goldwater, who was then the frontrunner for the 1964 Republican nomination, that the two candidates would travel the nation appearing in a series of campaign debates prior to the 1964 election. But Lyndon Johnson, the Democratic candidate in 1964, did all he could to reinstate the equal time rule so that he could avoid debating Goldwater. Johnson was not a good debater, not telegenic, and somewhat less than physically attractive.[56] In 1968 Nixon refused to debate the Democratic candidate Hubert Humphrey, and in 1972 he refused to debate George McGovern. It was not until 1976, when President Gerald Ford debated the Democratic candidate Jimmy Carter that presidential debates returned to the campaign trail. They have continued uninterrupted since then.

It was the debates that best characterize the 1960 campaign as the first modern campaign. For the first time in American history, the candidates could be seen and heard by nearly all Americans; they could be judged, criticized, and interpreted in ways they had never been before. Almost certainly, the election would have gone a different way had there not been the debates that year. Kennedy, the apparent "winner"—and of course the winner of the election in November—wrote just after the debates ended: "The network television debates between Mr. Nixon and myself have been a great service by the television industry to the American people."[57] Nixon made similar statements in the wake of the campaign. But in later years, he began to see the debates differently, and probably with good reason. In his 1978 memoir, he wrote: "As for television debates in general, I doubt that they can ever serve a responsible role in defining the issues of a presidential campaign. Because of the nature of the medium, there will inevitably be a greater premium on showmanship than on statesmanship."[58] Nixon was always the sorest of losers and these may sound like the words of a sore loser, but the Great Debates of the 1960 presidential campaign were a turning point in American political history, from one type of campaign to another.

Perhaps many Americans would agree that at some point in American history image replaced substance in the national electoral process. The accusatory fingers might well be pointed at the 1960 presidential campaign and the use of television.

~

CHAPTER NINE

Campaign Two

What infuriated Nixon the most about the campaign was that he had to defend the Eisenhower administration's policies and record when he really had little to do with making policy. Ike had kept the major decisions to himself, and Nixon did little more than tag along. At the same time, the administration had wracked up a number of failings that gave Kennedy all the ammunition he needed to attack Nixon. A good example is the economy. Kennedy had developed no cohesive economic program, which normally would have made him vulnerable, but he only had to point to the failings of the Eisenhower administration on economic issues. And there were many. During the Eisenhower years, there had been two severe recessions and economic growth had averaged a paltry 2.4 percent a year. Between 1939 and 1953, the postdepression years in which the Democrats were in office, the economy had grown at 5.8 percent. That weak growth was causing the United States to lag behind the growth levels of much of the industrialized world. Western Europe and Japan were growing more rapidly, and according to CIA reports, the Soviet Union was growing at a rate near 7 percent. There was also rising unemployment and underemployment, increasing inflation, and an alarming trade imbalance.[1] A third recession began in April 1960 and lasted throughout the campaign, giving Kennedy's mantra "Let's get the country moving again" all the more significance.

The situation was much the same in foreign policy. Eisenhower had suffered a series of foreign policy setbacks just as his administration was winding down and the campaign was beginning. The Soviet launch of the

Sputnik satellite in 1957 (along with U.S. failures in its launch attempts), the U-2 incident, the collapse of the subsequent Paris summit, and the "loss" of Cuba all played well into Kennedy's hands. He was able to emphasize international dangers while making Nixon responsible for those setbacks when the responsibility, of course, fell only on the president's shoulders.

Kennedy made the most out of this in his call that the Soviets were producing missiles more rapidly than the United States, or, what he called the "the missile gap." The issue allowed Kennedy to assert his toughness, while insisting that the Republicans had scaled back missile production at a time when the Soviets were producing ICBMs, as Khrushchev said, "like sausages." Kennedy first mentioned the missile gap in a speech before the Senate in 1958, explaining that the United States was on course to lose its supremacy over the Soviets in both nuclear weapons and in weapons delivery systems. He insisted that the Soviets had (or would soon have) the capability of destroying "85 percent of our industry, 43 of our 50 largest cities, and most of the Nation's population." Then he attacked the Eisenhower administration for cutting military spending in order to balance the budget. "We tailored our strategy and military requirements," he added, "to fit our budget." The speech was so successful, and it so annoyed Republicans, that Kennedy repeated the argument incessantly over the next two years, and it became a key component of his campaign.[2]

By most accounts, there was, in fact, no missile gap, and Eisenhower had that information from U-2 flyovers of Soviet air space; and he believed he could not respond to Kennedy because of the secrecy of those intelligence missions. Nixon, possibly seeing what was to come in the campaign, tried to convince Eisenhower to neutralize the issue by going public with the information. But the president refused, insisting that it would provoke the Soviets to begin an ICBM buildup that the United States would have to match—and fund.[3]

In an obvious attempt to defuse the issue during the campaign, the Eisenhower administration held a series of briefings in which they tried to convince Kennedy that there was, in fact, no missile gap. The first was a Joint Chiefs of Staff briefing in September, followed by a briefing by the Strategic Air Command and then a briefing by Allen Dulles of the CIA. Either the briefings did not convince Kennedy that a gap did not exist, or more likely, the candidate saw the advantage of the issue in the campaign and simply ignored the information. Either way, the secret briefings had no impact on the campaign.[4]

The result of this "missile gap" campaign issue was the frightening arms race of the next decade. Kennedy as president came under immediate public pressure to close the missile gap—whether there was one or not. The Soviets, then, responded by initiating a nuclear buildup to match. At least in part, Kennedy's "missile gap" charge during the 1960 campaign led to the dangerous arms race of the early 1960s.

Kennedy also floated statistics about economic growth that he surely knew were not true. He often claimed that the Soviets enjoyed a growth rate that was two or three times that of the United States and that in 1959 the United States had the lowest percentage of growth of any of the major industrialized societies.[5] As a member of the Senate Foreign Relations Committee, Kennedy surely knew that the Soviets often manipulated and exaggerated their figures, and if there was any significant growth in the Soviet Union, it was only because Russia was still growing out of the World War II collapse. At the same time, the United States was in a recession. Still, in 1960, the United States produced fully one-third of the world's goods, and the Soviet economy was barely a fraction the size of the U.S. economy.

All this boxed Nixon in. He could not repudiate the administration. In fact, he was bound to defend it. And he could not disclose U-2 intelligence. At the same time, he agreed with Kennedy on several issues, such as the need to increase conventional forces. But even on that point, to agree with Kennedy was to repudiate Eisenhower, something he refused to do. In foreign affairs, where Nixon was supposed to hold most of the cards, he continued to lose ground to Kennedy throughout the campaign.

⌢

For several reasons, Nixon might have chosen a better running mate in 1960 than Henry Cabot Lodge. Among other things, he was not a strong campaigner, he had no ability to deliver to the ticket any states or regions, and he was often described as dull. But perhaps more importantly, Lodge contrasted physically with Nixon. Lodge was tall and thin. As a *Time* reporter noted, when Nixon and Lodge appeared together, "He towers above him, mak[ing] Nixon look slight, hunched and physically unimpressive. At one point, Nixon appeared to be trying to stand on tiptoe to cut down the difference in height."[6] Lodge was undoubtedly a drag on the Nixon campaign. Of the four candidates, he was the least energetic, made the fewest speeches, drew the smallest crowds, and finally attracted the least number of voters. In 1964, Lodge grabbed a surprise victory in the New Hampshire primary, but party support for his candidacy that year was barely measurable; most party leaders refused to support him because they believed he had done more damage in 1960 than he had aided the ticket.

Part of the Nixon strategy was to present himself as a national candidate and not to try and appeal to various interest or minority groups. That was the province of the Democrats, and Nixon had concluded that he would not try and outdo the Democrats in that venue. He left that to Lodge, the U.N. ambassador who dealt daily with the world's minorities, who was photographed with world leaders of all ethnicities and colors, and was seen as sympathetic to minority groups in the United States. Lodge was also perceived as popular in the Northeast industrial states, and undoubtedly Nixon hoped that with Lodge on the ticket, he would have a good chance to pull some of those states. But Lodge in the final analysis had little appeal.

The 1960 Lodge campaign is known for little more than a statement he made in East Harlem, on October 12, that Nixon, if elected, would name an African-American to his cabinet: "[T]here should be a Negro in the cabinet," Lodge told the primarily African-American audience. He also promised to end segregation in public schools and in public facilities and to support legislation to guarantee African-Americans the right to vote. "It is part of our program," Lodge added in Nixon's name, "and it is offered as a pledge."[7] These were solid campaign promises that Lodge had failed to run by Nixon.

Again, Nixon was boxed in. He had hoped to continue Eisenhower's advances of 1952 and 1956 into the southern electorate, and that, of course, meant winning southern white votes. At the same time, he was actually doing well, generally, with black voters in the North. In fact, Nixon had done a good job of walking that very narrow fence line between the nation's blacks and whites, between civil rights for African-Americans and southern segregationists. And he had a fairly good civil rights record. He had chaired Eisenhower's committee to insure nondiscrimination in federal contract jobs; he had supported rulings against the filibuster in the Senate, and he had supported the 1957 civil rights bill. In addition, several of the nation's civil rights leaders supported his candidacy. Most importantly, Martin Luther King, Jr. had accepted Nixon's offer to lead a voter registration drive among African-Americans. Nixon had no hope of winning a majority of the northern black vote, but he did have a reasonable hope of combining a significant minority of black votes with white suburban and rural votes to win the electoral votes of such states as Pennsylvania and Illinois. But if he let Lodge's statement stand, he would lose southern white votes, and presumably the South. In fact, polls in the days following Lodges statements showed Nixon's numbers dropping fast in the South. At the same time, if he repudiated the Lodge promise, northern black votes would disappear.

Then to make matters worse, Kennedy appeared just a few days later on *Meet the Press* and, in answer to a question about Lodge's statement, said all jobs should go to the most qualified person, "If the best person is Negro, if he is white, if he is of Mexican descent or Irish descent or whatever he may be.

. . . But," Kennedy added, "I do believe we should make a greater effort to bring Negroes into participation in the higher branches of government. There are no Federal district judges—there are 200-odd of them; not one is a Negro. We have about 26 Negroes in the entire Foreign Service of 6,000, so that particularly now with the importance of Africa, Asia, and all the rest, I do believe we should make a greater effort to encourage fuller participation on all levels, of all the talent we can get—Negro, white, of any race."[8]

Four days after Lodge's statement, at a meeting of the Republican minds in Hartford Connecticut, Lodge was disciplined. "Whoever recommended that Harlem speech," said one Republican operative from the South, "should be thrown out of an airplane at 25,000 feet." Lodge was told to moderate his enthusiastic cultivation of minority groups, and a statement was issued by Herb Klein that Nixon had made no such promise, and that cabinet members would be chosen following the election—and that the decisions would be made based on merit, not on race.[9] The result was that Nixon was damaged among black voters and northern moderates and among southern white voters who no longer trusted him. It was his biggest disaster of his campaign. "It hurt us in the South unquestionably," Nixon recalled. "And it did us no good in the North. To Negroes and other voters it appeared to be a crude attempt to woo the support of Negroes without regard to the qualifications an individual might have for high office." Lodge's statement, Nixon added, "continued to plague us for the balance of the campaign."[10]

Much of this was reinforced when, just a few days later on October 19, Martin Luther King Jr. and about fifty other African-American protesters were arrested for sitting-in at a segregated restaurant in Atlanta. Most of those arrested were soon released, but on October 26, King was sentenced to four months at hard labor on a trumped up probation violation charge of driving in Georgia with an Alabama license—which was not illegal. He was clasped in chains and hustled off to a state prison in the Georgia backwoods. The immediate outcry made the incident an issue in the campaign. King's wife was five months pregnant, and she feared for her husband's life.

King was mostly outside the political scene in 1960. His father, an influential Baptist minister, had announced for Nixon, based purely on the Catholic issue. Martin Jr. had stayed away from the campaign, though he had praised Nixon. At the same time, Kennedy had done nothing to cultivate King.

The morning after King's sentencing, Kennedy received a call from his civil rights advisor, Harris Wofford, who knew King, and suggested that Kennedy might want to consider intervening on King's behalf. According to Richard Goodwin, Kennedy polled his staff: "What do you think?" Ken O'Donnell, Ted Sorensen, and Pierre Salinger, and others in the room argued that Kennedy had no such authority. "It's a local concern," they said. "Our position in the South is already precarious," O'Donnell added, "and this can only antagonize the white political leaders whose organizations are essential to electoral success."[11] While this discussion was going on in Chicago, Bobby Kennedy nearly jumped down Wofford's throat. "Do you know that three southern governors told us that if Jack supported Jimmy Hoffa, Nikita Khrushchev or Martin Luther King they would throw their votes to Nixon? Do you know that this election may be razor close and you have probably lost it for us?" Then he added, the civil rights section "isn't going to do another damn thing in this campaign."[12]

John Kennedy then found himself in much the same position as Nixon: walking that narrow fence between the votes of white southerners and northern African-Americans. But instead of being forced into a decision, Kennedy made a conscious one. It was Sargent Shriver who convinced Kennedy to place a call to Mrs. King. Kennedy agreed and made the call. The two spoke for less than two minutes. Kennedy expressed his shock and outrage at Dr. King's imprisonment and then pledged to do everything he could to gain her husband's release.[13] As the incident raged on in the press, Bobby apparently felt compelled to follow his brother's lead and phoned the Georgia judge who had sentenced King. The judge was already under great pressure from Georgia's governor, Ernest Vandiver, to use Kennedy's intervention to release King as a way of getting out from under a no-win political situation. The judge relented, and King was released on a $2,000 bond.[14]

King gave Kennedy public credit for his release, and Kennedy emerged from the incident as a civil rights advocate. Then, in a much-publicized statement, Dr. King's father ended his suspicion of Catholics and urged his followers to vote for Kennedy. "I had expected to vote against Senator Kennedy because of his religion. But now he can be my President, Catholic or whatever he is. It took courage to call my daughter-in-law at a time like this. He has the moral courage to stand up for what he knows is right."[15] Perhaps the most important aspect of the event was Nixon's silence. When Nixon's campaign manager Herb Klein asked Nixon for a statement to give to the press on the issue, Nixon told Klein: "I think Dr. King got a bum rap. But despite my strong feelings in this respect, it would be completely improper for me or any other lawyer to call the judge. And Robert Kennedy should have known better than to do so." Klein relayed that to the press as "no comment." As Nixon reported in Six Crises, "This incident was widely interpreted by Negro leaders both North and South as indicating that I did not care about justice in the King case." "[I]n retrospect," Nixon admitted, the situation "might have been avoided or at least better handled."[16]

Kennedy was by no means a champion of civil rights, but the incident, and the favorable press that went with it, brought him the nation's black vote. It was only a minor story in the national mainstream press, but in the African-American newspapers, Kennedy became a black hero, a candidate who had done the right thing and was worth black support in November.[17] On the Sunday before the election, two million handbills were distributed outside African-American churches. On one side of the handbill it said "Jack Kennedy called Mrs. King." On the other side it said, "Richard Nixon did not."[18] And African-Americans turned out. In 1956, Stevenson won about 60 percent of the African-American vote. Four years later, Kennedy took a whopping 80 percent. In Illinois, a state which was so close that the outcome is still questioned, Kennedy took some 250,000 black votes and officially won the state by only 9,000 votes. Without strong voting from African-Americans, he may well have lost New Jersey, Michigan, South Carolina, and Delaware.[19]

~

It was Theodore White's thesis that John Kennedy won the 1960 election because he did just about everything right and that Nixon lost because he did just about everything wrong. On one point where that thesis holds true is in the two candidates' choices of running mates. Lodge did almost nothing for Nixon. Johnson, however, accomplished everything that the Kennedy campaign wanted.

Arthur Schlesinger and others on the Left in the Kennedy circle winced at the choice of Johnson, but they soon realized that he was necessary— whether they liked him or not. Reinhold Niebuhr, one of the doyens of the postwar liberal Left, saw the genius in the Johnson choice and told the doubting Schlesinger that he needed to get on board. Niebuhr "pointed out," Schlesinger wrote, "that the Democratic Party had pledged itself to the strongest civil rights plank in history." If the party had chosen a left-wing northern liberal as Kennedy's running mate, it would "only have confirmed the South in its sense of isolation and persecution. But the nomination of a southern candidate who accepted the platform, including the civil rights plank, restored the Democrats as a national party and associated the South with the pursuit of national goals." Schlesinger concluded that the choice was both "brave and wise."[20]

The original campaign strategy was for Johnson to be the regional candidate, to take the campaign to the South and the West—areas where he was most popular. Kennedy was to be the national candidate, showing himself in all regions while focusing on the swing states. But several of Johnson's advisors, particularly Jim Rowe, opposed that strategy. Rowe believed that both candidates should confront their demons, show themselves in areas where they were least known. Johnson should be seen outside the South, in New York, Chicago, and California, while Kennedy should campaign in the South to show that the ticket was truly a national ticket. Rowe, who had been writing strategy memos for Democratic Party candidates since the 1930s, also had considered that Kennedy might lose the election, opening the door for a Johnson run in 1964. As Johnson's close advisor, Rowe wanted his man to be seen as a national candidate, not another son of the South.[21] Although Johnson campaigned outside the South and Kennedy did campaign in the South, it was Johnson's southern campaigns, particularly in his home state of Texas, that swayed the tide in the end. Johnson pulled his weight.

In August, Johnson was stuck dealing with the month-long rump session of the 87th Congress. Johnson and Rayburn had originally arranged the session in July under the assumption that it would aid Johnson's anticipated run for the presidency. But by the time Congress met, the plan was to push through a Kennedy-Johnson program that would aid the party ticket in November. LBJ introduced or supported bills that would increase the minimum wage, medical care for the aged, aid to education, and a federal housing bill. All failed. A coalition of Republicans and conservative southern Democrats (nearly the same coalition that would bottle up Kennedy's domestic agenda after he took office) bolstered by a threat of a presidential veto, managed to kill all the initiatives. Rather than increase his stature, Johnson had done little more than annoy the members of Congress, most of whom wanted to return to their districts to campaign. Through the remainder of the campaign, Kennedy insisted that Congress had shirked its responsibility in not passing the bills, while Nixon argued that the Democratic initiative was so liberal that even with Democrats controlling of both houses of Congress, it could not push the bills through.

The failure of the Kennedy-Johnson initiatives was seen by the Kennedy campaign as a serious defeat, even an embarrassment. But apparently few Americans paid much attention. Most likely, they only saw it as an attempt to pass a controversial series of bills in an election year by a candidate who was not yet in office. The failed initiative had no discerning impact on the election.

At James Rowe's insistence, Johnson headed off to campaign in the Northeast, spending most of his time in New Jersey and New York. The strategy was surprisingly successful, owing mostly to Johnson's down home-type campaign skills that, apparently, he did not moderate for the Northeastern crowds. His most important effort was a speech he delivered to the Liberal Party's Trade Union Council, a mostly Jewish labor group in New York City.

Many Jews were skeptical of Kennedy because of his father's supposed dalliances with Nazism before the war, but Johnson was able to smooth over much of that doubt and distrust with mostly a personal appeal and several strong statements on civil rights. "I will never," he said, "speak as a Southerner to Southerners, as a Protestant to Protestants, or as a white to whites." The *New York Times* called his appearance an "old fashioned stem-winder of a political speech." Afterward, he toured Queens, shaking hands, kissing babies, and nibbling on kosher pickles. His wife Lady Bird even picked up some press attention by meeting with local ladies' groups and discussing such things as where she bought her clothes.[22] Eisenhower had received the support of 49 percent of the city in 1956 and carried the state. It was a must-win for Kennedy-Johnson in 1960.

Nixon toured the city's garment district the next day, introduced often by Rockefeller and New York senator Jacob Javits. Nixon thanked Rockefeller for writing the civil rights plank into the Republican Party Platform, and Javits, several times, used the word "liberal" to describe the platform, which must have brought tears of anger to the eyes of Republican conservatives. The mostly liberal *New York Times* called Nixon's visit "lukewarm."[23]

From New York, Johnson headed off on his southern trip, a three-week excursion by train covering some three thousand miles through eight states. Johnson chose to send out an advance team of women, headed by Lindy Boggs, the wife of Louisiana congressman Hale Boggs. Johnson decided, Boggs recalled, "that in the South in a year when there were civil rights difficulties the only way he could send a team out and be sure it was met with politeness was if he had women on it." "What southern gentleman," she added, "is not going to receive southern ladies when they are coming to his state and his city?"[24]

Johnson's eleven-car train pushed through the South. The candidate met with hundreds of congressmen, senators, mayors, and other local officials. Occasionally, the receptions were not enthusiastic; it was not a popular ticket in the South. Often, local politicians were conspicuous only by their absence. Others agreed to support the ticket but denounced the platform and its civil rights plank. Both Alabama and Mississippi were expected to go for Nixon, and in those states the local politicians did not want to damage their political futures by cavorting with the Democrats. But generally Johnson's southern campaign was successful, at least in part because his campaign style was successful. As Sorensen recalled, Johnson traveled through the South "decrying the religious issue, deriding Nixon's experience, detailing Republican shortcomings, warning of the dangers of divided government, praising Kennedy, mixing in a few homely Texas stories . . . and refusing to back down on civil rights."[25]

Johnson's theme was religion. He pushed the issue hard, arguing that one should not make an issue of another man's religion, and comparing anti-Catholic bigotry to prejudice against the South. He would often tell the PT-109 story, adding the point he had made in San Antonio a month before that religion was not an issue during the hard days and nights while the boat's crew waited to be rescued in the Pacific. He also told a similar story about John Kennedy's older brother, Joe, whose plane went down over the English Channel during the war. His copilot, Johnson said, was from New Braunfels, Texas, and "I'm sure they didn't ask each other what church they went to. They both died for their country."[26]

Johnson knew that his political future relied on his ability to deliver the South. But even more importantly, he had to deliver his home state. Texas had gone to Eisenhower in 1952 by seven percentage points and in 1956 by eleven points. As the 1960 campaign moved toward Election Day, Texas was too close to call. Texas liberals had stayed away from the campaign, and many of the state's conservative Democrats, led by former governor Allen Shivers, had crossed over to join the very active "Democrats for Nixon." The prospect of losing Texas weighed heavily on Johnson.

But on November 4, just four days before the election, an incident occurred in Dallas that may well have been significant enough to tip the Texas scales. While attending a rally at the Adolphus Hotel, Johnson and Lady Bird were attacked by hundreds of hostile, mostly female, screaming Nixon supporters. Shrieking "We want Nixon, we want Nixon," the crowd enveloped the Johnsons as they moved slowly through the lobby of the hotel. While television cameras rolled, the candidate and his wife were spat on, yelled at, and cursed. A hostile woman grabbed Lady Bird's white gloves and threw them in a ditch. Another hit her on the head with a sign that read "Let's Ground Lady Bird" and then spit in her face. It took the Johnsons thirty minutes to move seventy-five feet. Other signs read, "Let's Beat Judas," and "LBJ—Counterfeit Confederate."[27]

By most accounts, Johnson knew exactly what he was doing. In fact, at one point he asked the police to leave the scene, telling one policeman, "If the time has come when I can't walk through the lobby of a hotel in Dallas with my lady without a police escort, I want to know it."[28] At one point, Lady Bird was about to retaliate on her own, when Lyndon grabbed her and placed his hand over her mouth. He knew he had to survive the incident with dignity. A Johnson aide recalled the incident: "LBJ and Lady Bird could have gone through that lobby and got on that elevator in five minutes, but LBJ took thirty minutes to go through that crowd, and it was all being recorded and photographed for television and radio and the newspapers, and he knew it and played it for all it was worth. They say he never learned how to use the media effectively, but that day he did."[29]

That evening, film of the event appeared on network news reports all over Texas and on the front pages of the nation's newspapers the next morning. The incident worked in favor of the Kennedy-Johnson ticket by showing what many had come to fear as the growing extremism within the Republican Party. It also turned Johnson's image from a boisterous southern conservative into a sympathetic figure under attack by the far Right—and protecting his wife. Immediately after the incident, and just days before the election, polls showed a significant jump in support for the Kennedy-Johnson ticket in Texas.

The incident was also the deciding factor in pulling Georgia senator Richard Russell into the campaign. Russell was one of the Democratic Party's biggest guns in the Senate. He was also a conservative Democrat and one of Johnson's best friends. Johnson had hoped that the appearance of a conservative southerner like Russell in Texas would pull votes from the state's conservative Democrats who were leaning toward Nixon. But over and over, Russell had rejected Johnson's requests to get involved in the campaign—partly because of the civil rights plank in the party platform and partly because he did not like Kennedy. But Russell had a particular fondness for Lady Bird, and when he read about the Adolphus Hotel incident, he finally told Lyndon he would campaign for the ticket in Texas. He stumped the state, speaking highly of Johnson and agreeing to accept Kennedy as "the lesser of two evils." When the election was over and Texas went for Kennedy-Johnson, several of Johnson's aides believed that Russell's last-minute contribution played a key role in the victory.[30]

〜

In the fourth debate, Kennedy had said that he thought the situation in Cuba could best be dealt with by arming anti-Castro Cubans, who might overthrow the Castro government. Following the debates, in the last week of October, the two candidates jousted over the Cuba issue. Kennedy had made a statement on Cuba that appeared stronger than anything Nixon had said. It immediately became a question of who was the strongest on Cuba—and thus who was the softest. In the end, however, the back-and-forth banter did little to clarify the issue. Nixon began the squabble by insisting that Kennedy's plan for supporting a revolution in Cuba "is the most shocking reckless proposal ever made in our history by a presidential candidate during a campaign. . . ." Nixon went on to refer to Kennedy's proposal as "shooting from the hip." He argued that the United States could not aid anti-Castro

Cubans because "We do not break our treaties. We do not work against the United Nations." "What we must do, is quarantine him . . . quarantine him diplomatically; quarantine him economically." Nixon then referred to a situation that he saw as similar, the U.S. overthrow of Guatemalan president Jacobo Arbenz during the Eisenhower administration in 1954. Nixon intended to explain that Arbenz had been quarantined and then overthrown by the people of Guatemala. But to anyone who truly understood the Guatemalan revolution in 1954, the events that led to the overthrow of Arbenz amounted to little more than a CIA covert operation that removed a government that had threatened to nationalize banana plantations owned by American corporations. Nixon's reference to these events as a model for what might be done in Cuba upset just about every Latin American government.[31] James Reston of the *New York Times* wrote that Nixon's "solution of the Cuban problem creates little more enthusiasm in the embassies of our friends. . . . This is the joke of the weekend in the Latin-American Embassies. For every official who knows anything about the fall of the Arbenz Government in Guatemala knows that the United States Government, through the Central Intelligence Agency, worked actively with, and financed, and made available arms, with which the anti-Arbenz forces finally 'threw him out.'" In fact, Reston added, the Eisenhower administration "did in Guatemala what Senator Kennedy is proposing to do in Cuba. . . ."[32]

Kennedy immediately backpedaled on his original statement, insisting on *Face the Nation* that the United States should only "encourage" the anti-Castro Cubans with Voice of America transmissions into Cuba and do nothing that would violate any treaties with the Latin American states or compromise the U.N. Charter.[33]

At just that moment, anti-Castro Cubans were training in Honduras for an invasion of Cuba—an invasion that would become the Bay of Pigs Incident six months later at the beginning of the Kennedy administration. For Nixon's many detractors, it was the height of hypocrisy for the vice president to criticize Kennedy for suggesting a policy that he had advocated as a member of the Eisenhower administration. But Nixon saw it as protecting the Cubans: "In order to protect the secrecy of the planning and the safety of the thousands of men and women involved in the operation, I had no choice but to take a completely opposite stand and attack Kennedy's advocacy of open intervention in Cuba. This," he added in the memoirs, "was the most uncomfortable and ironic duty I have had to perform in any political campaign."[34]

～

In the last days of October, Nixon finally brought Eisenhower into the campaign, whose absence had been conspicuous considering that the accomplishments of his entire administration were being questioned openly by the Democrats. But it had been Eisenhower's intention from the beginning that he would remain above the fray and allow Nixon to run his own campaign. The fear was, for both Nixon and Eisenhower, that the president would overshadow Nixon. At a meeting between the president and Nixon at Newport, Rhode Island, just after the convention, it was agreed that Eisenhower would give three televised speeches, designed mostly to appeal to independents and moderate Democrats. One speech would be in late September and designed as a fund-raiser. The second would be in early November, and the last would be on election eve. In addition, Eisenhower would make several nonpolitical speeches around the country, with a focus on peace and prosperity, and on the successes of his administrations. Beyond that, Nixon intended to be the only focus of his campaign. By most accounts, however, Eisenhower wanted to do more. The president's brother Milton said later that the president did not become more engaged simply because Nixon failed to ask.[35]

The Kennedy camp labored over the fear that Eisenhower would enter the campaign—or more specifically they worried about how to deal with him *when* he finally jumped in. The plans were simple. If he entered early, Kennedy would charge Nixon with hiding behind Eisenhower's favorable image, unable to stand on his own two feet because he had no discernable accomplishments of his own. If he entered late, Kennedy would accuse Nixon of bringing in a ringer at the last minute—a desperate call for the president's help. Either way, the plan was not to attack the president. His policies and accomplishments were, however, another matter.[36]

Most likely, Nixon did not call on Eisenhower for help for the simple reason that he wanted to win the election on his own. It was truly in his nature. He had labored in Ike's shadow for so long, considered by critics as little more than the general's lapdog, that he was chafing at the bit to get out on his own, to run his own campaign. The last thing he wanted was, again, to be carried along by Eisenhower's coattails. Theodore White quotes an anonymous Nixon aide who said, "All we want out of Ike is for him to handle Khrushchev at the UN and not let things blow up there. That's *all*." According to White, the aide stressed the word "all."[37]

But Eisenhower wanted in. Kennedy's attacks were hitting hard—on U.S. prestige abroad, on the missile gap, on the Eisenhower administration's handling of everything from the economy to Cuba and China. The "Let's get America moving again" theme must have felt like a personal attack. Finally, in late October, Nixon asked for the president's assistance for the last week of campaigning. Eisenhower seemed to jump out of his box. The plan was for the president to speak in Minneapolis on the 18th, then in Philadelphia ten days later. On November 2, he would meet Nixon and Lodge in New York, followed by visits to Pittsburgh and Cleveland and then again to New York. But on October 30, just eight days before the election, Mamie Eisenhower called Pat Nixon and told the candidate's wife that she was worried about the president's health, that he was not up to the strain campaigning might put on his heart, but that he was determined to get out on the campaign trail and answer the attacks on his record. The next morning, Nixon received a call from Dr. Howard Snyder, the White House physician, who refused to approve a heavy campaign schedule for the president. "I know what he wants to do," Snyder told Nixon, "and he usually won't take my advice. Please," he added "either talk him out of it or just don't let him do it—for the sake of his health." That afternoon, Nixon met the president at the White House. "I had rarely seen Eisenhower more animated. . . ." He had, in fact, scheduled an expanded itinerary that included Illinois, upstate New York and parts of Michigan. But Nixon talked him out of it. "I opened the discussion with half a dozen rather lame reasons for his not carrying out the expanded itinerary." Eisenhower protested, but Nixon held his ground and insisted that the president keep to the original schedule. "He finally acquiesced," Nixon recalled in his memoir. "His pride prevented him from saying anything, but I knew that he was puzzled and frustrated by my conduct."[38] Nixon later speculated that had Eisenhower campaigned in Illinois and Missouri, states the candidate lost by razor thin margins, that he might have won the election.[39]

But Nixon was not through with Eisenhower. On November 6, just two days before the election, Nixon went on television and announced that, once he became president, he would send Eisenhower on a goodwill tour of Eastern Europe and that he would send ex-presidents Hoover and Truman along to accompany him. He even added that he had consulted with the president, who had agreed and that it was Eisenhower's idea to invite Truman and Hoover.[40] If this was intended as Nixon's ninth inning surprise, it fell pretty flat. The New York Times led with the story the next day, giving Nixon the publicity he wanted, but he had enraged the president.[41] Just two days before, Nixon had asked the president if he would agree to tour Eastern Europe after the election, and Eisenhower responded with an emphatic no. He referred to his revulsion for "auctioning off the Presidency" and complained of the difficulties of traveling overseas without the benefit of government protection or transportation. Eisenhower was livid following Nixon's announcement. Nixon had not only committed him but had done so after he had made it clear that he would not go. Eisenhower tried to get Nixon to make a statement retracting the promise, but the president's press secretary, James Hagerty, convinced him that with only twenty-four hours left before the election, such a move could badly damage Nixon's campaign.[42] He decided to forget about the incident.

～

There were, of course, many deciding factors in the 1960 campaign. Possibly one of the most important was the manner in which the two candidates treated the press. In 1960, the nation wanted information about these men. Of the four candidates, three were truly fascinating characters, larger than life, with distinctive and interesting backgrounds. What the press delivered, the nation absorbed—from television, newspapers, and radio. The candidates, it would seem, would have done all they could to foster strong relationships with the press, keep them close, and feed them—both food and information. But Nixon never saw it that way. In 1962, when he announced his first retirement from politics, Nixon delivered one of several famous statements associated with him: "You won't have Nixon to kick around anymore." That statement was directed at the press. Nixon never liked the press, and the feeling was generally mutual. Whatever the origins of this antagonistic relationship, it was clear in 1960, and it damaged Nixon's campaign.

Theodore White saw the relationship between Nixon and the press this way: "I believe . . . that the sense of dignity of these [reporters] . . . was abused by Mr. Nixon and his staff—and not by accident, but by decision. The brotherhood of the press was considered by Mr. Nixon and his press staff, not as a brotherhood, but a conspiracy, and a hostile conspiracy at that. . . . What he planned, what he wished to express, Nixon kept to himself, believing (until too late in the campaign) that he could reach the American people over the heads of the press. . . . What Mr. Nixon really felt, what he wished truly to clarify, he made no effort to communicate to the reporters, who were his amplifiers." White noted that when the campaign began, the press was generally divided evenly in their loyalty to the two candidates. As the campaign progressed, that changed quickly; the Kennedy campaign became the preferred assignment. White also recalled the differences in working with the two campaigns, and how moving from the Nixon campaign to the Kennedy campaign was like being "transformed in role from leper and outcast to friend and battle companion." The result, White added, was that the "cultivation of the press colored all the reporting that came from the Kennedy campaign, and then contrast adversely the reporting of the Nixon campaign."[43]

Ben Bradlee, who was a writer and editor at *Newsweek*, recounted much the same experience. "The difference" between the two candidates, Bradlee wrote in his memoirs, "was the difference between night and day. In the first place, the men around Nixon cordially disliked the press and simply spoke a different language, where the men around Kennedy genuinely liked the press and spoke the same language. At any time during the Kennedy campaign, a reporter could get to Larry O'Brien, Ken O'Donnell, Ted Sorensen, Bobby, all of them, often for a drink, always a bull session. During the Nixon campaign, it took an all-day siege to get a few minutes with the men around Nixon, and they made reporters feel like lepers during those few minutes."[44] "He wouldn't see us," said Peter Lisagor of the *Chicago Daily News*. And conservative journalist Robert Novak has written, "it was easier to gain an audience with the Pope than to see Nixon privately during the 1960 campaign."[45] Nixon went through the motions of meeting with the press in obligatory press briefings and press conferences, but he clearly believed that he could never sway the press to his side and he knew that he lacked the relationship with the press that Kennedy enjoyed.

Despite the animosity between Nixon and the press, the vast majority of the nation's newspapers endorsed Nixon—by as much as 80 percent. But an official endorsement did not always translate into support on the page. That was true of the *New York Times*, which officially supported Nixon and had not supported a Democratic presidential candidate since 1944. But in fact, the primary editors at the *New York Times* and most of the reporters supported Kennedy.

Perhaps for just this reason Nixon came to believe that the press was intrinsically liberal and against him, and as the campaign progressed, he pushed the press farther and farther away from his campaign. He may well have had good reason to dislike the press, but it was still necessary to cultivate reporters in order to get his message across to the American people—and he simply refused to do so. "I completely reject the theory," he wrote after the campaign, "that I might have received better treatment from the press had I 'courted' them more, or had Herb [Klein] provided the more elaborate facilities for entertainment than [Kennedy's press secretary Pierre] Salinger, with greater funds at his disposal, was able to provide." Then he added that the problem was not the manner in which the press was treated, but that the press was simply not sympathetic to the Republican agenda. "Republicans will get better treatment in the press only if and when more reporters . . . take a more favorable or at least a more tolerant view of Republican policies and principles—and not before."[46]

Eisenhower, however, had gotten along agreeably with the press. He treated them well and with respect within certain parameters. They, in turn, admired and respected him—and it showed in their stories and reports. It was, in fact, a fairly good relationship. Following the 1960 campaign Republicans would do battle with the press. Barry Goldwater in 1964 grew to hate the press and following that election, his supporters came away with a terribly bitter taste in their mouths. Only 368 newspapers endorsed Goldwater, to 445 newspapers for Johnson in that campaign, reversing a trend that went back to the beginning of the century. In 1968 and 1972 Nixon was devastated by the press.[47] And even Ronald Reagan, who possibly handled the press better than any president or presidential candidate since Kennedy, warred with the press through much of the 1980s and often expressed his belief that newsmen were constantly waiting in ambush to destroy his presidency.[48]

Whatever the cause, by the end of the 1960s the Republican Party (particularly the Republican Right) and the national media were at war and with only a few exceptions, that war carried on through the remainder of the century. Much of that animosity began with Nixon's 1960 campaign and his relationship with the press.

∼

By mid-October, Kennedy was pushing out in the polls—possibly as a result of the debates, possibly as a result of his intervention in Martin Luther King's arrest and imprisonment. Gallup showed Kennedy with a solid 51 to 45 percent lead.[49] That was reason enough for the Kennedy people to initiate what Nixon called a "victory blitz," an attempt to convince the press and the American people that the election was headed for a landslide. It was a "time worn but highly effective campaign technique," Nixon recalled.[50] He immediately ordered his people to respond with a similar blitz, which seemed to confuse just about everyone. As the election approached, Nixon closed the gap—most likely because of Eisenhower's entrance into the campaign—and the two candidates went into the last days of the campaign with most polls showing close to a 50–50 dead heat.[51]

Nixon flew to California to vote and wait for the results. He expected to get the first returns at about 3:30 when polls began closing in the East. To fill the time, Pat Nixon took her two girls, Tricia and Julie, to Beverly Hills to have their hair done. Nixon went for a drive with aides Don Hughes and Jack Sherwood, heading south along the Pacific Coast Highway, first to San Diego and then on to Tijuana in Mexico where they got some "authentic Mexican" food. In his memoirs, Nixon found great humor in a presidential candidate having lunch in a foreign country on Election Day. On the return trip, they stopped off at San Juan Capistrano and visited the mission before returning to the Ambassador Hotel in Los Angeles to watch the returns come in.[52]

Nixon believed he had done all he could do. "I had traveled over 65,000 miles and visited all fifty states. I had made 160 scheduled speeches and delivered scores of impromptu talks and informal press conferences. . . . I did not let up once, nor did my staff."[53]

Kennedy met Jackie at their legal residence, their apartment on Bowdoin Street on Beacon Hill in Boston, and that morning the two went to their local voting place at the West End Library. Jackie was eight months pregnant, and Jack worried that she would be unduly jostled as they pushed through the cheering crowds. Afterward, they flew to the Cape and then drove on to Hyannis where the entire Kennedy entourage checked into the Yachtsman Hotel and then on to Bobby's house to wait for the election returns.[54]

Bobby Kennedy's house had been converted into "a communications and vote analysis center," as Ken O'Donnell described it. There were thirty telephones, each with an operator, connected to the various Democratic headquarters around the country, and four teletype machines. As the information flowed in, it was analyzed by Kennedy's personal pollsters, Lou Harris and his staff. Reports from what were called "indicator" precincts were received hourly, and experts projected voting trends.[55]

At the Ambassador Hotel, Nixon was surrounded by his chief aides, his wife, and daughters. The first returns, which began coming in at just after five o'clock Pacific Coast time, showed little. The first final numbers, and Nixon's first disappointment of several to come, came from Connecticut, which Kennedy took by 90,000 votes. Nixon expected to lose Connecticut, but not by that much.[56] Connecticut had been the telltale of 1956. When several of the state's factory towns repudiated Stevenson—areas that he should have carried easily—it was instantly clear by 7:30 on election night that Eisenhower would sweep the country.[57] Nixon may have seen it coming early.

The Kennedy compound probably received the numbers from Connecticut at about the same moment. "The three Kennedy sisters were jumping with glee," O'Donnell recalled, "assuming that Jack had already been elected. . . ." But there was a long way to go. "Jack surveyed the joyous scene without saying much, knowing that later in the night, when returns came in from the Midwest and the West, everybody would be in a quieter mood." Kennedy left to have dinner. O'Donnell added, "When he returned . . . after ten o'clock, nobody was laughing. He was losing in Ohio, Wisconsin, Kentucky, Tennessee, and in the farm belt west of the Mississippi, and he was not doing as well as he expected in Michigan and Illinois."[58] But as Ted Sorensen recalled, Kennedy had not lost his sense of humor. He told those around him of a phone call to Johnson: "Lyndon says, 'I hear *you're* losing Ohio, but *we're* doing fine in Pennsylvania.'"[59]

Nixon began to worry when CBS computers, analyzing early returns, put Kennedy's odds of victory at seven-to-one; and at six o-clock, CBS predicted a Kennedy victory even before the polls closed in the West, and with less than 8 percent of the votes counted. At 6:30, NBC's computer gave Kennedy fifteen-to-one odds, and John Chancellor announced that he thought Ohio would go to Kennedy even though Nixon held a comfortable lead there. At 6:45, Eric Sevareid of CBS predicted a Kennedy victory. But fifteen minutes later, the polls closed in Indiana, Kentucky, Vermont, and Oklahoma with Nixon victories.[60]

The numbers from the big electoral states began to trickle in after about 7:30. Nixon had a big state strategy. Of the seven biggest states (New York, Pennsylvania, Ohio, Michigan, Illinois, Texas, and California) he believed he could win the election if he carried three of the seven, but that Kennedy would need at least five to win. He was right. In the final analysis, Kennedy took five (New York, Pennsylvania, Michigan, Illinois, and Texas), while Nixon took only two (Ohio and California).[61]

By eight o'clock, Nixon recalled, "we had thought everything would be over but the shouting. But eight came and went [and] the fight was far from over." However, by then, all three television stations were predicting a Kennedy victory.[62] To stem the tide, to keep party workers from giving up in the face of what looked like a Kennedy victory, Eisenhower appeared on television and appealed to Republican Party workers to "keep fighting to the last minute." By that time, the president had become angry at the day's events. He believed that Nixon had lost the election because he had run a poor campaign, and he disliked Kennedy.[63] Of course, had he gotten more involved in Nixon's campaign, Nixon might well have won.

An hour later, the problems were in New York and California. New York was slow to report from upstate, which was expected to go Republican as opposed to the predominantly Democratic downstate. And California's numbers were being recorded late simply because polls closed three hours later on the West Coast. But by nine o'clock, a call from Tom Dewey forced Nixon to give up on New York. It would go for Kennedy by almost 400,000 votes. Then Pennsylvania fell to Kennedy, as a result of a stronger than expected showing for Kennedy in Philadelphia.[64]

At about ten o'clock, Johnson called Kennedy to let him know that Texas was running close, but safe.[65] He was right. As Nixon recalled, "Texas had been a ding-dong battle from the beginning but with most all of the vote in, it appeared that Kennedy would carry the state by about 40,000 [votes]." It was "another plus," Nixon added, "for the 'corn pone special,'" the phrase used by both Republicans and Democrats for the Johnson campaign.[66]

As the night went on, and poll closings moved west with the setting sun, the race got steadily closer. It was an American political axiom in the postwar era: The nation becomes very Republican at about midnight on Election Day when some of the most conservative states in the nation begin reporting their numbers. The farm states from Oklahoma to the Dakotas went for Nixon. That was a big disappointment for Kennedy who had hoped that the near-hatred for Eisenhower's farm policies and the administration's agriculture secretary, Ezra Taft Benson, might pull those states his way.[67] Then Nixon carried Washington, Wyoming, and Colorado. The race was tightening.

By three in the morning, it all seemed to boil down to four states: California, Illinois, Michigan, and Minnesota. Chicago Mayor Richard Daly called Ken O'Donnell to spell out the situation in Illinois: "We're trying to hold back our returns," Daly said. "Every time we announce two hundred more votes for Kennedy in Chicago, they come up out of nowhere downstate with another three hundred votes for Nixon."[68]

At the same time, Nixon's aides were talking to party leaders in Illinois who were insisting that the state could go either way. Nixon concluded that he had to win California, Illinois, and one other state—possibly Minnesota—in order to win. Then Nixon received word from a supporter at the Chicago *Sun-Times* who told him that Illinois was lost. Nixon still held out hope for Illinois, but "it just wasn't in the cards for us to take the state," he recalled.[69] It was a turning point.

The time had come. "At 11:30, Pat walked into my room. . . . Both Pat and Tricia were wearing the new dresses they had bought for the occasion, Tricia in blue and Pat in a gray-green flowered print. . . . All evening long, Pat had been telling Tricia and Julie . . . that the news would get better as the West came in. Tricia greeted me with, 'Hi, Daddy, how is the election going? . . . I replied, almost too bluntly, 'I'm afraid we have lost, honey.'"[70] It was premature. The trends were definitely in that direction, but it was not over yet.

At about 12:30 Pacific daylight time, Nixon spoke to a crowd of supporters at the Ambassador Hotel. He said, "there are still some results to come in. . . . [I]f the present trend continues, Senator Kennedy will be the next President of the United States." Then he concluded his short speech, "My congratulations to Senator Kennedy for a fine race in this campaign." To some, it sounded like a concession, but Nixon had not intended to concede, only thank his supporters.[71] Some of Kennedy's aides were furious that Nixon had not conceded; the trends by then were obvious, they believed. Kennedy would win. But it was still too early, and Kennedy snapped: "Why should he [concede]? I wouldn't under these circumstances."[72]

Kennedy watched Nixon's speech. Pierre Salinger, one of his ever-present aides and advisors, had been trying to convince Kennedy to make a similar appearance before a large group of supporters that had gathered at the armory in Hyannis. But Kennedy, with his eye on the 1960 campaign bottom line—image—sneered back at Salinger, "You want me to put on a performance like that at this hour of the night? Not me. I'm going to bed, and all of you had better do likewise."[73] Bobby stayed up manning the phones and keeping the last hours of the campaign going.

Nixon still held hope for Illinois—and just about any other state to go with it. At 4:00 a.m. Pacific daylight time, Kennedy's popular vote margin had been whittled down to almost nothing, to about 600,000 votes. There were reports coming in to UPI and other news agencies of voter fraud in Cook County, Illinois, and CBS had begun hedging on its earlier prediction of a Kennedy victory. Nixon finally went to bed, hoping he would wake up to victories in California, Illinois, and Minnesota. But two hours later, when he woke up, he had won California but lost the other two. Some around him wanted to contest Illinois, where the Daley machine was suspect in voter fraud. "Even if we were to overturn the Illinois outcome" he wrote later, "we would still need 15 more electoral votes to win." With a phone call or two to campaign operatives in Minnesota, it was clear that Minnesota was lost. It was over. He sent a formal concession wire to Kennedy.[74]

Kennedy woke up at 9:00 a.m. and headed downstairs. He was greeted by Sorensen. "What happened in California," Kennedy asked. Sorensen told him he had won California (he had not), along with Minnesota, Michigan, and Illinois. Sorensen also told him that the Secret Service had surrounded the house. The president-elect got dressed and went to the Hyannis armory to acknowledge his victory before a crowd of family, supporters, and friends. Nixon's concession came at about noon, Eastern time.[75]

~

CHAPTER TEN

Epilogue and Analysis

Immediately after the campaign, the two candidates took time off to rest. In a twist of fate, they both ended up in southern Florida, Kennedy at the Kennedy family compound at Palm Springs and Nixon at the estate of his friend Bebe Rebozo on Key Biscayne. On Friday, November 11, Joe Kennedy called Herbert Hoover and suggested that he use his influence to bring the two candidates together in a public show of national unity. Hoover immediately put in the call to Nixon who was having dinner at the Jamaica Inn on Key Biscayne. Without mentioning Joe Kennedy's intercession, Hoover suggested that Nixon and Kennedy meet. He said that he believed the election had split the nation badly, and he saw a need for the two candidates to at least put on some show of unity, even if it was artificial. According to Hoover, as Nixon recalled the conversation, "some indications of national unity are not only desirable but essential." Nixon immediately called Eisenhower and asked what he should do. The president, who was on the links at Augusta, told Nixon that if he refused to go he "would look like a sorehead."[1] So Nixon agreed to the meeting; the two candidates met on November 14 at the Key Biscayne Hotel.

The meeting was inauspicious, exhibiting more animosity and differences in personality and character than national or political unity. The plan was for the two to meet quietly at a small, private villa behind the hotel. Nixon arrived first and waited calmly for his adversary. When Kennedy arrived, the two greeted each other and then walked from the hotel lobby to the villa. Nixon recalled in his memoirs that he insisted that Kennedy walk to his right, "as his rank now entitled him to do." They sat on the porch of the hotel villa, and Nixon made up two soft drinks.[2] They asked each other about their biggest surprise of the election. Nixon said he thought he would take Texas; Kennedy said he was surprised by Ohio. The conversation must have been fairly dull because Ken O'Donnell, who sat with the two men, could only recall that "I cannot remember either of them saying anything that was interesting or amusing." And O'Donnell, apparently daydreaming and assuming that Kennedy was also bored, thought the president-elect might be thinking, "how did I manage to beat a guy like this by only a hundred thousand votes?"[3]

But Kennedy and Nixon did have points of discussion. They talked about China. Nixon counseled that the United States should not extend recognition to the Peoples Republic of China, and that Beijing should not be allowed to join the United Nations because, Nixon said, the U.N. Charter only allowed "peace-loving nations." Kennedy talked about how he expected to have trouble with Congress because of the "natural coalition of conservative southern Democrats and most of the Republicans. . . ."[4]

One of the primary reasons for the meeting was that there were stories in the press that, because of the closeness of the election, Kennedy might be willing to bring Nixon into his administration, possibly at the cabinet level.[5] Kennedy had no intention of making such an offer, and Nixon had no intention of accepting. But Kennedy did suggest that he might appoint Lodge and Eisenhower insider Douglas Dillon to ambassadorships abroad.[6] Then Kennedy, rather sheepishly, added, "I wondered, in fact, if after a few months you yourself might want to undertake an assignment abroad on a temporary basis." It was not much of an offer, and Nixon sensed that Kennedy was making it because "he thought it was expected of him—'the thing to do.' . . . " Nixon demurred, explaining that after such a close election he needed to stay close to his party.[7] Most likely, Kennedy was relieved.

If the true purpose of the meeting was to put on an air of unity and healing (artificial or not) it did that. The *New York Times* called the meeting "cordial" and referred to the two adversaries as "friends." But as Ken O'Donnell observed, Kennedy and Nixon were not that cordial. As O'Donnell and the president-elect climbed back into the helicopter for the ride back to Palm Beach, O'Donnell recalled Kennedy's last words on the meeting, "It was just as well for all of us that he didn't quite make it."[8]

～

One reason for the tensions surrounding the Key Biscayne meeting was that accusations of election fraud were still hanging thick in the air. Nixon had conceded the morning after the election, and for most Americans that ended it and made Kennedy the president-elect. But Nixon was under great pressure from his family, friends, and advisors to contest the election and demand a recount—at least in several states. Even Eisenhower wanted him to contest the election. In his memoirs, Nixon listed seven specific examples of corruption and fraud, three in Texas and four in Illinois. If Nixon could force a recount and win those states, he would win the election. "From the evidence I examined," he wrote, "there was no question that there was real substance to many of these charges.[9] Nixon, of course, did not implicate, by name, Chicago mayor Richard Daly or Johnson's behind-the-scenes manipulators in Texas, but by identifying Illinois and Texas as states where the fraud took place, he certainly had Johnson and Daly on his mind.

Nixon finally decided to spare the nation the recount process. A recount in Cook County, Illinois, where most of the accusations of fraud occurred, could take as long as eighteen months, and Nixon refused to hold up the transition for that long. He certainly considered that to set such a precedent might, in fact, have damaged the American tradition of an orderly transfer of power. "The situation within the entire Federal Government would be chaotic," he wrote.[10] And in Texas, there were no state provisions for a recount; a recount might not even be possible there. Nixon was also concerned about the American image abroad. Asia and Africa were in the throes of decolonization; new nations were being formed out of the old system. "I could think of no worse example for nations abroad, who for the first time were trying to put free electoral procedures into effect, than that of the United States wrangling over the results of our presidential election, and even suggesting that the presidency itself could be stolen by thievery at the ballot box."[11] He may also have been worried about strong evidence that downstate Illinois Republicans had initiated their own election fraud on his behalf. For all those reasons, Nixon refused to support those who where trying to push for a recount, and eventually the matter was dropped. Right or wrong, Nixon was statesmanlike in defeat.

On January 6, 1961, Nixon, as president of the Senate, presided over the official Electoral College count and, in effect, announced his own defeat to the nation. That was the first time since vice president and presidential candidate John C. Breckinridge, as president of the Senate, announced Abraham Lincoln's victory just one hundred years before.

⌣

The 1960 election was the closest in seventy-six years. In 1886, Grover Cleveland won with a plurality of only 30,000 votes, beating the Republican

James G. Blaine. Protestant ministers that year claimed that the Democrats were the party of "rum, Romanism and rebellion." Irish Catholics in the Northeast were offended. They voted Democratic in big numbers and Cleveland won.

The 1960 election was the highest recorded voter participation in America's history. Over 64 percent of the people voted, or about 68.8 million out of a total 107 million who were eligible to vote. From those numbers, Kennedy received 34,221,463 votes or 49.9 percent of the total. Nixon received just 112,881 votes less for a total of 34,108,582 or 49.6 percent of the total. "This margin" of difference, Theodore White wrote, "is so thin as to be, in all reality, nonexistent."[12]

In the afterlife of election statistics, however, it is the count in the Electoral College that decides the outcome. And here, Kennedy was a clear winner, taking 303 electoral votes to Nixon's 219. Fifteen electoral votes in Mississippi (8 of 8) and Alabama (6 of 11) and Oklahoma (1 of 8) were pledged to neither Nixon nor Kennedy and were finally cast for Senator Harry F. Byrd of Virginia. To round out the basic numbers, thirteen minority party candidates received about a half million votes, or 0.7 percent of the total and no electoral votes.

In Congress, the Republicans gained two Senate seats and twenty-two seats in the House. That pushed the totals to 64 Democrats to 36 Republicans in the Senate, and 261 Democrats to 174 Republicans in the House.

Exactly how close was it? Eighteen states were decided by a 2 percent margin or less.[13] Among the "what ifs," had 4,500 votes in Illinois and 28,000

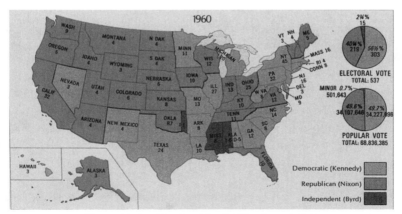

Figure 10.1. The Presidential Election of 1960

Table 10.1. 1960 Presidential Election Data

State	Total Vote	Kennedy	Nixon	JFK (%)	RMN (%)	EV JFK	RMN
Alabama	570,225	324,050	237,981	56.39	42.16	5*	
Alaska	60,762	29,809	30,953	49.06	50.94		3
Arizona	398,491	176,781	221,241	44.36	55.52		4
Arkansas	428,509	215,049	184,508	50.19	43.06	8	
California	6,506,578	3,224,099	3,259,722	49.55	50.10		32
Colorado	736,246	330,629	402,242	44.91	54.63		6
Connecticut	1,222,863	657,055	565,813	53.73	46.27	8	
Delaware	195,963	99,590	96,373	50.63	49.00	3	
Florida	1,544,180	748,700	795,476	48.49	51.51		10
Georgia	733,349	458,638	274,472	62.54	37.43	12	
Hawaii	184,705	92,410	92,295	50.03	49.97	3	
Idaho	300,450	138,853	161,597	46.22	53.78		
Illinois	4,757,409	2,377,846	2,368,988	49.98	49.80	27	
Indiana	2,135,360	952,358	1,175,120	44.60	55.03		
Iowa	1,273,810	550,565	722,381	43.22	56.71		10
Kansas	928,825	363,213	561,474	39.10	60.45		8
Kentucky	1,124,462	521,855	602,607	46.41	53.59		10
Louisiana	807,891	407,339	230,980	50.42	28.59	10	
Maine	421,767	181,159	240,608	42.49	57.05		5
Maryland	1,055,346	565,808	489,538	53.61	46.39	9	
Massachusetts	2,469,480	1,487,174	976,750	60.22	39.55	16	
Michigan	3,318,097	1,687,269	1,620,428	50.85	48.84	20	
Minnesota	1,541,887	779,933	757,915	50.58	49.16	11	
Mississippi	298,171	108,362	73,561	36.34	24.67	0*	0*
Missouri	1,934,422	972,201	962,221	50.26	49.74	13	
Montana	277,579	134,891	141,841	48.60	51.10		4
Nebraska	613,095	232,542	380,553	37.93	62.07		6
Nevada	107,267	54,880	52,387	51.16	48.84	3	
N. Hampshire	295,761	137,772	157,989	46.58	53.42		4
New Jersey	2,773,111	1,385,415	1,363,342	49.96	49.16	16	
New Mexico	311,107	156,027	153,733	50.15	49.41	4	
New York	7,380,075	3,830,085	3,446,419	52.53	47.27	45	
N. Carolina	1,368,556	713,136	655,420	52.11	47.89	14	
North Dakota	278,431	123,963	154,310	44.52	55.42		4
Ohio	4,161,859	1,944,248	2,217,611	46.72	53.28		25
Oklahoma	903,150	370,111	533,039	40.98	59.02		7*
Oregon	775,462	367,402	408,060	47.32	52.56		6
Pennsylvania	5,006,541	2,556,282	2,439,956	51.06	48.74	32	
Rhode Island	405,535	258,032	147,502	63.63	36.37	4	
South Carolina	386,688	198,129	188,558	51.24	48.76	8	
South Dakota	306,487	128,070	178,417	41.79	58.21		4
Tennessee	1,051,792	481,453	556,577	45.77	52.92		11
Texas	2,311,084	1,167,567	1,121,310	50.52	48.52	24	
Utah	374,709	169,248	205,361	45.17	54.81		4
Vermont	167,324	69,186	98,131	41.35	58.65		3
Virginia	771,449	362,327	404,521	46.97	52.44		12
Washington	1,241,572	599,298	629,273	48.27	50.68		9
W. Virginia	837,781	441,786	395,995	52.73	47.27	8	
Wisconsin	1,729,082	830,805	895,175	48.05	51.77		12
Wyoming	139,882	63,331	77,451	44.99	55.01		3
Total	68,836,385	34,220,984	34,108,157	49.72	49.55	303	219

Total votes designated as "other": 503,341.

15 electoral votes (6 from Alabama, 8 from Mississippi, and 1 from Oklahoma) were designated as "unpledged."

Source: Benjamin Guthrie and Ralph Roberts, *Statistics of the Presidential and Congressional Election of November 8, 1960* (Washington, DC: USGPO, 1961), 50–51.

*In Mississippi, the state's 8 electors voted for Virginia Senator Harry Byrd. In Atlanta, 5 of 11 electors voted for Kennedy. The remaining 6 voted for Byrd.

votes in Texas shifted, both of those states would have gone to Nixon, and he would have won the election by 3 electoral votes.

Nixon wrote in *Six Crises*, "When the election is this close . . . no one can say for certain what caused us to lose."[14] There are, of course, several statistics that are telling. Perhaps the most glaring is that Kennedy carried seven of the nine biggest states: New York, Pennsylvania, Michigan, Illinois, Texas, New Jersey, and Massachusetts while Nixon carried only two: Ohio and California. Most of those states (with the significant exceptions of Massachusetts, Ohio, and New York) were so close that they could have gone either way.[15]

These deciding figures owe mostly to Kennedy's strategy of focusing his energies on the big states, and in October directing that strategy even more closely by visiting the suburbs—particularly around Chicago, New York, Philadelphia, and Baltimore—where his youth played well among young baby boomers. These areas had been traditionally Republican and after about 1968, they would become a bastion of the Republican Party's growing power, but in 1960 Kennedy won the suburbs. In the suburban regions of the top fourteen metropolitan areas of the Northeast, Kennedy increased Democratic voter strength from 38 percent for Stevenson in 1956 up to 49 percent. This was a huge jump, and it was important in his victory.[16] This strategy also allowed Kennedy to hand over the responsibility of the urban vote to the city bosses and let Johnson focus on the South. The strategy worked well—while Nixon traveled the nation trying to make good on his promise to visit all fifty states.

Of all Kennedy's strategies, it was his choice of running mate that truly reaped the most rewards. Johnson held Texas when it certainly would have gone to Nixon. That alone was worth the choice. But Johnson also allowed Kennedy to hold on to much of the remainder of the South, including the Carolinas, Georgia, Louisiana, Arkansas, and the border states of Missouri, Maryland, and West Virginia. Kennedy's biggest victory was to win back Texas, Louisiana, and Maryland, states that had gone over to the Republicans in the 1956 Eisenhower onslaught. Johnson toured the South by rail, traveling nearly three thousand miles, making about sixty speeches. Adding to that, he used his political flare to twist arms and secure endorsements from reluctant party leaders. Then near the end of the campaign, he focused all his energies on Texas. He was a loyal lieutenant, and he did all he was asked to do.

The most interesting aspect of the southern vote was the Republican Party gains. And that would be a telltale for the future. Democrats had assumed that it had been Eisenhower's personal appeal that had given him big sections of the South in 1952 and 1956. But Nixon's numbers in 1960 revealed that the South was in transition into the Republican Party—and that the transition was continuing, even picking up steam. Not only did Nixon increase Republican voter strength throughout the South, he outran Eisenhower's 1956 numbers in four southern states: Alabama, Georgia, Mississippi, and South Carolina. Although he lost all four of those states, he won Virginia, Kentucky, Florida, Oklahoma, and Tennessee. And in a national losing effort, he maintained Eisenhower's 1956 strength in three of those states: Virginia, Florida, and Tennessee.[17] Possibly more important, Nixon's numbers in the South did not come from the rural and small town areas (portions of the electorate where he did so well in the Midwest and the Plains) but from the New South cities of Atlanta, Birmingham, Dallas, and Houston and their suburbs. All this was a portent for the future. In 1968 Nixon would lose much of the South to third party candidate, George Wallace. But in 1972 he would sweep the South. Georgia Democrat Jimmy Carter would bring the South back to the Democrats briefly in 1976. But from 1980 to 1992 the South would remain firmly in Republican hands.

At least for the Republicans, the future of the American political system was coming into focus in 1960. A new Republican coalition was forming. The conservative South was joining with the Midwest and generally rejecting the moderate northeastern wing of the party. By 1964 that coalition would bring in the West in a losing cause, but by 1968 the regional coalition of the South, the Midwest, and the West was in place. And it had added the nation's big city suburbs. It was a strong coalition, and it would stay in place for the remainder of the century.

The reason for the South's slow postwar shift into the Republican Party was, of course, race. As the Democrats became more committed to civil rights, southern whites became more and more distrustful of the Democratic Party. The Republicans, and their strong belief in states' rights, seemed like a more natural home. As the Democrats threatened to force a reorganization of the southern social structure through federal legislation, the Republican policy of states' rights allowed the South to maintain its segregated system without federal interference. Generally, Republicans were not racists, but their political philosophy allowed southern racists to maintain a racist system.

At the beginning of the campaign, the African-American vote was a problem for Kennedy. He had done almost nothing for African-Americans at any level of his government service, and he had barely managed even a kind word for African-Americans. By all accounts, he had no knowledge of the African-American condition, but he did understand fluently the need to keep southern whites in his camp, particularly white southern legislators who held the balance of power in Washington. When Kennedy went to the convention in Los Angeles he was, among all the Democratic hopefuls there, the least acceptable to the nation's black population. Even Lyndon Johnson scored higher than Kennedy among the nation's African-American voters.[18] But Kennedy set up a civil rights "division" within his campaign structure and placed two very capable men there: Harris Wofford and Sargent Shriver. Through hard work, they put Kennedy's name before the nation's black community. Their efforts succeeded, but it was the manner in which Kennedy dealt with Martin Luther King's arrest in mid-October that shifted the black vote. Kennedy's call to Mrs. King and then Bobby's call to the Georgia judge that affected Dr. King's release during the campaign was one of several great turning points in the postwar civil rights movement—at least from a political standpoint; possibly no other event pushed black voters out of the Party of Lincoln and into the Democratic Party. Gallup reported that seven out of ten African-Americans nationwide voted for Kennedy. In 1956, 64 percent of New York City's African-American population voted for Stevenson. In 1960, that number jumped to 74 percent. The numbers went from 63 to 78 percent in Chicago, 68 to 78 percent in Pittsburgh, 48 to 74 percent in Baltimore, 36 to 64 percent in Atlanta, and 19 to 65 percent in the rural areas of the South.[19]

Perhaps the most telling statistic is that had African-Americans cast their votes in 1960 the same as they had in 1956, Kennedy would most likely have lost Illinois, New Jersey, Michigan, South Carolina, and Delaware.[20]

The Republicans did not come away as big losers in 1960. They not only added two Senators and twenty-two Congressmen, they won complete control of seven state legislatures and added one of two houses in the legislatures of six other states. Although the Democrats controlled both houses of Congress, Kennedy did not come to office with a working majority. Of their number, 101 Democrats were from the South, and more than half of those voted with the Republicans on most domestic issues. In fact, the sixty-three freshmen Congressmen who went to Washington in the class of 1960 voted against Kennedy's domestic programs at a rate that averaged about 44 to 19. Theodore White called it "the most conservative Congress in six years."[21]

The Catholic issue has always been difficult to unravel. Was Kennedy hurt by his religion, or helped? One point is clear: The concentration of Catholics in several Northeastern and Midwestern states helped Kennedy win those states; Catholic voters in Detroit, New York City, and Chicago pushed Kennedy over the top in the big electoral states of Michigan, New York, and Illinois. At the same time, Kennedy's religion probably cost him California, and he lost more votes than he gained because of his religion in the South and in heavily Protestant Midwestern states like Ohio and Indiana.[22]

Nixon always believed that the Kennedy lieutenants were trying to keep religion at the forefront of the campaign, while accusing Nixon of deliberate religious bigotry. "And they were using it," Nixon added, "where it would do them the most good." Nixon's insiders insisted he confront the issue with a speech and accuse Kennedy of "reverse bigotry." Nixon refused, insisting that such a speech would "substantially set back" the cause of religious tolerance in the United States. He probably knew he could never win that battle, that any such statement could only brand him a bigot.[23]

A study at the Massachusetts Institute of Technology concluded that religion may have cost Kennedy as many as 1.5 million votes, or 2.3 percent, and given to Nixon the states of California, Kentucky, Oklahoma, and Tennessee. At the same time, however, the same study concluded that Kennedy won—because of his religion—the heavily weighted Catholic states of New York, Connecticut, Illinois, and Pennsylvania, giving him a net gain of 22 electoral votes as a direct result of the religious issue.[24] Lou Harris, Kennedy's personal pollster, told the *New York Times* that Kennedy's electoral edge can be attributed to three states he won by close margins: New Jersey (37 percent Catholic), Michigan (22 percent Catholic), and Minnesota (23 percent Catholic). Kennedy ran ahead of the Democratic Party ticket in all three of those states, which finished just under 50 percent of the total vote.[25] In the final analysis, Catholics voted for Kennedy, and they cast their votes in the big states.

⌢

In many ways the 1960 campaign was the first modern presidential campaign. Never again would voters look at their candidates or their election process quite the same way. The obvious contrast is Truman's 1948 run. The most significant image that has emerged from the lore of that campaign is Truman whistle-stopping his way across the country, taking his campaign to the nation, trying to put his face before as many people as possible. The campaign worked; Truman won the election, at least in part because thousands of Americans saw their president and voted for him. Certainly, for the vast majority of those American voters it was the first time they had seen a president in the flesh. But by 1960 television would change that and change the nature of American politics. What Truman achieved in months of whistle-stop campaigning, Kennedy and Nixon, in 1960, could achieve with one televised speech or one Sunday morning interview on national television.

Eisenhower had made some use of television in the 1956 campaign against Stevenson. Stevenson, however, refused to make any significant use of television, and it damaged his campaign. In that year, about half the nation's households had television sets. Four years later, in 1960, 80 percent of Americans could tune in to the three television network stations. By then, television had already become a part of the American way of life, a part of society, and a part of the nation's political landscape.

It was Kennedy who made the most use of television in the 1960 campaign—and he received the most from it. Kennedy was not as well known as Nixon, so he entered the primaries to keep his face on TV and his name in the news. The debates, later that year, made Kennedy a household name, at least in part because they were televised. But Nixon also understood television and the possibilities it held for his own candidacy. It was Nixon who had, himself, changed the very nature of the relationship between politics and television when, in 1952, he delivered his nationally televised "Checkers Speech." There were few televisions in 1952, but enough people saw the speech that the response forced Eisenhower to keep Nixon on the ticket. Because of that event Nixon, at least up until 1960, always believed that television was his friend.

And then there was the image of the candidates. Of course, 1960 was not the first campaign in which image played a part. Eisenhower's image was, in fact, at the very foundation of his own appeal with voters. Truman, again by contrast, had a very poor image. His speaking style was often called "wooden," and "boring," and his advisors constantly pushed him to speak extemporaneously, away from his prepared texts. On his whistle-stop tours in 1948, he bantered with the crowds, and they loved it. But by 1960 American voters could view their presidential candidates on television and make critical judgments they could have never made before. Of course it was in 1960 that Kennedy's image seemed to explode onto the television screen and into the nation's living rooms. Just as importantly, Nixon's image did not. Because the 1960 election was so close, image, perhaps for the first time in U.S. history, became a deciding factor in a presidential election.

Americans seemed to want to project movie star qualities onto John Kennedy. Certainly an attractive young man with a casual manner, he was often described as charismatic, and his speaking style was strong and clear. All that projected onto the TV screen in 1960. Nixon's messages were always strong, well presented, and thoughtful, but he simply could not measure up to Kennedy's image. The message was clear to any candidate who wanted to run for office in the future: An image would be projected to voters through television. That image had to be appealing or the American people might not respond. Not surprisingly, then, 1960 set the stage for manufactured political candidates and manufactured images.

Image in the 1960 campaign was certainly significant, but there were other factors that made 1960 the first truly modern presidential contest—and much of that comes from Kennedy's campaign and his success as a candidate. Kennedy's massive organization changed the way campaigns would be run in the future. Surrounding the candidate was a close-knit command structure made up of a few political insiders who strategized and planned, a group of brain trusters who kept the candidate well informed; speechwriters, private pollsters, and an almost limitless array of volunteers and campaign workers who saturated the primary states and then the nation in the general campaign. His people were never out of touch with the local politicos who had their fingers on the voters' pulse, and his research people compiled mountains of information on the public's voting patterns and habits. He used movie stars and popular theme songs. Kennedy's 1960 campaign was by far the biggest campaign operation to that time, and it brought an end to the old time front porch campaign, and even to the Truman-style campaign of the candidate and a few advisors and press people traveling the nation and making speeches.

Throughout American history it was almost expected that a candidate (particularly a popular candidate) would play a game of reticence, insisting that he did not want to run for the presidency. In an almost ritual dance, candidates would deny that they wanted the nomination, but they would always leave the door open to a candidacy by agreeing to run "if called" by the party as a service to the party and to the nation. As the 1952 campaign approached, the two eventual candidates, Eisenhower and Stevenson, seemed to try and outdo each other in denouncing their candidacies; both men insisted that they would not run for the presidency. Stevenson had been denying interest since he was elected governor of Illinois in 1948; Eisenhower had been rejecting all such notions at least since the end of the war. Both men continued to play coy, saying often that they would run if "drafted," or if their party insisted, or as a service to the nation. The 1960 campaign brought an end to that. After that year candidates had to announce their candidacy and run for the nomination and the office. There was no time—and no real appeal anymore—for a candidate to feign his disinterest or wait for a party draft. After 1960 the best candidates wanted the job. Both John Kennedy and Richard Nixon wanted to be president, and the American people wanted their candidates to want to be president.

The 1960 campaign also brought an end to the short run campaign that traditionally began on Labor Day and ended eight or nine weeks later on the first Tuesday in November. Kennedy began running for the 1960 nomination almost immediately after the 1956 campaign, with no apologies, and with no disclaimers that he would "accept the nomination if offered." After 1960, it would take a flat-out and early run to garner the votes necessary to win a party's nomination, to enter the primaries, draw publicity, and build momentum for the general election.

As the 1952 campaign approached, Truman was asked what he thought of primaries. He called them "eye-wash," meaning that, to him, they held no significance. Like so many other things, that remark identified Truman as a true symbol of the past, one of America's great politicians who was not changing with the political times. After 1960, presidential candidates could not afford to bypass the primaries—unless, of course, their nomination was not contested. Kennedy won his party's nomination by putting together a long string of primary victories, collecting delegates, and then winning the nomination on the first ballot. That would be the way of the future. Candidates running in contested races could not, like Lyndon Johnson in 1960, attend the convention as a favorite son and hope to grab the nomination as a compromise candidate following several ballots. In 1940 Wendell Willkie took the Republican nomination under just those circumstances, and for years afterward, long-shot candidates from both parties seemed to want to look back at that event and hope for such a miracle in the nominating process. But after 1940 nothing like that would ever happen again. After 1960 the nation's political conventions began moving away from those contentious political brawls and toward the modern political convention style, which is little more than a huge advertising event and a rallying point for party unity.

It cannot be said that 1960 produced any significant political realignments. It is, however, important that Kennedy's candidacy was the first departure in the Democratic Party from the New Deal-Fair Deal years that began in 1933 and carried on almost unabated for twenty years under Roosevelt and Truman. The Kennedy administration may not have been a great digression from the political coalition and economic philosophy of those years, but Kennedy did present an image of something new, different, and forward looking. For the Republicans, however, 1960 was a true turning point that would change the nature of that party for the future—although it may not have been apparent at the time. At the 1960 convention Barry Goldwater emerged as the darling of the Right when he insisted that conservatives stop being passive and take the party back from the moderates. For many conservatives that event was a milestone in the party's future. Immediately, conservative groups began organizing, intent on convincing Goldwater to make a run in 1964. That election was an ignominious defeat for conservatives, but they succeeded in expelling the moderates from the party and building a new majority coalition of the Midwest, the South, and the West. The campaign also seemed to have spawned Ronald Reagan, who emerged almost immediately as the leader of the Republican Right and was elected governor of California just two years later. The stage was set for a new majority Republican Party that would emerge in 1980.

For these several reasons, 1960 was the first modern presidential election. The electoral process would never be the same again. The Truman-style campaigns were over.

~

Endnotes

Preface

1. Perhaps the best example is Zachary Karabel, *The Last Campaign: How Harry Truman Won the 1948 Election* (New York, 2001).

2. See particularly, Joyce Hoffmann, *Theodore H. White and Journalism as Illusion* (Columbia, MO, 1995).

3. It was White who interviewed Jackie just weeks after the Kennedy assassination and, in a *Life* article, invented the image of the Kennedy presidency as Camelot after the popular musical stage play then on Broadway. Theodore H. White, "For President Kennedy: An Epilogue," *Life*, Dec. 6, 1963, 158–60.

Chapter One

1. Karl Hess, *In a Cause That Will Triumph: The Goldwater Campaign and the Future of Conservatism* (New York, 1967), 6.

2. M. Stanton Evans, *The Future of Conservatism: From Taft to Reagan and Beyond* (New York, 1968), 223.

3. *Newsweek*, Nov. 18, 1946.

4. *U.S. News*, Nov. 15, 1946.

5. Paul Walter to Taft (July 30, 1947) two letters, Political Files, Robert Taft Papers, LC; "Taft Story," (n.d.), campaign pamphlet; and Bill McAdams to Clarence Brown, "Confidential Memo," titled "Outline of Public Relations and Publicity Program" (n.d., fall 1947?), both in Political Files, Robert Taft Papers, LC. See also, James T. Patterson, *Mr. Republican: A Biography of Robert A. Taft* (Boston, 1972), 396–99; and Gary Donaldson, *Truman Defeats Dewey* (Lexington, KY, 1999), 129.

6. Quoted in Gary Reichard, *Politics as Usual: The Age of Truman and Eisenhower* (Arlington Heights, IL, 1988), 131.

7. See Arthur Larson, *A Republican Looks at His Party* (New York, 1956); and Emmet John Hughes, *The Ordeal of Power: A Political Memoir of the Eisenhower Years* (New York, 1963).

8. William A. Rusher, *Rise of the Right* (New York, 1984), 64–65.

9. *New York Times*, July 11, 12, 13, 1952.

10. Quoted in Stephen Ambrose, *Eisenhower: Soldier and President* (New York, 1990), 307. To a friend Eisenhower wrote, "It is a sorry mess; at times one feels almost like hanging his head in shame. . . ." DDE to Harry Bullis (May 18, 1953), Diary Series, Papers as President, 1953–1961, Ann Whitman File, EP, DDEL, Abilene, Kansas.

11. Gallup data quoted in Robert Griffin, *Politics of Fear: Joseph R. McCarthy and the Senate*, 2d ed. (Amherst, MA, 1987), 263.

12. DDE to (governor of Indiana) George Craig (March 26, 1954), Diary Series, Papers as President, 1953–1961, Ann Whitman File, EP, DDEL, Abilene.

13. DDE to William Robinson (March 12, 1954), ibid.

14. *Cong. Rec.*, 82d Cong., 1st sess., 6556-6603. McCarthy's entire argument against Marshall is in Joseph McCarthy, *America's Retreat from Victory: The Story of George Catlett Marshall* (New York, 1951).

15. DDE to Harry Bullis (May 18, 1953), Diary Series, Papers as President, 1953–1961, Ann Whitman File, EP, DDEL, Abilene. See also DDE interview (July 28, 1964), Princeton University Oral History Collection.

16. The question of Bohlen's statements about Yalta and that he is "pro-Democratic," can be seen in Legislative Leadership Meeting (March 9, 1953), Legislative Meeting Series, Papers as President, 1953–1961, Ann Whitman File, DDEL, EP, Abilene.

17. *U.S. News and World Report* (April 3, 1955); Charles E. Bohlen, *Witness to History, 1929–1969* (New York, 1973), 309–36. This quote can also be found in William S. White, *The Taft Story* (New York, 1952), 239.

18. DDE Diary (April 1, 1953), Diary Series, Papers as President, 1953–1961, Ann Whitman File, EP, DDEL, Abilene. Those Republicans who voted against the Bohlen appointment were the Senate's most conservative members, including William Jenner, Styles Bridges, John Bricker, Everett Dirksen, McCarthy, and Barry Goldwater. Eisenhower was surprised by the Bricker and Goldwater vote because, he wrote in his April 1 diary entry, he thought they "seemed to me a bit more intelligent than the others."

19. Quoted in William Manchester, *The Glory and the Dream: A Narrative History of America, 1932–1972* (Boston, 1973), I, 812.

20. DDE Diary (May 1, 1953), Diary Series, Papers as President, 1953–1961, Ann Whitman File, EP, DDEL, Abilene. In the official report of the Legislative Leadership Committee, it is stated that "Sen. Taft then stated [that] he could not possibly

express the deepness of his disappointment at the program the Administration presented today." Minnich, Legislative Leadership Committee, Proceedings (May 9, 1953), EP, DDEL, Abilene.

21. DDE Diary (April 1, 1953), Diary Series, Papers as President, 1953–1961, Ann Whitman File, EP, DDEL, Abilene.

22. *National Review*, June 27, 1956.

23. Stephen E. Ambrose, *Nixon*, vol. 1, *The Education of a Politician, 1913–1962* (New York, 1987), 374. See *New York Times*, Sept. 26, 1955.

24. Ambrose, *Eisenhower: Soldier and President*, 399. There were also rumors that Milton Eisenhower might step in. See *Time*, Sept. 19, 1964; and Milton Eisenhowner, *The President Is Calling* (Garden City, NY, 1974), 315.

25. Eisenhower always told friends and family that he would not run for a second term. See particularly DDE to Swede Hazlett (Dec. 24, 1953), Diary Series, Papers as President, 1953–1961, Ann Whitman File, EP, DDEL, Abilene; and DDE to Milton Eisenhower (Dec. 11, 1953), ibid.

26. *National Review*, Nov. 5, 1955; *Cong. Rec.*, 83d Cong., 2d sess., 16039; John Judas, *William F. Buckley, Jr.: Patron Saint of the Conservatives* (New York, 1988), 128–33.

27. DDE to Milton Eisenhower (Dec. 11, 1953), Diary Series, Papers as President, 1953–1961, Ann Whitman File, EP, DDEL, Abilene. And DDE to Hazlett (Dec. 24, 1953), ibid.

28. Sherman Adams interview, Oral History Collection, Eisenhower Library, Abilene.

29. DDE Diary (March 13, 1956), Diary Series, Papers as President, 1953–1961, Ann Whitman File, EP, DDEL, Abilene. See also DDE Diary (Feb. 9, 1956 and Feb. 13, 1956), ibid. In these entries, Eisenhower considers appointing Nixon secretary of state. For the suggestion of secretary of defense, see Earl Mazo, *Richard Nixon* (New York, 1959), 147

30. DDE to Hazlett (Mar. 2, 1956), Diary Series, Papers as President, 1953–1961, Ann Whitman File, EP, DDEL, Abilene.

31. DDE Diary (March 13, 1956), ibid.

32. DDE Diary (March 13, 1956), ibid.

33. Milton Eisenhower always argued that the president liked Nixon and hoped that a cabinet post would be a better stepping stone to the presidency than the vice presidency. See Milton Eisenhower interview, COHC.

34. Richard Nixon, *RN: The Memoirs of Richard Nixon* (New York, 1978), 171–72.

35. DDE Diary (entry April 26, 1956), Diary Series, Papers as President, 1953–1961, Ann Whitman File, EP, DDEL, Abilene. Much of this is also quoted in Nixon, *Memoirs*, 172; and Ambrose, *Nixon*, 397–99. *New York Times*, April 27, 1956.

36. Quoted in Ken Schuparra, *Triumph of the Right: The Rise of the California Conservative Movement, 1945–1966* (Armonk, NY, 1998), 25.

37. *Life*, Sept. 3, 1956.

38. *New York Times*, Nov. 7, 1960.

39. DDE to William Robinson (Mar. 12, 1956), Diary Series, Papers as President, 1953–1961, Ann Whitman File, EP, DDEL, Abilene.

40. This "rumor" is borne out in Rusher, *Rise of the Right*, 66. Knowland committed suicide in 1974. See Trotton Anderson, "The 1958 California Election," *Western Political Science Quarterly* 12 (March 1959), 276–300.

41. *New York Times*, Nov. 6, 1958.

42. Brent Bozell, "Coroner's Report," *National Review* (Nov. 12, 1958).

Chapter Two

1. Richard Chesteen, "'Mississippi Is Gone Home!' A Study of the 1948 Mississippi States' Rights Bolt," *Journal of Mississippi History* 32 (Feb. 1970), 43–59; Donaldson, *Truman Defeats Dewey*, 164.

2. Harry S. Truman, *Memoirs*, vol. 2, *Years of Trial and Hope* (Garden City, NY, 1956), 491–92.

3. Robert H. Ferrell, *Harry S. Truman: A Life* (Columbia, MO, 1994), 375–76; Clark Clifford (with Richard Holbrooke), *Counsel to the President: A Memoir* (New York, 1991), 282–84.

4. Walter Johnson, ed., *The Papers of Adlai E. Stevenson: Governor of Illinois, 1949–1953* (Boston, 1973), 580, 585.

5. *New York Times*, July 27, 1952. For another analysis of Stevenson's "moderate" politics in the popular press, see Ernest K. Lindly in *Newsweek*, Nov. 21, 1955. See also George Reedy interview, JLOHC.

6. William C. Berman, *The Politics of Civil Rights in the Truman Administration* (Columbus, OH, 1970), 231; Nancy J. Weiss, *Farewell to the Party of Lincoln: Black Politics in the Age of FDR* (Princeton, NJ, 1983), 209–35; Dewey Grantham, *The Life and Death of the Solid South: A Political History* (Lexington, KY, 1988), 177–203.

7. Quoted in William H. Chaffe, *Unfinished Journey: America since World War II* (New York, 1993), 3d ed., 154.

8. Press Release (n.d.), "Statement by Adlai Stevenson Regarding the 'Declaration of Constitutional Principles,'" 1956 Presidential Campaign Series, AES Papers, Mudd Library, Princeton.

9. See particularly, *PPP, Eisenhower, 1957*, 431, 435, and 476–79.

10. Robert Dallek, *Lone Star Rising: Lyndon Johnson and His Times, 1908–1960* (New York, 1991), 478.

11. Reedy interview, JLOHC. The liberals, led by Hubert Humphrey, did not trust LBJ at first, but he was able to include the liberals in his united party. Humphrey said he was "of a different cut" from other southerners. Humphrey interview, JLOHC.

12. Reedy interview, JLOHC. Another good description of "the treatment" by one who was on the receiving end is in the Steward Alsop interview, JLOHC. See also James Reston, "Yodels for a Texan," *New York Times* (Aug. 12, 1958).

13. Reedy interview, JLOHC.

14. Johnson was back at work by mid-December; Eisenhower by mid-February.

15. A good example of Johnson's insistence that he was not a candidate is Johnson's speech transcript (March 28, 1956), Senate Political Files, 1949–1961, Convention, 1956, LBJA, LBJL, Austin.

16. Reedy interview, JLOHC. Johnson's reticence is documented in a number of places. See Robert A. Caro, *The Years of Lyndon Johnson: Master of the Senate* (New York, 2002), 812.

17. See Johnson's own account of this in Lyndon Johnson, *The Vantage Point: Perspectives of the Presidency, 1963–1969* (New York, 1971), 3; James Rowe to LBJ (Oct. 26, 1955), Select Names Files, LBJA, LBJL. See also, Dallek, *Lone Star*, 490–91; Robert Dallek, *An Unfinished Life: John Kennedy, 1917–1963* (Boston, 2003), 204; and Doris Kearns Goodwin, *The Fitzgeralds and the Kennedys: An American Saga* (New York, 1987), 780–81.

18. Stevenson to Schlesinger (Sept. 16, 1955), 1956 Presidential Campaign Series, Adlai Stevenson Papers, Mudd Library, Princeton.

19. Strategy memo by Arthur Schlesinger, "The Political Problem: 1956" (Sept. 6, 1955), ibid.

20. Stevenson's campaign announcement speech (Dec. 15, 1955), ibid. Stevenson had said he would run in Minnesota a month earlier. See *New York Times*, Nov. 17, 1955.

21. Press Release on Minnesota Primary Results (n.d., March 20–22), 1956 Campaign Series, Stevenson Papers, Mudd Library, Princeton. This press release claims that 125,000 Minnesota Republicans crossed over in an effort to stop Stevenson; in some precincts the Democratic voter turnout was 300 percent over 1952.

22. *Washington Post* (Aug. 20, 1956); Porter McKeever, *Adlai Stevenson: His Life and Legacy* (New York, 1989), 375–76.

23. John Sparkman to Robert Kendall (July 17, 1956), 1956 Presidential Campaign Series, Stevenson Papers, Mudd Library, Princeton.

24. *New York Times*, August 13, 1956, for Humphrey's statement, and ibid., August 3, 1956, for Eleanor Roosevelt's statement. See also Joseph P. Lash, *Eleanor: The Years Alone* (New York, 1972), 241.

25. Reedy interview, JLOHC.

26. Kenneth P. O'Donnell and David F. Powers, *"Johnny We Hardly Knew Ye": Memories of John Fitzgerald Kennedy* (Boston, 2d ed., 1973), 135–36. As early as July 1, Kennedy had said on the television news program *Face the Nation* that he was not a candidate for vice president. Transcript of *Face the Nation* (July 1, 1956), Pre-Presidential Papers, JFKL, Boston.

27. Herbert Parmet, *Jack: The Struggles of John F. Kennedy* (New York, 1980), 361–62.

28. McKeever, *Adlai Stevenson*, 357. See also Reedy interview, JLOHC.

29. Arthur Schlesinger, Jr., *A Thousand Days: John F. Kennedy in the White House* (Boston, 1965), 9.

30. Arthur Schlesinger, Jr., *Robert Kennedy and His Times* (Boston, 1978), 133–36.

31. "Campaign Analysis, 1956" (Aug. 7, 1956), 1956 Campaign Series, Stevenson Papers, Mudd Library, Princeton.

32. "Public Opinion and Campaign Strategy" (Sept. 13, 1956), unpublished memo, no stated author, ibid. The poll information was gathered from several sources, but mostly Gallup Polls. Lou Harris, *Is There a Republican Majority? Political Trends, 1952–1956* (New York, 1954). The Democratic National Committee came to many of the same conclusions. See Research Division of the DNC, "Analysis of the 1956 Election" (Feb. 12, 1957), copy in LBJA—Famous Names, LBJL, Austin. See also, Samuel Lubell, *Revolt of the Moderates* (New York, 1956), 73. Another work at the time that was asking and answering many of these same questions was Angus Campbell, et al., *The Voter Decides* (New York, 1954) and the *New York Times* (Nov. 3, 1960). This is a discussion of many of these trends just before the 1960 election.

33. Copy of DNC announcement in "Statements by Adlai Stevenson Concerning 1960 Presidential Nomination" (n.d.), Theodore Sorensen Papers, JFKL, Boston. Also included here are a number of statements by Stevenson insisting that he will not run in 1960, including several transcripts from *Meet the Press*. A second collection of Stevenson denials has been collected in the David Powers Papers, JFKL, Boston. See particularly, *Time*, Sept. 23, 1957; *U.S. News and World Report*, Nov. 29, 1957: "I will never run again for the presidency," *New York Times*, Feb. 22, 1959, "I've had enough." *New York Times*, April 21, 1959, "It's time for someone else to have a chance."

34. James Rowe to Johnson (Aug. 11, 1956), LBJA—Select Names, LBJL, Austin.

35. Gilbert C. Fite, *Richard B. Russell, Jr., Senator from Georgia* (Chapel Hill, NC, 1991), 333.

36. Reedy interview, JLOHC.

37. The president made this statement in a White House legislative meeting, (April 17, 1956), Minnich, Legislative Meeting Series, Papers as President, 1953–1961, Ann Whitman File, EP, Abilene.

38. James Rowe to Johnson (July 3, 1957), LBJA—Selected Names, LBJL, Austin. In August, after the bill passed, LBJ thanked Rowe for his advice earlier in the summer. Johnson to Rowe (Aug. 8, 1957), ibid.

39. Summary of telephone call, Eisenhower to Johnson (June 15, 1957), DDE Diary Series, Ann Whitman File, Papers as President, 1953–1961, EP, Abilene. These are Whitman's notes from the conversation.

40. Reedy interview, JLOHC.

41. Ibid.

42. Merle Miller, *Lyndon: An Oral Biography* (New York, 1980), 211.

43. Quoted in Dwight Eisenhower, *The White House Years: Waging Peace* (Garden City, NY, 1965), 160. Reedy insisted that a stronger bill would have been impossible in 1957. See Reedy interview, JLOHC.

44. Byrd to Johnson (Aug. 2, 1957), LBJA, Congressional File, Harry F. Byrd, LBJL, Austin.

Chapter Three

1. Greg Mitchell, *Tricky Dick and the Pink Lady: Richard Nixon vs. Helen Gahagan Douglas—Sex, Politics and the Red Scare, 1950* (New York, 1998), 99–100. Arthur Schlesinger has written that Kennedy always regretted the speeches he made regarding the "loss" of China. See Schlesinger *Thousand Days*, 13.

2. For much of the McCarthy-Kennedy connection, see Thomas C. Reeves, *The Life and Times of Joe McCarthy* (Lanham, MD, 1997), 162, 203.

3. Quoted in Dallek, *John Kennedy*, 162.

4. JFK interview, Martin Papers, JFKL. Dallek, *John Kennedy*, 191. Schlesinger insists that Kennedy and the Kennedy family did not have a particularly strong relationship with McCarthy. He also argues that Kennedy was ill the day of the vote to censure McCarthy. See Schlesinger, *Thousand Days*, 13.

5. *Face the Nation* transcripts (March 30, 1959), Pre-Presidential Papers, JFKP, JFKL, Boston.

6. Al Smith Dinner Speech (Oct. 22, 1959), ibid.

7. Transcript, *College News Conference* (Dec. 8, 1958). Theodore Sorensen Papers, JFKL, Boston.

8. The entire exchange between JFK and Eleanor Roosevelt can also be found in ibid. See also, JFK to Eleanor Roosevelt (Dec. 11, 1958), President's Office Files, JFKL, Boston.

9. Eleanor Roosevelt to JFK (Dec. 18, 1958), Sorensen Papers, JFKL, Boston.

10. JFK to Eleanor Roosevelt (Dec. 29, 1958), ibid.

11. Eleanor Roosevelt to JFK (Jan. 6, 1959), ibid; *New York Herald-Tribune*, Jan. 6, 1959.

12. Eleanor Roosevelt to JFK (Jan. 20, 1959), Sorensen Papers, JFKL, Boston.

13. Eleanor Roosevelt to JFK (Jan. 29, 1959), ibid. Kennedy discussed the entire incident on *Face the Nation* in late February. See *Face the Nation* transcript (February 22, 1959), Lawrence Spivak Papers, Library of Congress, Washington, DC.

14. *Face the Nation* (Feb. 22, 1959), ibid.

15. *New Leader*, Dec. 11, 1959.

16. Richard Fox, *Reinhold Niebuhr: A Biography* (New York, 1986); Steven M. Gillon, *Politics and Vision: The ADA and American Liberalism, 1947–1985* (New York, 1987), 9.

17. Kennedy to Neibuhr (Feb. 11, 1959), Sorensen Papers, JFKL, Boston.

18. Neibuhr to Kennedy (Feb. 16, 1959), ibid.

19. Kennedy to Neibuhr (Feb. 17, 1959), ibid.

20. Schlesinger, *Thousand Days*, 23.

21. *Newsweek*, January 11, 1960; *New York Times*, May 6, 1960.

22. Theodore H. White, *Making of the President, 1960* (New York, 1961), 56.

23. "Dear Stevenson Supporters" (May 16, 1960), 1960 Presidential Campaign Series, Stevenson Papers, Mudd Library, Princeton; "Excerpts from Some of the Letters Received in Response [to the *Saturday Review* ad]," (May 20, 1960), ibid.

24. Arthur Schlesinger, Jr., to Stevenson (May 16, 1960), President's Office Files, JFKP, JFKL, Boston.

25. Stevenson to Schlesinger (May 21, 1960), Schlesinger Papers, JFKL, Boston; and Stevenson to Schlesinger (May 27, 1960), ibid.

26. Stevenson to Schlesinger (June 7, 1960), ibid.

27. Schlesinger to JFK (June 6, 1960), President's Office Files, JFKP, JFKL, Boston.

28. "Statement by Mrs. Roosevelt" (June 10, 1960), 1960 Presidential Campaign Series, Stevenson Papers, Mudd Library, Princeton; "Petition to Delegates to the DNC on Behalf of the Nomination of Adlai Stevenson" (June 13, 1960), ibid.

29. "An Important Message to All Liberals" (June 17, 1960), Sorensen Papers, Box 23, Campaign Files, JFKL, Boston.

Chapter Four

1. Dallek, *John F. Kennedy*, 248.

2. In 1960, only Florida, Maryland, Ohio, Wisconsin, New Hampshire, Oregon, and California bound their delegates to the result of their states' primaries. Indiana bound its delegates only on the first ballot.

3. Joseph P. Kennedy to Count Enrico Galeazzi (Mar. 31, 1960), Joseph P. Kennedy Papers, JFKL, Boston.

4. *Meet the Press* transcripts (Jan. 3, 1960), Lawrence Spivak Papers, LC; "Wisconsin" file (n.d.), Box 26, Powers Papers, JFKL, Boston.

5. "Kennedy Charges 'Gang-up' by Foes," *New York Times*, April 19, 1960; *New York Times*, May 1, 1960.

6. Hubert H. Humphrey, *Education of a Public Man: My Life and Politics* (Minneapolis, 1991), 149.

7. Ibid., 150.

8. James Doyle to William McC. Blair (April 5, 1960), 1960 Presidential Campaign Series, Stevenson Papers, Mudd Library, Princeton.

9. See as example, "Candidates Cautioned: Truman Hopes West Virginia Rivals Won't Get Hurt," *New York Times*, May 1, 1950.

10. *St. Louis Post-Dispatch* May 1, 1960.

11. Humphrey, *Education of a Public Man*, 150.

12. *New York Times*, April 15, 1960.

13. O'Donnell and Powers, *"Johnny, We Hardly Knew Ye,"* 175.

14. Humphrey, *Education of a Public Man*, 152.

15. O'Donnell and Powers, *"Johnny, We Hardly Knew Ye,"* 178.

16. Humphrey, *Education of a Public Man*, 151.

17. Ibid., 151.

18. Ibid., 152.

19. Ibid., 152; Dallek, *John F. Kennedy*, 250.

20. Theodore C. Sorensen, *Kennedy* (New York, 1965), 153.

21. "Wisconsin Attacks" (April 4, 1960), Pre-Presidential Papers, JFKP, JFKL, Boston.

22. Quoted in Dallek, *John F. Kennedy*, 251.

23. Dave Powers, "1960 Presidential Primaries" (n.d.), Powers Papers, JFKL, Boston; O'Donnell and Powers, "*Johnny, We Hardly Knew Ye*," 183.

24. Humphrey, *Education of a Public Man*, 156; "'Stop Kennedy' Drive Led by Byrd of West Virginia," *New York Times*, April 11, 1960; "Lewis Backs Move to Stop Kennedy," *New York Times*, April 13, 1960; "Kennedy Charges 'Gang-up' by Foes," *New York Times*, April 19, 1960; "Stevenson Is Back Again Haunting Campaign," *New York Times*, April 13, 1960. John L. Lewis of the United Mine Workers was a significant member of the stop-Kennedy organization in West Virginia, *New York Times*, April 13, 1960; Sorensen, *Kennedy*, 141; O'Donnell and Powers, "*Johnny, We Hardly Knew Ye*," 186.

25. "Activities of R. P. McDonough in West Virginia . . . in the Interest of Then Senator John F. Kennedy" (n.d.), Box 26, Sorensen Papers, JFKL, Boston; White, *Making of the President, 1960*, 120–21, 123.

26. Ibid., 120. On early Kennedy interests in Wisconsin, see Louis Harris Polling Data (June 1958), Pre-Presidential Papers, JFKP, JFKL, Boston.

27. That all this was a concern to the Kennedys, see "1960 Presidential Primaries" (n.d.), Powers Papers, JFKL, Boston. He writes in his notes, "The Wisconsin victory was not decisive enough to beat Humphrey, and it showed that religion was a factor." See also Sorensen, *Kennedy*, 139.

28. "1960 Presidential Primaries" (n.d.), Powers Papers, JFKL, Boston.

29. Humphrey, *Education of a Public Man*, 156.

30. "Meeting of Kennedy Men" (April 8, 1960), Pre-Administration Files, Political Files, Robert F. Kennedy Papers, JFKL, Boston.

31. Sorensen to JFK, "Possible Vice Presidential Nominees" (June 29, 1960), Powers Papers, JFKL, Boston.

32. "Lewis Backs Move to Stop Kennedy," *New York Times*, April 13, 1960. The Kennedys thought it was in retaliation for Bobby and Jack's work on the McClellan Senate Racketeering Committee that investigated Jimmy Hoffa among other union leaders. See O'Donnell and Powers, "*Johnny, We Hardly Knew Ye*," 187.

33. Ibid., 184; White, *Making of the President, 1960*, 103–4; *New York Times*, May 1, 2, 1960.

34. Ken O'Donnell contacted UAW chief Walter Reuther and Humphrey's closest advisor James Rowe. According to O'Donnell, both agreed that Humphrey should withdraw and gave that advice to Humphrey. Orville Freeman and Pat Brown also tried to convince Humphrey to withdraw. O'Donnell and Powers, "*Johnny, We Hardly Knew Ye*," 185; White, *Making of the President, 1960*, 115.

35. A good accounting of most of these people—by name—can be found in White, *Making of the President, 1960*, 124.

36. Dave Powers, "Recollections: West Virginia" (n.d.), Powers Papers, JFKL, Boston.

37. "Reuther Backs Kennedy Drive," *New York Times*, May 15, 1960; White, *Making of the President, 1960*, 130–31; Humphrey, *Education of a Public Man*, 156; "Humphrey Cites Wealth of Foes," *New York Times*, April 26, 1960.

38. White, *Making of the President, 1960*, 130–31. White wrote that "My memory tells me that the sum of that check was $750." See also, Humphrey, *Education of a Public Man*, 160. For some of Humphrey's bitterness over his money problems, see *New York Times*, April 26, 1960.

39. It was not until April 8, 1960, that the Kennedys decided to recruit Franklin, Jr. See David Powers, "Recollections: West Virginia" (n.d.), Powers Papers, JFKL, Boston; O'Donnell and Powers, *"Johnny, We Hardly Knew Ye,"* 189.

40. Ibid., 189.

41. David Powers, "Recollections: West Virginia;" Sorensen, *Kennedy*, 142. Humphrey was turned down for the military service because of a physical disability.

42. *New York Times*, May 3, 1960; *Time*, May 9, 1960; Lawrence F. O'Brien, *No Final Victories: A Life in Politics: John F. Kennedy to Watergate* (Garden City, NY, 1974), 72–73; *Washington Post*, May 29, 1987; Doris Kearn Goodwin, *The Fitzgeralds and the Kennedys: An American Saga* (New York, 1987), 799.

43. Donaldson, *Truman Defeats Dewey*, 139. Lash, *Eleanor: The Years Alone*, 146–47.

44. Humphrey, *Education of a Public Man*, 161. The *New York Times* agreed, see "West Virginia Debate" (May 5, 1960).

45. David Powers, "Recollections: West Virginia."

46. Humphrey, *Education of a Public Man*, 161.

47. Richard N. Goodwin, *Remembering America: A Voice from the Sixties* (New York, 1989), 87.

48. Carol V. R. George, *God's Salesman: Norman Vincent Peale and the Power of Positive Thinking* (New York, 1993), 196. For more on Peale and Graham in the campaign, see Thomas J. Carty, *A Catholic in the White House: Religion, Politics, and John F. Kennedy's Presidential Campaign* (New York, 2004), 49–58.

49. *New York Times*, April 19, 25, 1960.

50. White, *Making of the President, 1960*, 128–29.

51. Goodwin, *Remembering America*, 89. Theodore White agreed that Kennedy believed he would lose. White, *Making of the President, 1960*, 136. On O'Donnell and Bobby Kennedy's fears, see O'Donnell and Powers, *"Johnny, We Hardly Knew Ye,"* 196.

52. *New York Times*, May 11, 1960.

53. Goodwin, *Remembering America*, 90.

Chapter Five

1. Nixon to John Bricker (April 18, 1960), Vice Presidential Papers, Box 102, RMNP, NARA, Laguna Niguel, CA. See also *Time*, May 16, 1960.

2. Milton Eisenhower interview, COHC

3. The press saw Nixon's dilemma. See *Time*, May 16, 1960; and *New York Times*, March 7, 1960.

4. Ambrose, *Nixon*, 548.

5. Ambrose, *Eisenhower*, 559, 596–97; Ambrose, *Nixon*, 547–48.

6. *PPP, Eisenhower*, (1960), 144, 147.

7. Ambrose, *Eisenhower*, 560; Herbert S. Parmet, *Richard Nixon and His America* (Boston, 1990), 263. Other names considered were Tom Dewey, Charles Halleck, William Rogers, Sherman Adams, Herbert Brownell, economist Gabriel Hauge, and even Milton Eisenhower. Most of these names came up (instead of Nixon) while the president was convalescing following his heart attack. *Newsweek* Jan. 4, 1960.

8. Mazo, *Richard Nixon*, 243.

9. *Newsweek* Jan. 25, 1960. For another recount of Nixon's change, see ibid., (Jan. 11, 1960).

10. Ibid. Jan. 25, 1960.

11. Mazo, *Richard Nixon*, 241–42.

12. Lou Cannon, *President Reagan: The Role of a Lifetime* (New York, 1991), 74; William Pemberton, *Exit with Honor; The Life and Presidency of Ronald Reagan* (Armonk, NY, 1998), 51.

13. Nixon to Reagan (June 17, 1959), Reagan to Nixon (June 27, 1959), and Nixon to Reagan (July 6, 1959), all in General Correspondence Files, Box 621, Pre-Presidential Papers, RMNP, NARA, Laguna Niguel, CA.

14. Cannon, *President Reagan*, 74. By September 1960, Nixon was trying to get Reagan to campaign for him. See Stanley McCaffrey to Jules Alberti (Sept. 2, 1960), General Correspondence Files, Box 621, Pre-Presidential Papers, RMNP, NARA, Laguna Niguel, CA.

15. *New York Times*, July 25 and 27, 1959; *Time*, Aug. 10, 1959; *Newsweek*, Aug. 3, 1959; *Life*, Aug. 10, 1959. A good account of all this is Milton S. Eisenhower, *The President is Calling*, 328–32. Milton accompanied Nixon to the Soviet Union and was in the "Kitchen" with Nixon at the time of the debates.

16. Ambrose, *Nixon*, 533; Richard M. Nixon, *Six Crises* (Garden City, NY, 1962), 303.

17. Reagan to Nixon (Sept. 7, 1959), General Correspondence Files, Box 621, Pre-Presidential Papers, RMNP, NARA, Laguna Niguel, CA.

18. Mazo, *Richard Nixon*, 239; McWhorter to Nixon (Aug. 27, 1959), Vice Presidential Papers, RMNP, Box 505, NARA, Laguna Niguel, CA.

19. *Newsweek*, Jan. 4, 1960; *New York Times*, March 7, 1960. A copy of Rockefeller's June 7 speech is in General Correspondence, Box 650, Pre-Presidential Papers, RMNP, NARA, Laguna Niguel, CA. See also *New York Times*, June 8, 1960.

20. Joseph E. Persico, *The Imperial Rockefeller: A Biography of Nelson A. Rockefeller* (New York, 1982), 39

21. Rockefeller statement (Dec. 26, 1959), Vice Presidential Papers, Box 650, RMNP, NARA, Laguna Niguel, CA. The 10-point plan and the Rockefeller speech

that accompanied it were written by John Emmet Hughes, a journalist and one-time Eisenhower speechwriter. This outraged Eisenhower even more. It was Hughes who wrote the "I will go to Korea" speech in 1952.

22. Ambrose, *Nixon*, 539; Parmet, *Richard Nixon*, 372.

23. *Newsweek*, June 6, 1960.

24. Summary of telephone call, DDE to Rockefeller (June 11, 1960), DDE Diary Series, Ann Whitman File, Papers as President, 1953–1961, EP, Abilene. This analysis is from Whitman's notes.

25. Robert Alan Goldberg, *Barry Goldwater* (New Haven, CT), 142–44.

26. *Time*, May 16, 1960.

27. *Time*, July 11, 1960.

Chapter Six

1. Truman refused to attend the convention because, he said, it had been "fixed." See that quote in *Time*, July 11, 1960. To most observers that meant he thought the Kennedy family had purchased the nomination. As the convention approached it appeared he would attend, then he did not. See "Resignation" statement, Speech files, Post-Presidential Papers, Box 731, HSTP, HSTL, Independence, Missouri.

2. John Steele to Stevenson, quoted in John Bartlow Martin, *Adlai Stevenson and the World: The Life of Adlai Stevenson* (Garden City, NY, 1977), 521. Other political figures saw the dawning of a new era. See Clifford, *Counsel to the President*, 315.

3. Merle Miller, *Plain Speaking: An Oral History of Harry S. Truman* (New York, 1964), 199–201; Alonzo Hamby, *Man of the People* (New York, 1995), 624.

4. O'Donnell and Powers, *"Johnny We Hardly Knew Ye,"* 205; Miller, *Plain Speaking*, 201. Truman's speech endorsing Symington is in Post-Presidential Papers, Speech Files, Box 731, HSTP, HSTL, Independence.

5. O'Donnell and Powers, *"Johnny We Hardly Knew Ye,"* 205–6.

6. Hamby, *Man of the People*, 625.

7. Quoted in Martin, *Adlai Stevenson*, 521.

8. *New York Times*, May 6, 1960. Kennedy and his advisors thought that all this was an attempt to get the nomination for Johnson and not Stevenson. See O'Donnell and Powers, *"Johnny We Hardly Knew Ye,"* 204–5.

9. Ibid., 205.

10. *Time*, July 18, 1960.

11. *New York Times*, May 6, 1960; *Time*, July 18, 1960. Others believed that Johnson was actually supporting Stevenson in hopes of derailing Kennedy. See Clifford, *Counsel to the President*, 315.

12. *New York Times*, April 9, 1960; *Time*, July 18, 1960.

13. Quoted in O'Donnell and Powers, *"Johnny, We Hardly Knew Ye,"* 207.

14. White, *Making of the President, 1960*, 192; *Time*, July 7, 1960.

15. White, *Making of the President, 1960*, 195.

16. See John Forbes, "The 1960 Democratic and Republican Conventions" (n.d. late July, 1960), 1960 Campaign Series, Box 330, Stevenson Papers, Mudd Library, Princeton.

17. Schlesinger, *Thousand Days*, 38

18. The quote is from Agnes Meyer, in Martin, *Adlai Stevenson*, 525. See also John Forbes, "The 1960 Democratic and Republican Conventions"; White, *Making of the President, 1960*, 195–97. Stevenson went to the convention hall to take his seat as a delegate. That, according to his biographer John Bartlow Martin, was intended to show that he was, in fact, not a candidate. Traditionally, candidates do not appear on the convention floor before nominations are concluded. Martin, *Adlai Stevenson*, 534.

19. Schlesinger, *Thousand Days*, 38; O'Donnell and Powers, *"Johnny, We Hardly Knew Ye,"* 211.

20. Ibid., 210. *Time*, July 18, 1960.

21. Schlesinger, *Thousand Days*, 39. McCarthy's speech is excerpted in *Time*, July 25, 1960.

22. White, *Making of the President, 1960*, 203. The final tally was Kennedy 806, Johnson, 409, Symington, 86, Stevenson, 79, and all others 140. Following the Wyoming vote, Kennedy received votes from Puerto Rico and the Virgin Islands to carry him over 800. See also, *Time*, July 25, 1960.

23. *Time*, July 25, 1960. *Time* made much the same statement before the convention. *Time*, July 11, 1960.

24. Milton Gwertzman to Mike Feldman and Theodore Sorensen, "Counterattack Sourcebook" (Aug. 10, 1960), Pre-Presidential Papers, Box 991, JFKP, JFKL, Boston.

25. *Time*, July 25, 1960.

26. Richard Taylor, "Pressure Groups and the Democratic Platform: Kennedy in Control," in Paul Tillett, ed., *Inside Politics: The National Conventions, 1960* (Dobbs Ferry, NY, 1962), 93–94.

27. Dallek, *Lone Star Rising*, 571–72.

28. Phil Graham memo, "Notes on the 1960 Democratic Convention" (July 19, 1960), Reference File, LBJA, LBJL, Austin.

29. Dallek, *Lonestar Rising*, 576. According to Dallek, LBJ's reluctance helped appease some of his Texas friends who did not want him to run in the number-two spot; and it might have been part of a plan to force Kennedy to make the vice presidency a more effective position. See ibid., 577–78.

30. Arthur Krock, "Private Memorandum" (Sept. 22, 1960), Arthur Krock Papers, Box 1, Mudd Library, Princeton; Clifford, *Counsel to the President*, 318. This offer, and then Symington's acceptance, was done through Clifford as intermediary. Clifford writes that this event occurred on Thursday, July 14. Almost certainly it was the day before. See also James C. Olson, *Stuart Syminton: A Life* (Columbia, MO, 2003), 358–59.

31. See Johnson's account in Johnson Diary entry (July 14, 1960), Reference File, LBJA, LBJL, Austin. See R. Kennedy's account in Edwin O. Guthman and Jeffrey

Shulmann, eds., *Robert Kennedy In His Own Words* (New York, 1988), 316–17. Phil Graham witnessed most of these events from Johnson's room. See Graham memo, "Notes on the 1960 Democratic Convention."

32. On who was trying to convince Kennedy and Johnson to accept these offers, see Arthur Krock, "Private Memorandum," Arthur Krock Papers, Box 1, Mudd Library, Princeton; and "Drew Pearson Memo" (n.d.), Drew Pearson Papers, Box G287, LBJL, Austin. Also, Graham memo, "Notes on the 1960 Democratic Convention."

33. *Time*, July 25, 1960; *Newsweek*, July 25, 1960.

34. O'Donnell and Powers, *"Johnny, We Hardly Knew Ye,"* 220–21; Jeff Shesol, *Mutual Contempt: Lyndon Johnson, Robert Kennedy, and the Feud That Defined a Decade* (New York, 1997), 51; Dallek, *Lone Star Rising*, 579; Schlesinger, *Robert Kennedy*, 208–9.

35. Edwin O. Guthman, *We Band of Brothers* (New York, 1971), 47; Shesol, *Mutual Contempt*, 51.

36. See Johnson's own account: Johnson Diary Entries (July 13 and 14, 1960), Reference File, LBJA, LBJL, Austin. Jeff Shesol generally follows this account. See Shesol, *Mutual Contempt*, 51–53. And Schlesinger, *Thousand Days*, 43.

37. Krock does mention that Bobby's first visit was misconstrued by Rayburn and Johnson as an attempt to force Johnson off the ticket. But that issue was ironed out quickly. See Arthur Krock, "Private Memorandum" (Sept. 22, 1960), Arthur Krock Papers, Box 1, Mudd Library, Princeton.

38. Kennedy Acceptance Speech (July 15, 1960), Pre-Presidential Papers, Box 1027, JFKP, JFKL, Boston. The speech is excerpted in *Time*, July 25, 1960.

39. Schlesinger, *Thousand Days*, 59.

40. Nixon to George Sokolsky (July 13, 1960), Vice Presidential Papers, Box 712, RMNP, NARA, Laguna Niguel, CA.

41. Reagan to Nixon (July 15, 1960), General Correspondence Files, Pre-Presidential Papers, Box 621, ibid.

42. *Time*, July 11, 1960.

43. *New York Times*, Oct. 20, 1967; Robert A. Divine, *The Sputnik Challenge: Eisenhower's Response to the Soviet Satellite* (New York, 1993), xv; Robert A. Divine, *Since 1945: Politics and Diplomacy in Recent American History* (New York, 1985), 85.

44. *Time*, July 18, 1960

45. Ibid., Aug. 1, 1960; *Newsweek*, Aug. 1, 1960.

46. Nixon, *Six Crises*, 314.

47. *Time*, Aug. 1, 1960; *Newsweek*, Aug. 1, 1960.

48. Nixon, *Memoirs*, 215.

49. Rockefeller statement (July 23, 1960), "Republican Party Platform," Robert Merriam Papers, EL, Abilene; Memorandum on the Joint Nixon-Rockefeller Statement of July 23, 1960, 1960 Election Chapter (Sept. 15, 1960), Vice Presidential Papers, Box 1, RMNP, NARA, Laguna Niguel, CA. A more easily accessible copy of the Nixon-Rockefeller agreement is in White, *Making of the President, 1960*, 464–67.

For the response from the Right, see Rusher, *Rise of the Right*, 88. For Nixon's recol-lections, see Nixon, *Memoirs*, 215. See also *Newsweek*, Aug. 1, 1960; *Time*, Aug. 1, 1960.

50. *Time*, Aug. 1, 1960.

51. *Newsweek*, Aug. 8, 1960; Barry Goldwater, *Goldwater* (New York, 1988), 256.

52. Reagan to Nixon (July 23, 1960), Pre-Presidential Papers, Box 621, RMNP, NARA, Laguna Niguel, CA.

53. Rusher, *Rise of the Right*, 88; *New York Times*, July 24, 1960; *National Review*, Aug. 6, 1960; *Time*, Aug. 1, 1960.

54. White, *Making of the President, 1960*, 238.

55. *Time*, Aug. 1, 1960.

56. *Newsweek*, Aug. 8, 1960.

57. Nixon to Eisenhower, summary of telephone conversation (July 24, 1960), Di-ary Series, Papers as President, 1953–1961, Ann Whitman File, EP, Abilene. *Time*, Aug. 8, 1960.

58. Percy to Eisenhower (July 24, 1960), ibid. By this time Percy, who could not stave off the pressure from the Right, had been replaced by Melvin Laird. *Time* called Laird a "hard-nosed Wisconsin Congressman." *Time*, Aug. 8, 1960.

59. The best discussion of these issues and events is John H. Kessel, "Political Leadership: The Nixon Version," in Tillett, ed., *Inside Politics*, 43–49.

60. *Time*, Aug. 1, 1960.

61. Barry Goldwater, *With No Apologies: Personal and Political Memoirs of Barry Goldwater* (New York, 1979), 112.

62. Ibid., 111–12; *New York Times*, July 28, 1960.

63. Lodge believed this is why he was chosen. See Henry Cabot Lodge, *The Storm Has Many Eyes* (New York, 1971), 183–84. Eisenhower wanted Lodge, see William J. Miller, *Henry Cabot Lodge: A Biography* (New York, 1967), 319.

64. *Time*, July 25, and Aug. 8, 1960; *Newsweek*, Aug. 1, 1960.

65. Ibid., Aug. 1, 1960; *Time*, July 25, 1960.

66. Quoted in Miller, *Henry Cabot Lodge*, 320. For a discussion of this meeting, see Kessel, "Political Leadership," 51–52.

67. *Time*, July 11, 1960.

Chapter Seven

1. George Gallup, *The Gallup Poll: Public Opinion, 1935–1971* (New York, 1972), 1680–82. *Time*, July 11, 1960.

2. Herbert S. Parment, *JFK: The Presidency of John F. Kennedy* (New York, 1983), 35.

3. Schlesinger to Kennedy (Aug. 30, 1960), Box 32, President's Office Files, JFKP, JFKL, Boston.

4. Sorensen, *Kennedy*, 187–88.

5. Ambrose, *Nixon*, 557.

6. Ann Whitman Diary (Aug. 30, 1960), Ann Whitman File, DDEL, Abilene.

7. White, *Making of the President, 1960*, 516–29.

8. Ambrose, *Nixon*, 561.

9. Schlesinger to Kennedy (Aug. 26, 1960), 1960 Presidential Campaign Series, Box 329, Stevenson Papers, Mudd Library, Princeton. Four days later, Schlesinger made many of the same points in another letter: Schlesinger to Kennedy (Aug. 30, 1960), President's Office Files, JFKP, JFKL, Boston.

10. Stevenson to Marietta Tree, quoted in McKeever, *Adlai Stevenson*, 467–68.

11. *New York Times*, Aug. 1, 1969; *Time*, Aug. 15, 1960.

12. "Dear Friend" (Sept. 19, 1960), 1960 Presidential Campaign Series, Box 328, Stevenson Papers, Mudd Library, Princeton.

13. Lash, *Eleanor: The Years Alone*, 297.

14. *The Speeches, Remarks, Press Conferences, and Statements of Senator John F. Kennedy, August 1 through November 7, 1960*, Report of the Committee on Commerce, U.S. Senate, 87th Cong. (Washington, DC, 1961), Part I, 18–21.

15. Eleanor Roosevelt to Mary Lasker (Aug. 15, 1960) President's Office Files, Box 32, JFKP, JFKL, Boston. The letter to Lasker was sent to Kennedy with a note enclosed from Mrs. Roosevelt: Eleanor Roosevelt to Kennedy (Aug. 16, 1960), in ibid. See also, Martin, *Adlai Stevenson*, 535–36.

16. Kennedy to Eleanor Roosevelt (Aug. 26, 1960), President's Office Files, Box 32, JFKP, JFKL, Boston. President Kennedy appointed Stevenson as ambassador to the United Nations, a position largely considered ministerial and ceremonial. George Ball, a Stevenson friend and advisor, told Stevenson that if he turned down the appointment, it would embarrass the administration. Stevenson was consulted during the Cuban Missile Crises, but he was considered "soft" and his opinions were not taken. See McKeever, *Adlai Stevenson*, 466.

17. Truman to Dean Acheson (Aug. 26, 1960) [letter unsent], in Robert H. Ferrell, ed., *Off the Record: The Private Papers of Harry S. Truman* (New York, 1980), 390.

18. Clifford to Kennedy (July 19, 1960), President's Office Files, Box 29, JFKP, JFKL, Boston; and Kennedy to Clifford (July 29, 1960), in ibid.

19. *The Speeches, Remarks, Press Conferences, and Statements of Senator John F. Kennedy*, Part I, 24. Clifford, *Counsel*, 322. See also David McCullough, *Truman* (New York, 1992), 974.

20. Steven Gillon, *Politics and Vision: The ADA and American Liberalism* (New York, 1987), 133–34.

21. Schlesinger to Kennedy (Aug. 30, 1960) President's Office Files, Box 32, JFKP, JFKL, Boston.

22. *The Speeches, Remarks, Press Conferences, and Statements of Senator John F. Kennedy*, Part I, 238–42. Copy of speech to the Liberal Party of New York (Sept. 14, 1960), Pre-Presidential Papers, Box 911, JFKP, JFKL, Boston.

23. Nixon, *Six Crises*, 320.

24. Ibid., 320.

25. See Nixon's schedule in *The Speeches, Remarks, Press Conferences, and Statements of Vice President Richard M. Nixon, August 1 through November 7, 1960*, Report

of the Committee on Commerce, U.S. Senate, 87th Cong. (Washington, DC, 1961), Parts II, III–VIII.

26. Ibid., 322.

27. Dwight D. Eisenhower, *Waging Peace* (Garden City, NY, 1965), 598–99.

28. *PPP, Eisenhower* (1960), 622–27.

29. *The Joint Appearances of Senator John F. Kennedy and Vice President Richard M. Nixon and Other 1960 Campaign Presentations*, Report of the Committee on Commerce, U.S. Senate, 87th Cong. (Washington, DC, 1961), Part III, 2. Kennedy thought Nixon's appearance on *Tonight* was undignified and cancelled his own scheduled appearance. Sorensen, *Kennedy*, 195.

30. *PPP, Eisenhower* (1960), 651, 653, 657–58. Nixon believed that Eisenhower had meant, "Ask me at next week's conference." See Nixon, *Memoirs*, 219.

31. Ann Whitman Diary (Oct. 4, 1960), Ann Whitman File, DDEL, Abilene. Eisenhower tried to explain his statement to the press. See *Time*, Oct. 10, 1960.

32. Truman speech, Reno, NV (Oct. 20, 1960), 1960 Presidential Campaign File, David Stowe Papers, HSTL, Independence, MO.

33. Ambrose, *Eisenhower*, Vol. 2, 601.

34. Nixon, *Six Crises*, 325.

35. *The Speeches, Remarks, Press Conferences, and Statements of Vice President Richard M. Nixon*, Part II, 5.

36. Nixon, *Six Crises*, 325–26.

37. *New York Times*, Sept. 8, 1960; *Time*, Oct. 31, 1960.

38. Nixon, *Six Crises*, 327.

39. Ibid., 327–28; *The Speeches, Remarks, Press Conferences, and Statements of Senator John F. Kennedy*, Part I, 183–84. *Meet the Press* transcript (Sept. 9, 1960), Lawrence Spivak Papers, LC.

40. Nixon to Claire Booth Luce (Sept. 7, 1960), Vice Presidential Papers, Box 465, RMNP, NARA, Laguna Niguel, CA.

41. O'Donnell and Powers, *"Johnny, We Hardly Knew Ye,"* 237.

42. Miller, *Lyndon*, 342.

43. Quoted in Christopher Mathews, *Kennedy and Nixon: The Rivalry That Shaped Postwar America* (New York, 1996), 142.

44. *The Speeches, Remarks, Press Conferences, and Statements of Senator John F. Kennedy*, Part I, 206–10.

45. O'Donnell and Powers, *"Johnny, We Hardly Knew Ye,"* 239–40.

46. *The Speeches, Remarks, Press Conferences, and Statements of Senator John F. Kennedy*, Part I, 211–18; O'Donnell and Powers, *"Johnny, We Hardly Knew Ye,"* 240.

Chapter Eight

1. Nixon, *Six Crises*, 330–32.

2. White, *Making of the President, 1960*, 335; Sorensen, *Kennedy*, 197. The *New York Times* estimated that 60 million watched, some 53 percent of the populations of the eastern urban areas. *New York Times*, Sept. 27, 1960.

3. Sorensen, *Kennedy*, 197–98.

4. *New York Times*, Sept. 28, 1960.

5. Mazo, *Richard Nixon*, 243.

6. Eisenhower, *Waging Peace*, 598–99.

7. Nixon, *Six Crises*, 323.

8. Ibid., 323. In 1968 and again in 1972, Nixon refused to debate his Democratic opponents, Hubert Humphrey and George McGovern, most likely because of the outcome of the 1960 debates.

9. White, *Making of the President, 1960*, 335.

10. In 1964, Lyndon Johnson worked to have the temporary change in the law lifted, which kept him from having to debate the Republican candidate, Barry Goldwater. I discuss this in some detail in *Liberalism's Last Hurrah: The Presidential Campaign of 1964* (Armonk, NY, 2003), 243–44.

11. Ibid., 339–40. Sorensen, *Kennedy*, 196–97.

12. Don Hewett, *Tell Me a Story: Fifty Years and 60 Minutes in Television* (New York, 1999), 67.

13. Nixon, *Six Crises*, 336–37.

14. Hewitt, *Tell Me a Story*, 67.

15. Nixon, *Six Crises*, 337; White, *Making of the President, 1960*, 42.

16. White, *Making of the President, 1960*, 340.

17. Goodwin, *Remembering America*, 113. Sorensen recalled many of the same events. See Sorensen, *Kennedy*, 198.

18. Ibid., 198.

19. Klein's recollection is quoted in Mathews, *Kennedy and Nixon*, 148. See also White, *Making of the President, 1960*, 343. The *New York Times* noted the incident in the next morning's issue, but stated that Nixon "gave no indication that it bothered him." The *Times* also noted that moments later, Nixon rose to greet Kennedy in the reception room and cracked his head on a microphone. *New York Times*, Sept. 27, 1960.

20. Mathews, *Kennedy and Nixon*, 148.

21. Later, however (and behind closed doors), Kennedy allowed a light coat of makeup. See Sorensen, *Kennedy*, 198.

22. Hewitt, *Tell Me a Story*, 68. White called the stuff "Lazy Shave." White, *Making of the President, 1960*, 344.

23. *The Joint Appearances of Senator John F. Kennedy and Vice President Richard M. Nixon*, Part III, 74. The transcript is also available in the *New York Times* the next day, Sept. 27, 1960.

24. See particularly Sorensen, *Kennedy*, 199.

25. *The Joint Appearances of Senator John F. Kennedy and Vice President Richard M. Nixon*, Part III, 77–78. Russell Baker discusses these issues in the *New York Times*. *New York Times*, Sept. 27, 1960.

26. *The Joint Appearances of Senator John F. Kennedy and Vice President Richard M. Nixon*, Part III, 78.

27. *New York Times*, Sept. 27, 1960. Nixon said that Kennedy's plan would cost between $13.2 billion and $18 billion.

28. *The Joint Appearances of Senator John F. Kennedy and Vice President Richard M. Nixon*, Part III, 81, 82, 85.

29. Ibid., Part III, 86–88.

30. *New York Times*, Sept. 27, 1960.

31. White, *Making of the President, 1960*, 346.

32. Ibid., 346–47. *Time* reported that Nixon won "only to those who listened to the radio." *Time*, Oct. 10, 1960.

33. Quoted in Anthony Summers, *The Arrogance of Power: The Secret World of Richard Nixon* (New York, 2000), 208

34. *New York Times*, Sept. 28, 1960.

35. *The Wall Street Journal*, Sept. 28, 1960.

36. *New York Times*, Oct. 8, 1960. The candidates also argued over lighting. The *Times* even went so far as to identify Nixon's makeup artist and confirm that he was, in fact, a Republican. Apparently, there were rumors that Nixon's makeup in the first debate had been applied by a Democrat.

37. Ibid., Oct. 8, 1960.

38. Nixon, *Six Crises*, 324. The first debate began with, of course, a great deal of anticipation before the event and a saturation of analysis after. As many as 66 million watched the first debate. In the second and third debates the numbers dropped to about 60 million, and in the last debate some 70 million watched. *Time* also explored the question of the thermostat. *Time*, Oct. 17, 1960.

39. *New York Times*, Oct. 8, 1960.

40. *The Joint Appearances of Senator John F. Kennedy and Vice President Richard M. Nixon*, Part III, 146–65. *Time* opined that Nixon won the Quemoy and Matsu argument and thus the second debate. *Time*, Oct. 17, 1960.

41. *New York Times*, Oct. 8, 1964.

42. *The Joint Appearances of Senator John F. Kennedy and Vice President Richard M. Nixon*, Part III, 204.

43. *New York Times*, Oct. 14, 1960.

44. *The Joint Appearances of Senator John F. Kennedy and Vice President Richard M. Nixon*, Part III, 204–22.

45. White, *Making of the President, 1960*, 349; *New York Times*, Oct. 22, 1960.

46. *The Joint Appearances of Senator John F. Kennedy and Vice President Richard M. Nixon*, Part III, 263–66

47. Ibid., 266.

48. Ibid., 260–78.

49. *New York Times*, Oct. 8, 1960.

50. *The Joint Appearances of Senator John F. Kennedy and Vice President Richard M. Nixon*, Part III, 264. Nixon believed he did his best in the last debate. See Nixon, *Six Crises*, 324.

51. Gallup Polls cited in White, *Making of the President, 1960*, 383.

52. Ibid., 349.

53. Quoted in Schlesinger, *A Thousand Days*, 64.

54. Ambrose, *Nixon*, 589.

55. *Washington Post*, Oct. 25, 1960.

56. Donaldson, *Liberalism's Last Hurrah*, 243–44.

57. Quoted in Sidney Kraus, ed., *The Great Debates: Kennedy vs. Nixon, 1960* (Bloomington, IN, 1962), n.p.

58. Nixon, *Memoirs*, 221.

Chapter Nine

1. These economic figures were compiled by the Council of Economic Advisors, headed by Walter Heller. See particularly, Heller memo (Oct. 4, 1960), Box 4, Walter Heller Papers, JFKL, Boston.

2. *Cong. Rec.* (Aug. 14, 1958), 85th Cong. 2d sess. Kennedy's speech so infuriated Indiana Republican Homer Capehart that he threatened to initiate a rule that would close down Congress if Kennedy or any other Democrat spoke on the subject again. *New York Times*, Aug. 15, 1958. Kennedy repeated the missile gap argument so many times that in September 1960 John Kenneth Galbraith complained to Lou Harris that Kennedy "has made the point that he isn't soft. Henceforth he can only frighten." See Galbraith to Harris (Sept. 27, 1960), Box 74, John Kenneth Galbraith Papers, JFKL, Boston.

3. Michael Beschloss, *The Crisis Years: Kennedy and Khrushchev, 1960–1963* (New York, 1991), 25–26.

4. Ibid., 26–27. For the argument that there was a missile gap (or at least that Kennedy believed there was) see Dallek, *Kennedy*, 289.

5. *The Speeches of Senator John F. Kennedy: Presidential Campaign of 1960*, 87th Cong. 1st sess., rept. 994 (Washington, DC, 1961), 112, 262. Kennedy made these statements in Detroit on September 5, 1960 and in Greenville, North Carolina on September 17, 1960.

6. Quoted in Miller, *Henry Cabot Lodge*, 322.

7. Lodge statement quoted in Nixon, *Six Crises*, 350.

8. *The Speeches of Senator John F. Kennedy*, 244. See also, *Meet the Press* transcript (Oct. 16, 1960), Pre-Presidential Papers, Box 780, JFKP, JFKL, Boston.

9. White, *Making of the President, 1960*, 355–56; Ambrose, *Nixon*, 580; Miller, *Henry Cabot Lodge*, 325. *Time*, Oct. 31, 1960. Nixon defended Lodge's statement in *Six Crises*, arguing that Lodge had reached a misunderstanding that Nixon had intended to name Ralph Bunche to his cabinet. See Nixon, *Six Crises*, 350–51.

10. White, *Making of the President, 1960*, 351.

11. Quoted in Goodwin, *Remembering America*, 121.

12. Quoted in Harris Wofford, *Of Kennedys and Kings* (Pittsburgh, 1992), 19.

13. The statements of Kennedy and Mrs. King can be found in *The Speeches of Senator John F. Kennedy, 1201*.

14. Goodwin, *Remembering America*, 122. According to Goodwin, Robert Kennedy did not make the call: "Someone called someone. Someone called the judge." By most other accounts, however, Bobby did make the call. See particularly, Dallek, *Kennedy*, 293. And, Schlesinger, *Thousand Days*, 74.

15. Quoted in Wofford, *Of Kennedys and Kings*, 22–23. See also Ronald Steel, *In Love with the Night: The American Romance with Robert Kennedy* (New York, 2000), 59.

16. Nixon, *Six Crises*, 362.

17. See particularly *Jet*, Nov. 10, 1960; Pittsburgh *Courier*, Nov. 5, 1960.

18. Sorensen, *Kennedy*, 216; Sargent Shriver interview ("Kennedy's Call to King"), JFKL.

19. For a contemporary analysis of these events and their significance, see *New York Times*, Nov. 3, 1960. For an extended look at this entire event, see Taylor Branch, *Parting the Waters: America in the King Years, 1951–1963* (New York, 1988), 351–70.

20. Schlesinger, *Thousand Days*, 58.

21. James Rowe interview, LBJL. Miller, *Lyndon*, 340–41.

22. *New York Times*, Oct. 5 and 6, 1960.

23. Ibid., Oct. 6, 1960.

24. Miller, *Lyndon*, 343.

25. Sorensen, *Kennedy*, 189.

26. Miller, *Lyndon*, 344. The quote is from James Blundell's recollection of Johnson's speeches in the South.

27. Ibid., 349. The quote is from Carl Phinney.

28. *New York Times*, Nov. 6, 1960; Jan Jarboe Russell, *Lady Bird: A Biography of Mrs. Johnson* (New York, 1999), 207.

29. Miller, *Lyndon*, 349. The quote is from D. B. Hardeman.

30. *New York Times*, Nov. 10, 1960; Fite, *Richard Russell*, 379.

31. *The Speeches of Vice President Richard Nixon, 710–11.* Nixon made these statements on October 22 in Allentown, Pennsylvania.

32. *New York Times*, Oct. 24, 1960. Nixon discusses this in *Six Crises*, 356.

33. *Joint Appearances of Senator John F. Kennedy and Vice President Richard M. Nixon: Presidential Campaign of 1960*, 340. This is a transcript from *Face the Nation*, October 30, 1960.

34. Nixon, *Memoirs*, 220.

35. Milton Eisenhower, COHC; White, *Making of the President, 1960*, 369–70. *Time*, Aug. 15, 1960.

36. O'Donnell and Powers, *"Johnny, We Hardly Knew Ye,"* 248–49.

37. White, *Making of the President, 1960*, 370.

38. Nixon, *Memoirs*, 222.

39. Ibid., 222. Theodore White speculates a great deal on what might have changed had Eisenhower entered the campaign earlier. See White, *Making of the President, 1960*, 371–72. *Time* speculated after that election that Nixon would have won had the president entered the campaign earlier. See *Time*, Nov. 14, 1960.

40. *The Speeches of Vice President Richard Nixon*, 1058.

41. *New York Times*, Nov. 7, 1960.

42. Ann Whitman Diary (Nov. 8, 1960), DDEL.

43. White, *Making of the President, 1960*, 402–5.

44. Benjamin C. Bradlee, *Conversations with Kennedy* (New York, 1975), 17–18.

45. Quoted in Herbert S. Parmet, *Richard Nixon and His America* (Boston, 1990), 432–33; Robert D. Novak, *Agony of the GOP: 1964* (New York, 1965), 8.

46. Nixon, *Six Crises*, 396–97.

47. See James Keogh, *President Nixon and the Press* (New York, 1972), 172; Edith Efron, *News Twisters* (Los Angeles, 1971), 47; Nixon, *Memoirs*, 330.

48. Ronald Reagan, *An American Life* (New York, 1990), 209–10.

49. Gallup, *The Gallup Poll*, 1689–90.

50. Nixon, *Six Crises*, 358.

51. Gallup, *The Gallup Poll*, 1689–90.

52. Nixon, *Six Crises*, 377–78; Nixon, *Memoirs*, 223.

53. Ibid., 223.

54. O'Donnell and Powers, "*Johnny, We Hardly Knew Ye*," 255; White, *Making of the President, 1960*, 4

55. Ibid., 255–56; Sorensen, *Kennedy*, 211.

56. Nixon, *Six Crises*, 380.

57. White, *Making of the President, 1960*, 11.

58. O'Donnell and Powers, "*Johnny, We Hardly Knew Ye*," 256–57.

59. Sorensen, *Kennedy*, 211.

60. Nixon, *Six Crises*, 380. Kennedy had little faith in these predictions. See Sorensen, *Kennedy*, 213.

61. Ibid., 380–81.

62. Ibid., 381–82. Huntley and Brinkley, however, were still using the word "cliff-hanger" at eight o'clock Eastern time. Sorensen, *Kennedy*, 212.

63. White, *Making of the President, 1960*, 15–16. In the 1964 campaign, Eisenhower became upset because he did not do more to keep Barry Goldwater from getting the Republican nomination. See Donaldson, *Liberalism's Last Hurrah*, 166–67.

64. Nixon, *Six Crises*, 382–83.

65. O'Donnell and Powers, "*Johnny We Hardly Knew Ye*," 257.

66. Nixon, *Six Crises*, 382.

67. Sorensen, *Kennedy*, 220.

68. O'Donnell and Powers, "*Johnny, We Hardly Knew Ye*," 358. There has been much made of the "theft of Chicago" and thus Illinois, by Mayor Daley. Daley-controlled wards went for Kennedy in unprecedented numbers. Kennedy won the state by fewer than 9,000 votes of over 4.7 million votes cast. Daley blocked an official recount. Years later, Chicago mobster Sam Giancana claimed to have stuffed ballot boxes in Chicago for Kennedy and thus allowed him to carry Illinois and win the election. See *Report of the Senate Select Committee on Improper Activities in the Labor or Management Field: Hearings*, 86th Cong., 1st sess. See also Thomas C. Reeves, *A Question of Character: The Life of John F. Kennedy* (New York, 1991), 214.

69. Nixon, *Six Crises*, 385.
70. Ibid., 386.
71. Ibid., 390.
72. Quoted in Sorensen, *Kennedy*, 212.
73. O'Donnell and Powers, "*Johnny, We Hardly Knew Ye,*" 258. Sorensen, *Kennedy*, 212.
74. Nixon, *Six Crises*, 397–98. Nixon allowed his press secretary, Herb Klein, to read his concession to network television. Several of Kennedy's aides insisted that Nixon should have delivered the concession himself. Kennedy supposedly responded, "He went out the way he came in—no class." This is perhaps an indication of how raw the campaign had gotten near the end. The quote is in Pierre Salinger, *With Kennedy* (Garden City, NY, 1966), 51.
75. Sorensen, *Kennedy*, 212; White, *Making of the President, 1960,* 415.

Chapter Ten

1. Nixon, *Six Crises*, 404
2. Ibid., 406–7.
3. O'Donnell and Powers, "*Johnny, We Hardly Knew Ye,*" 263.
4. Nixon, *Six Crises*, 409.
5. There were two articles in the *New York Times* on November 15 that suggested this as a possibility. See W. H Lawrence, "Talk is Cordial," on page 1; and Arthur Krock, "In the Nation," on page 38.
6. Douglas Dillon had been Eisenhower's ambassador to France and then undersecretary of state. He would be named secretary of the treasury by Kennedy in 1961 and serve until 1974. Lodge would become Kennedy's ambassador to Vietnam.
7. Nixon, *Six Crises*, 409–10.
8. O'Donnell and Powers, "*Johnny, We Hardly Knew Ye,*" 263.
9. Nixon, *Six Crises*, 412.
10. Ibid., 413.
11. Ibid., 413
12. White, *Making of the President, 1960,* 420.
13. Kennedy won twelve; Nixon won six.
14. Nixon made this statement to his chauffeur who could not understand why Nixon had lost the election. Nixon, *Six Crises*, 403.
15.

Kennedy	margin of victory	Nixon	
New York	52.5%	Ohio	53.3%
Pennsylvania	51.1%	California	50.1%
Michigan	50.9%		
Illinois	50.0%		
Texas	50.5%		
New Jersey	49.9%		
Massachusetts	60.2%		

California was so close it had to be decided by absentee votes.

16. White, *Making of the President, 1960*, 423. This strategy failed in the Los Angeles suburbs, where Kennedy ran farther behind the Democratic ticket there than anywhere else in the country.

17. Throughout the South, Kennedy received 5.1 million votes to Nixon's 4.7 million. In 1956, Eisenhower received 4.2 million.

18. White, *Making of the President, 1960*, 424.

19. *New York Times*, Nov. 23, 1960.

20. White, *Making of the President, 1960*, 424.

21. Ibid., 433.

22. Carty, *A Catholic in the White House?*, 156–57.

23. Nixon, *Six Crises*, 367.

24. Ithiel de Sola Pool, Robert P. Ableson, and Samuel L. Popkin, *Candidates, Issues, and Strategies: A Computer Simulation of the 1960 Presidential Election* (Cambridge, MA, 1964), 115–17. For a quick breakdown of this statistical analysis, see Carty, *A Catholic in the White House?*, 157.

25. *New York Times*, Nov. 23, 1960.

~

Bibliography

Archival Collections

Lyndon Baines Johnson Papers, Lyndon Baines Johnson Library, Austin, TX
India Edwards Papers, Harry S. Truman Library, Independence, MO
Dwight Eisenhower Diary Series, Dwight Eisenhower Library, Abilene, KS
Dwight Eisenhower Papers, Dwight Eisenhower Library, Abilene, KS
Dwight Eisenhower Papers as President (Ann Whitman File), Dwight Eisenhower
  Library, Abilene, KS
Walter Heller Papers, John F. Kennedy Library, Boston, MA
John F. Kennedy Pre-Presidential Papers, John F. Kennedy Library, Boston, MA
Joseph P. Kennedy Papers, John F. Kennedy Library, Boston, MA
Robert F. Kennedy Pre-Administration Papers, John F. Kennedy Library, Boston, MA
Leon Keyserling Papers, Harry S. Truman Library, Independence, MO
Arthur Krock Papers, Mudd Lubrary, Princeton University, Princeton, NJ
Edwin Martin Papers, John F. Kennedy Library, Boston, MA
Richard M. Nixon Pre-Presidential Papers, Richard M. Nixon Library, Yorba Linda,
  CA
Richard M. Nixon Vice-Presidential Papers, NARA, Laguna Niguel, CA
Drew Pearson Papers, Lyndon Baines Johnson Library, Austin, TX
David F. Powers Papers, John F. Kennedy Library, Boston, MA
Joseph Rauh Papers, Library of Congress, Washington, DC
Arthur M. Schlesinger Papers, John F. Kennedy Library, Boston, MA
Theodore Sorensen Papers, John F. Kennedy Library, Boston, MA
Lawrence Spivak Papers, Library of Congress, Washington, DC.
Adlai Stevenson Papers, Mudd Library, Princeton University, Princeton, NJ

187

Robert Taft Papers, Library of Congress, Washington, DC
Harry S. Truman Post-Presidential Papers, Harry S. Truman Library, Independence, MO

Interviews

Everett Dirksen interview, Lyndon Baines Johnson Library Oral History Collection
Milton Eisenhower interview, Columbia Oral History Collection
Hubert Humphrey interview, Lyndon Baines Johnson Library Oral History Collection
Robert Nathan interview, Kennedy Library Oral History Collection
James Rauh interview, Kennedy Library Oral History Collection
James Rauh interview, Harry S. Truman Library, Independence, MO
George Reedy interview, Lyndon Baines Johnson Library Oral History Collection

Books and Articles

Alexander, Charles C. *Holding the Line: The Eisenhower Era, 1952–1961*. Bloomington: Indiana University Press, 1975.
Alsop, Joseph (with Adam Plant). *I've Seen the Best of It*. New York: W. W. Norton, 1992.
Ambrose, Stephen. *Nixon*. Vol. 1. *The Education of a Politician, 1913–1962*. New York: Simon and Schuster, 1987.
———. *Eisenhower: The President*, Vol. II. New York: Simon and Schuster, 1984.
———. *Eisenhower: Soldier and President*. New York: Simon and Schuster, 1990.
Anderson, Trotton. "The 1958 California Election," *Western Political Science Quarterly* 12 (March 1959), 276–300.
Armstrong, Richard. *The Next Hurrah: The Communications Revolution in American Politics*. New York: William Morrow, 1988.
Black, Earl, and Merle Black. *The Rise of Southern Republicans*. Cambridge, MA: Harvard University Press, 2002.
Bohlen, Charles E. *Witness to History, 1929–1969*. New York: W. W. Norton, 1973.
Bradlee, Benjamin. *Conversations with Kennedy*. New York: W. W. Norton, 1975.
Brauer, Carl M. *John F. Kennedy and the Second Reconstruction*. New York: Columbia University Press, 1977.
Brownell, Herbert (with John P. Burke). *Advising Ike: The Memoirs of Attorney General Herbert Brownell*. Lawrence: University of Kansas Press, 1993.
Burk, Robert F. *Dwight D. Eisenhower: Hero and Politician*. Boston: Twayne, 1986.
Burner, David. *John F. Kennedy and a New Generation*. New York: Harper Collins, 1988.
Carty, Thomas J. *A Catholic in the White House: Religion, Politics, and John F. Kennedy's Presidential Campaign*. New York: Palgrave, 2004.

Castello, William. *The Facts about Nixon: An Unauthorized Biography*. New York: Viking, 1959.

Cohadis, Nadine. *Strom Thurmond and the Politics of Southern Change*. New York: Simon and Schuster, 1993.

Dallek, Robert. *Lone Star Rising: Lyndon Johnson and His Times, 1908–1960*. New York: Oxford University Press, 1991.

———. *An Unfinished Life: John F. Kennedy, 1917–1963*. Boston: Little, Brown, 2003.

Donovan, Robert J. *Eisenhower: The Inside Story*. New York: Harpers, 1956.

Eisenhower, Milton S. *The President Is Calling*. Garden City, NY: Doubleday, 1974.

Evans, M. Stanton. *The Future of Conservatism: From Taft to Reagan and Beyond*. New York: Holt, Reinhart and Winston, 1968.

Ewald, William Bragg, Jr. *Eisenhower the President: The Crucial Days, 1951–1960*. Englewood Cliffs, NJ, 1981.

Ferrell, Robert H. *Harry S. Truman: A Life*. Columbia: University of Missouri Press, 1994.

———, ed. *Off the Record: The Private Papers of Harry S. Truman*. New York: Harper and Row, 1980.

Fite, Gilbert C. *Richard Russell, Jr.: Senator from Georgia*. Chapel Hill: University of North Carolina Press, 1991.

Frederickson, Kari. *The Dixiecrat Revolt and the End of the Solid South, 1932–1968*. Chapel Hill: University of North Carolina Press, 2001.

Gallup, George. *The Gallup Poll: Public Opinion, 1935–1971*. New York: Random House, 1972

Gellman, Irwin F. *The Contender: Richard Nixon, The Congress Years, 1946–1952*. New York: Free Press, 1999.

George, Carol V. R. *God's Salesman: Norman Vincent Peale and the Power of Positive Thinking*. New York: Oxford University Press, 1993.

Gillon, Steven M. *Politics and Vision: The ADA and American Liberalism, 1947–1985*. New York: Oxford University Press, 1987.

Goldman, Eric F. *The Tragedy of Lyndon Johnson*. New York: Dell, 1968.

Goodwin, Doris Kearns. *The Fitzgeralds and the Kennedys*. New York: Simon and Schuster, 1987.

Goodwin, Richard. *Remembering America: A Voice from the Sixties*. New York: Harper and Row, 1988.

Gould, Lewis L. *Grand Old Party: A History of the Republicans*. New York: Random House, 2003.

Griffin, Robert. *Politics of Fear: Joseph R. McCarthy and the Senate*. 2d ed. Amherst: University of Massachusetts Press, 1987.

Guthman, Edwin O. *We Band of Brothers*. New York: Harper and Row, 1971.

Hamby, Alonzo L. *Man of the People: A Life of Harry S. Truman*. New York: Oxford University Press, 1995.

Harris, Louis. *Is There a Republican Majority? Political Trends, 1952–1956*. New York: Harper and Row, 1954.

Hess, Karl. *In a Cause That Will Triumph: The Goldwater Campaign and the Future of Conservatism*. New York: Doubleday, 1967.

Himmelstein, Jerome L. *To the Right: The Transformation of American Conservatism*. Berkeley: University of California Press, 1990.

Hewitt, Don. *Tell Me a Story: Fifty Years and 60 Minutes in Television*. New York: Public Affairs, 2001.

Hoffmann, Joyce. *Theodore H. White and Journalism as Illusion*. Columbia: University of Missouri Press, 1995.

Hughes, Emmet John. *Ordeal of Power: A Political Memoir of the Eisenhower Years*. New York: Atheneum, 1963.

Hulsey, Byron C. *Everett Dirksen and His Presidents: How a Senate Giant Shaped American Politics*. Lawrence: University Press of Kansas, 2000.

Humphrey, Hubert. *Education of a Public Man: My Life and Politics*. Minneapolis: University of Minnesota Press, 1991. First published 1976.

Johnson, Walter. *How We Drafted Adlai Stevenson*. New York: Alfred Knopf, 1955.

Judas, John. *William F. Buckley, Jr.: Patron Saint of the Conservatives*. New York: Simon and Schuster, 1988.

Karabel, Zachary. *The Last Campaign: How Harry Truman Won the 1948 Election*. New York: Alfred Knopf, 2001.

Keogh, James. *President Nixon and the Press*. New York: Funk and Wagnalls, 1972.

Kramer, Michael, and Sam Roberts. *"I Never Wanted to Be Vice-President of Anything!": An Investigative Biography of Nelson Rockefeller*. New York: Basic Books, 1976.

Lodge, Henry Cabot. *The Storm Has Many Eyes: A Personal Narrative*. New York: W. W. Norton, 1973.

Lubell, Samuel. *The Future of American Politics*. Garden City, NY: Doubleday, 1956.

———. *Revolt of the Moderates*. New York: Harper and Brothers, 1956.

Manchester, William. *The Glory and the Dream: A Narrative History of America, 1932–1972*. Boston: Little, Brown, 1973.

Martin, John Bartlow. *Adlai Stevenson and the World: The Life of Adlai E. Stevenson*. Garden City, NY: Doubleday, 1977.

Martin, John Frederick. *Civil Rights and the Crisis of Liberalism: The Democratic Party, 1945–1976*. Boulder, CO: Westview Press, 1979.

Matthews, Christopher. *Kennedy and Nixon: The Rivalry That Shaped Postwar America*. New York: Simon and Schuster, 1996.

Mazo, Earl, and Stephen Hess. *Nixon: A Political Portrait*. New York: Popular Library, 1967.

———. *Richard Nixon: A Politician and Personal Portrait*. New York: Avon, 1969.

McCullough, David. *Truman*. New York: Simon and Schuster, 1991.

McGirr, Lisa. *Suburban Warriors: The Origins of the New American Right*. Princeton, NJ: Princeton University Press, 2001.

McKeever, Porter. *Adlai Stevenson: His Life and Legacy, a Biography*. New York: William Morrow, 1989.

Miller, Merle. *Lyndon: An Oral Biography*. New York: Ballantine, 1980.

Miller, William J. *Henry Cabot Lodge: A Biography*. New York: James H. Heinman, 1967.

Newfield, Jack. *Robert F. Kennedy: A Memoir*. New York: Penguin, 1969.

Nixon, Richard. *In the Arena: A Memoir of Victory, Defeat, and Renewal*. New York: Simon and Schuster, 1990.

——. *Six Crises*. Garden City, NY: Doubleday, 1962.

——. *RN: The Memoirs of Richard Nixon*. New York: Gossett and Dunlap, 1978.

O'Brien, Lawrence. *No Final Victories*. Garden City, NY: Doubleday, 1974.

O'Donnell, Kenneth P., and David F. Powers (with Joe McCarthy). *"Johnny, We Hardly Knew Ye": Memoirs of John Fitzgerald Kennedy*. Boston: Little, Brown, 1972.

Oshinsky, David. *A Conspiracy So Immense*. New York: Free Press, 1983.

Parmet, Herbert. *JFK: The Presidency of John F. Kennedy*. New York: Dell, 1983.

——. *Richard Nixon and His America*. Boston: Little, Brown, 1990.

Patterson, James T. *Mr. Republican: A Biography of Robert A. Taft*. Boston: Houghton Mifflin, 1972

Polsby, Nelson W., and Aaron Wildavsky. *Presidential Elections: Strategies and Structures of American Politics*. 10th ed. New York: Chatham House, 2000.

Reedy, George. *Lyndon B. Johnson a Memoir*. New York: Andrews McMeel, 1982.

Reeves, Thomas C. *The Life and Times of Joe McCarthy: A Biography*. Lanham, MD: Madison Books, 1997.

Reichard, Gary W. *Politics as Usual: The Age of Truman and Eisenhower*. Arlington Heights, IL: Harlan Davidson, 1988.

Reinhard, David W. *The Republican Right since 1945*. Lexington: University Press of Kentucky, 1983.

Rusher, William. *Rise of the Right*. New York: William Morrow, 1984.

Schapsmeier, Edward L., and Frederick H. Schapsmeier. *Dirksen of Illinois: Senatorial Statesman*. Urbana: University of Illinois Press, 1985.

Schlesinger, Arthur M., Jr. *A Thousand Days*. Boston: Houghton Mifflin, 1965.

Sevareid, Eric, ed. *Candidates 1960: Behind the Headlines in the Presidential Race*. New York: Basic Books, 1959.

Smith, Richard Norton. *Thomas E. Dewey and His Times*. New York: Simon and Schuster, 1982.

Solberg, Carl. *Hubert Humphrey*. New York: W. W. Norton, 1984.

Sorensen, Theodore C. *Kennedy*. New York: W. W. Norton, 1965.

Steel, Ronald. *Walter Lippmann and the American Century*. Boston: Little, Brown, 1980.

Tillett, Paul, ed. *Inside Politics: The National Conventions, 1960*. Dobbs Ferry, NY: Oceana, 1962.

Unger, Irwin, and Debi Unger. *LBJ: A Life*. New York: John Wiley and Sons, 1999.

Valenti, Jack. *A Very Human President*. New York: W. W. Norton, 1975.

White, Theodore, *The Making of the President, 1960*. New York: Atheneum, 1961,

White, William S. *The Taft Story*. New York: Harper and Row, 1954.

Wicker, Tom. *JFL and LBJ: The Influence of Personality upon Politics*. Chicago: Ivan R. Dee, 1968.

———. *One of Us: Richard Nixon and the American Dream*. New York: Random House, 1991.

Wills, Garry. *Nixon Agonistes*. New York: Signet, 1969.

Wiltcover, Jules. *Party of the People: A History of the Democrats*. New York: Random House, 2003.

———. *The Resurrection of Richard Nixon*. New York: Putnam, 1970.

Government Documents

The Joint Appearances of Senator John F. Kennedy and Vice President Richard M. Nixon: Presidential Campaign of 1960. Washington, DC: USGPO, 1961.

The Speeches of Senator John F. Kennedy: Presidential Campaign of 1960. Washington, DC: USGPO, 1961.

The Speeches of Vice President Richard M. Nixon: Presidential Campaign of 1960. Washington, DC: UDGPO, 1961.

Index

~

About the Author

Gary A. Donaldson holds the Keller Foundation Chair in American History at Xavier University in New Orleans, where he teaches twentieth-century U.S. History. His publications include *Dewey Defeats Truman: The Presidential Campaign of 1948*; *Liberalism's Last Hurrah: The Presidential Campaign of 1964*; *American Foreign Policy: The Twentieth Century in Documents*; and *Modern America: A Documentary History of the Nation since 1945*. He is also the university's director of undergraduate research.